Radical Fictions

Nick Bentley

Radical Fictions

The English Novel in the 1950s

PETER LANG

Oxford · Bern · Berlin · Bruxelles · Frankfurt am Main · New York · Wien

Bibliographic information published by Die Deutsche Bibliothek
Die Deutsche Bibliothek lists this publication in the Deutsche
Nationalbibliografie; detailed bibliographic data is available on
the Internet at ‹http://dnb.ddb.de›.

British Library and Library of Congress Cataloguing-in-Publication Data:
A catalogue record for this book is available from The British Library,
Great Britain, and from The Library of Congress, USA

ISBN 978-3-03910-934-0

© Peter Lang AG, International Academic Publishers, Bern 2007
Hochfeldstrasse 32, Postfach 746, CH-3000 Bern 9, Switzerland
info@peterlang.com, www.peterlang.com, www.peterlang.net

Printed in Germany

For Kenneth & Dorothy Bentley

Contents

Acknowledgements

This book began life as a PhD thesis and I am extremely grateful to my principal supervisors, Barry Taylor and Peter Brooker, for providing the sign posts and directions that have led to its final destination. They have provided invaluable support, advice and guidance along the way. I am also grateful for advice and guidance to Gail Low, Fiona Becket, Martin McQuillan, Shaun Richards, Scott Brewster, Laura Peters, Aidan Arrowsmith, Fred Botting, Roger Pooley and Simon Bainbridge. Thanks to Barry Taylor, Karla Smith, Aidan Arrowsmith and Sandra Courtman for proofreading sections of the book. Thanks also to Peter Widdowson and Susan Brook for their instructive insights and helpful comments. I would also like to thank Alexis Kirschbaum and Shirley Walker Werrett at Peter Lang, and Alan Mauro. I am grateful for the Research Scholarship provided by Staffordshire University to carry out most of the research for the book. I would also like to thank the University librarians at Keele, Birmingham and Staffordshire, and the British Library.

Versions of some of the chapters have already appeared in academic journals. Parts of chapters three and five have appeared in *The European Journal of Cultural Studies*. Parts of chapter five have appeared in *Literary London: Interdisciplinary Studies in the Representation of London* and *Connotations: A Journal for Literary Debate*. Parts of chapter six have appeared in *Wasafiri: The International Magazine of Contemporary Writing* and *Ariel: A Review of International Writing*.

I am very grateful for the love and support (emotional, financial and intellectual) of my mum and dad, and the rest of my family. Finally, I am indebted to Karla who has provided the love and encouragement that has been essential for me to complete this work.

Introduction
Back to the Fifties

Decade of Change

When, in 1960, Harold Macmillan gave his famous 'winds of change' speech to the South African Parliament in Cape Town, he was, of course, referring to the ongoing process of decolonization that was sweeping across Africa.[1] But the phrase 'winds of change' took on a much wider significance and came to represent the cultural and social revolution that was perceived to be emerging at the beginning of the new decade. According to the popular historical narrative evoked in the phrase, the 1960s are the years that represent the shake-up of the old order and the redrawing of the relationship between classes, genders and cultural ethnicities, whilst the 1950s are seen as the age of austerity: the last (and lost) decade during which Britain could still claim to be great, and its social order rested on an established class structure and a homogenous model of the nation.[2] The fifties are consequently recycled in our popular imagination with conservative

---

1   Harold Macmillan, 'Address given to Members of both Houses of the Parliament of the Union of South Africa', in *Pointing the Way, 1959–1961* (London: Macmillan, 1972), pp.473–82.

2   For an exposition of this reading of the relationship between the two decades see Bart Moore-Gilbert and John Seed, *Cultural Revolution?: The Challenge of the Arts in the 1960s* (London and New York: Routledge, 1992). Moore-Gilbert and Seed produce a binary model of cultural 'exhaustion' and 'revolution' between the fifties and sixties: 'Looking at the 1960s only in terms of what came after, and not also in terms of what went before, can obscure that significance. Focusing more precisely on the dominant values and cultural formations of the 1950s produces a different set of emphases [...] It was precisely a sense of exhausted potential of central institutions, practices, canons and definitions in sphere after sphere of cultural life that animated much of the activity and dissension of the 1960s', p.9.

myths of order, social stability, moral decency and restraint – the period before the experimentation, liberation and decadence of the 1960s. The 1950s are thereby understood as a period in which white, middle-class, middle-aged, heterosexual men still held sway, before the 'barbarians', of various subject positions, began to challenge the citadels of power.

This imaginative cultural construction of the 1950s still carries weight in the popular consciousness because there is an element of truth about it. However, this book is concerned to reveal an alternative range of texts and discourses that challenge this established view. This book will turn its attention to the range and diversity of radical and marginalized voices and positions being articulated during the period and show them as indicative of the immense social and cultural changes taking place in England. These subject positions find their clearest voices in the imaginative cultural output of the decade, and particularly in literary fiction. This alternative reading of the fifties will of course entail a shift in perspective of what I feel to be its most valuable literary texts and a subsequent re-shaping of the canon of 1950s novels and authors.

Doris Lessing registered something of this alternative view of the fifties, from the vantage point of 1969, in her novel *The Four-Gated City*:

> 1956, as everyone knows was a climactic year, a water-shed, a turning-point, a cross-roads: it has become one of the years one refers to: oh yes, that year of course! As if years were pegs in a wall, on which one hangs a certain type of memory, or gives stars to, like hotels and restaurants. 1956 was a five star year [...] So that now, looking back, the people who lived through it say, for the sake of speed and easy understanding: 1956, and what is conveyed is the idea of change, breaking up, clearing away, movement.
> Yet the air had cleared well before 1956.[3]

In this quotation, Lessing focuses on the symbolic power of 1956 as representative of the changes of the whole decade.[4] The sense of tran-

---

3   Doris Lessing, *The Four-Gated City* (Frogmore, St. Albans: Panther, 1972), first published in 1969, pp.303–04.

sition to which she refers, of breaking up and movement, indicates both the profound effects the decade had on those who lived through it, and the process of looking back and trying to find meaning and significance in those changes. In the quoted passage, Lessing views the 1950s from the end of the later decade, but suggests that the sources for the seismic changes in people's understanding of their recent cultural history occur at some period prior to 1956, at the beginning of the fifties.

Lessing's passage also identifies something about the way in which we interpret our own histories. As with Michel Foucault's conception of the way modern man develops structures of knowledge and history, Lessing identifies the artificial frameworks and categories upon which we construct or order our understanding of the past.[5] This idea of looking back historically to a specific cultural moment or 'occasion'[6] also invokes Walter Benjamin's powerful image of the historicist 'angel of history', projected into the future with its face turned backwards. Citing Klee's painting 'Angelus Novus', Benjamin writes: 'This is how one pictures the angel of history. His face is turned to the past. Where we perceive a chain of events, he sees one single catastrophe.'[7] This disconnection of ourselves from our past

4   Robert Hewison writes: 'Retrospectively, 1956 has become an annus mirabilis [...] the decade works towards a climacteric of change [...] the point of focus is 1956', In Anger: Culture in the Cold War 1945–60 (London: Weidenfeld and Nicolson, 1981), p.127. Also, the decision by Clive Bloom and Gary Day to split their three-volume history of literature and culture in the twentieth century at 1956 suggests something of the power of this year in the cultural imagination of the century. Literature and Culture in Modern Britain: Volume Three: 1956–1999, ed. by Clive Bloom and Gary Day (Harlow: Longman, 2000).

5   Michel Foucault, 'Preface', in The Order of Things: An Archaeology of the Human Sciences, trans. from the French (London: Routledge, 1970), pp.xv–xxiv.

6   Here, I am using the concept of historical 'occasion' as defined by Walter V. Spanos. See Walter V. Spanos, 'Overture in the Recursive Mode', in Repetitions: The Postmodern Occasion in Literature and Culture (Baton Rouge and London: Louisiana State University Press, 1987), pp.1–12.

7   Walter Benjamin, 'Theses on the Philosophy of History', in Illuminations, ed. by Hannah Arendt, trans. by Harry Zohn (London: Fontana, 1973), pp.245–55, (p.249).

produces problematic theoretical positions in terms of our power to 'write' history, problems identified, in particular, in much post-structuralist theory.[8] However, Benjamin also identifies the imperative and duty to rescue marginalized narratives from the dominant re-constructions of the past: 'For every image of the past that is not recognized by the present as one of its own concerns threatens to disappear irretrievably' (247). Benjamin identifies the intimate con-nections between the past and ourselves, rejecting what he defines as the 'historicist' attempt to objectify and distance a moment in history.[9] It is in the spirit of Benjamin's imperative, and his identification of the relevance of the past to the construction of meaning in the present, that this book attempts to 'read' important 1950s texts.

Cultural change, of course, is difficult to quantify. However, if we attempt to draw up a list of some of the specific events, move-ments and discourses we begin to get a sense of the immense social and cultural shifts of the period. Such a list might include the follow-ing: the Suez Crisis; the Hungarian Crisis; the death of Stalin; the Twentieth Party Congress of the Communist Party; the escalation of the Cold War in South-East Asia; the MacCarthy witch hunts in America; the first broadcast of ITV in 1955; the first exhibition of the British Pop Artists in 1956; the importation to Britain of American rock'n'roll; the media invention of the teenager; the rise in immi-gration from Britain's rapidly decolonizing empire; the rise of con-sumer capitalism and the shift from production to consumption as the basis for dominant economic theories; the affluent society; class-lessness; the New Left; the birth of CND; the Angry Young Man; the

8   See in particular theories of postmodern or post-structuralist history by Robert Young, Michel Foucault and Hans Kellner amongst others: Robert Young, *White Mythologies: Writing History and the West* (London and New York: Routledge, 1990); Michel Foucault, 'Nietzsche, Genealogy, History', in *Language, Counter-Memory, Practice* (Oxford: Blackwell, 1977), pp.139–64; and Hans Kellner, *Language and Historical Representation* (Madison: University of Wisconsin Press, 1989). See also *The Postmodern History Reader*, ed. by Keith Jenkins (London and New York: Routledge, 1997).

9   This, he claims, is the objective of 'historicist' approaches as opposed to the methodology of 'historical materialists', Benjamin, 'Thesis on the Philiospohy of History'.

Beats, the existentialists and jazz.[10] This list is, of course, partial, arbitrary and evocative rather than a direct indicator of change. Nevertheless, within it we can see some of the fundamental shifts occurring in the fifties that had profound effects on English society.

In terms of the dominant interpretation of literary production, however, the 1950s are often seen as a rather dull period, resting, so the literary grand narrative goes, between the peaks of European modernism in the twenties and thirties and the later avant-garde and postmodern experiments of the sixties, seventies, eighties and nineties.[11] Bernard Bergonzi, for example, reads the fifties as a period of 'consolidation' in terms of literary production.[12] There appears to be an anomaly here: the interpretation of 1950s literature as dominated by a 'return' to conventional realistic modes and away from the experiments of a previous generation of writers would suggest that the novel, in particular, was somehow out of tune with the profound cultural changes taking place during the decade. It could be suggested that the literature produced in the period lagged behind the large socio-cultural changes identified above. I would argue, however, that this anomaly is produced by the dominant critical interpretations of the period, rather than by the supposedly modest ambitions of fifties writing. It is my purpose in this book, therefore, to offer a re-reading of the 1950s novel, a reading that is sensitive to the articulation in fictional forms of the socio-cultural changes experienced during the decade. This will produce an alternative reading of the literature of the period that shifts the focus of the English novel from the traditional litany of fifties novelists: Evelyn Waugh, Graham Greene, C.P. Snow, Angus Wilson, Iris Murdoch, Kingsley Amis, and John Wain to alter-

---

10   See Alan Sinfield, *Literature, Politics and Culture in Postwar Britain* (Oxford: Basil Blackwell, 1989).
11   David Lodge is probably the primary critic in the dissemination of this view of fifties literature. See his *Modes of Modern Writing: Metaphor, Metonymy and the Typology of Modern Literature* (London: Edward Arnold, 1977).
12   Bergonzi writes: 'In a broader sense, too, the fifties were a period of consoliation, as when a convalescent has to consolidate his resources until his strength returns.' Bernard Bergonzi, *Wartime and Aftermath: English Literature and its Background 1939–1960* (Oxford: Oxford UP, 1993), p.207.

native, marginalized or 'radical' texts and writers such as Alan Silli-toe, Colin MacInnes, Sam Selvon and Muriel Spark.[13]

The main contention of the book in terms of literary history is that the dominant critical reading of fifties English literature as anti-modernist, anti-experimental and representing a return to traditional or conventional realist forms is a distortion of the actual heterogeneous nature of the novel produced during this period. By addressing this (mis) representation by contemporaneous cultural commentators and later literary critics such as Bernard Bergonzi, Rubin Rabinovitz, David Lodge, Malcolm Bradbury and, to a certain extent, Steven Connor and Andrzej Gasiorek, I will argue that there is, in fact, an identifiable 'group' of novelists who rather than corresponding to this dominant interpretation of the 1950s novel, represent what I will call a 'radical' literature. This 'radical' literature is constituted in two ways: first, as experimentation with narrative techniques as a response to a perceived inadequacy of conventional realist modes either to record lived experience faithfully, or to articulate the concerns of margin-alized groups within Britain; and second, to use the novel to produce a politically committed writing that challenges dominant power struc-tures and dominant socio-cultural ideologies, and represents an alter-native oppositional site to that offered in the committed novel, in traditional Marxist theoretical discourses and in those developed by the New Left. Although the 'group' of writers I identify as 'radical' were not working together in an organized literary movement, they correspond in their expressive response to contemporary anxieties and concerns within fifties culture and society. Similarities between the novels they produce can be identified in terms of the narrative tech-niques they employ and their attempt to produce empowering dis-courses for marginalized groups. However, it is also the case that despite similarities in the strategic deployment of narrative technique, there are distinctions in the specific marginalized discourses that are produced in each of the novels discussed. I will stress, therefore, that

13   John Brannigan attempts a similar project in his book *Literature, Culture and Society in Postwar England, 1945–1965* (New York: Edwin Mellen Press, 2002). Brannigan's book covers some of the same fiction as this book, although his scope is broader both in terns of period and genre.

there is often a lack of correspondence between different marginalized positions in these texts across the various categories of class, 'race', gender and age.[14] Defining this literature as 'radical' does not necessarily mean that there are not instances of the texts reproducing, rather than challenging, some dominant identity-constructions and ideologies. The texts I analyze reveal a play of ideological positions that, dependent upon the category of analysis foregrounded, generate different degrees of radicalism.

In particular, I focus on fiction produced by six writers who were working in England during the period, and whose works problematize the traditional reading of the fifties novel as identified above. Two of these writers, Kingsley Amis and John Wain, are discussed largely as representative of a certain kind of social criticism prevalent in the early 1950s associated with the group of writers that came to be known as the Movement. The other four, Muriel Spark, Alan Sillitoe, Colin MacInnes and Sam Selvon are more radical both in terms of form and the social and cultural issues they address. Each of them has their own political and philosophical agendas, but together they produced novels that offered a challenge to dominant literary paradigms, both formally and ideologically. I have chosen to discuss these writers as representative of a particular 'radical' tendency in 1950s writing. Other writers of the period could also be included within this group for example Doris Lessing, Gerald Kersch, Alexander Trocchi, John Berger, Keith Waterhouse and Clancy Sigal, but I have decided to pay particular attention to Spark, Sillitoe, MacInnes and Selvon and because they allow a focus on the articulation of contemporary anxieties and issues in relation to issues of class, youth, 'race' and gender, whilst each of them, in their different ways, are experimenting with narrative techniques and the form of the novel.

---

14   The term 'race' as a biological category has been problematized over the past few years. Throughout this book, therefore, the term will be placed in quotation marks to signify an awareness of this. The term ethnicity is, on the whole, a more satisfactory term as it includes a sense of cultural as well as biological difference. However, 'race' as a term of differentiation was widespread in the 1950s and needs to be addressed in its historical context.

Radical Fictions

Before continuing, however, it is necessary to define in what sense the term radical is to be understood in the book. Definitions of radical in the *Oxford English Dictionary* include 'forming the root, basis, or foundation; original, primary'; 'going to the root or origin; touching or acting upon what is essential and fundamental'; 'radical reform'; and 'characterized by independence of, or departure from, what is usual or traditional; progressive, unorthodox, or revolutionary'.[15] As we can see the definitions range from the philosophical and the linguistic to the political.

'Radical', as a political concept, is indefinite and historically relative. It operates as a signifier that promotes and celebrates an over-throwing of dominant social, political, economic and cultural relation-ships of power, but in terms of an abstract set of political positions is indeterminate. It cannot be finally appropriated by the political left or right: Thatcher's right-wing government of the 1980s was as 'radical' as Clement Attlee's 1945 administration. However, in the context of the 1950s, 'radical' assumes a political designation (although remain-ing undefined) that signifies a left-wing bias identified across a range of often distinct political discourses and models such as communism, socialism, Marxism, anarchism and even nihilism; each of which claim their own level and style of radicalism. In this context, John Lucas has traced the word back to the early nineteenth century where it 'acquired the meaning of "left-wing, revolutionary,"' and this

---

15   *The Oxford English Dictionary*, second edition (Oxford: Clarendon Press, 1989), Vol. xiii, pp.91–93. John Lucas's book *Writing and Radicalism* also begins with a definition of 'radical' from the *OED*. He chooses to include the definition of radical as 'advocating thorough or far-reaching change; represent-ing or supporting an extreme section of a party'. John Lucas, *Writing and Radicalism* (London and New York: Longman, 1996), p.1. Jonathan Dollimore defines the term: 'radical in the sense of going to their [prevailing beliefs] roots and pulling them up'. *Radical Tragedy: Religion, Ideology and Power in the Drama of Shakespeare and his Contemporaries* (Hemel Hempstead: Harvester Wheatsheaf, 1984), p.xxi.

remained the dominant political understanding of the term in the 1950s.[16]

In terms of cultural and aesthetic production, 'radical' is often used as a descriptive term suggesting newness and originality that combines an aesthetic with a political and ideological meaning. For example, the blurb on the 1960 Pan paperback edition of *Saturday Night and Sunday Morning* foregrounded the 'radical' nature of the text: 'A novel of today with a freshness and raw fury that makes *Room at the Top* look like a vicarage tea-party'.[17] An excess of radicalism is presumed here: to go beyond the radicalism of a previous 'radical' text. This suggests that the *more* radical the text, the better, and this reveals the cultural climate in which the term needs to be understood. The actual political and ideological constitution of the term is often left undefined, but it operates as a signal of change, and of a critique of the established political and cultural mores. It assumes an indefinite, though broadly 'left-wing' position, whilst refusing to define that position clearly.

The second definition of radical to be used in this book is more specific and relates to its use by Alan Sinfield in his model of the 'dominant', 'subordinate' and 'radical' functions of specific aesthetic and cultural practices. In this model, adapted from Frank Parkin, Sinfield defines the 'radical' as a 'meaning-system' that 'promotes an oppositional interpretation of the social order [...] articulated, historically, through the politically aware sectors of both the working class and the middle class'.[18] In this sense, cultural production can function politically to challenge dominant 'meaning-systems'. This book will accept Sinfield's model of the function of 'radical' texts, but will also

16   Lucas, *Writing and Radicalism*, 1.
17   Alan Sillitoe, *Saturday Night and Sunday Morning* (London: Pan, 1960), front cover.
18   Sinfield, *Literature, Politics and Culture*, p.34. It is apparent that Sinfield's model owes something to Raymond Williams's model of cultural forms which the latter defines as 'dominant', 'residual' and 'emergent', although Sinfield politicizes Williams's historicized model of the ideological delineation of aesthetic creation. The Sinfield/Parkin model also stresses the power relationships between various kinds of cultural production. See also Raymond Williams *Problems in Materialism and Culture* (London: Verso, 1980), pp.37–45.

suggest that the system of negotiation between dominant, subordinate and radical is registered not only in class terms, but also in terms of age, ethnicity, nation and gender. This definition of 'radical' suggests, therefore, that specific texts can be identified as either supporting or reproducing the dominant ideologies in place in society (dominant); challenging specific inconsistencies within the dominant ideology (subordinate); or foregrounding fundamental problems and injustices in dominant ideologies (radical). Following Sinfield's model, I will read the narrative techniques and strategies deployed in selected novels *ideologically* in relation to the culture from which they are produced, and also against a contemporary ideological framework that gives political significance to specific literary forms.

However, Sinfield's model has its limitations. He assumes that the concept of the 'radical' represents a primarily leftist concept that challenges the power structures of the dominant. This, of course, relies upon a fixed definition of 'radical' that this book denies for the reasons outlined above. Secondly, it is possible to identify separate discourses within a single text, some of which could be described as radical, but some of which are involved in reproducing dominant ideologies. It is the possibility of this multiple ideological reading that is of central interest to the methodology of this book. For example, MacInnes's *Absolute Beginners* can be read as a text that offers a radical discourse in terms of the representation of youth and black subcultures in Britain in the 1950s, but also as reproducing dominant discourses with respect to class and gender.

In the context of fifties literary debate, the term 'radical' needs further qualifying. In the terms used so far, 'radical' has referred to a political or ideological concept, highlighting the content of the text, and the way it can question or challenge dominant power frameworks. But 'radical' in literary terms can also relate more specifically to formal techniques. This is the sense in which a writer such as Alain Robbe-Grillet was using the term in the 1950s: 'But the present-day art of the novel is greeted with such apathy – which is recorded and discussed by all critics – that one can hardly believe that this art can survive much longer without some radical change.'[19] Robbe-Grillet here calls for a 'radical' re-working of the *form* of the novel away from the inherited formal structures and techniques upon which 'literature' and the novel have previously depended. Of course, Robbe-Grillet's definition of radical as a primarily aesthetic/formal concept cannot be detached from its ideological implications, but it adds a further dimension to the fifties understanding of the term.[20]

The term 'radical fictions' then, as used in the title of this book, refer to texts that engage with the constructions, reproductions and negotiations of particular formations of identity and ideology that are prevalent in 1950s culture. Fiction represents a site for the dissemination of these ideologically informed discourses in a specific cultural form. Alan Sinfield suggests that cultural meanings, ideologies and identities are produced through the 'stories we tell ourselves', and this focus on the narrative structure of the formation and reproduction of ideologies and identities makes the fiction of the period an interesting and self-reflexive site in this process.[21] The fifties novel produces 'stories' that negotiate and reformulate personal and collective identities and ideologies that are themselves re-articulated by the readers of those novels. This produces a doubling effect. On the one hand, novels announce or proclaim the existence of specific identifiable cultures and practices within a recognized community or sub-community in the 'real' world; on the other hand, and simultaneously, they are involved in the (re-) formation and (re-) construction of those identities and ideologies.

One other term needs to be addressed before we continue and that is the 'English' in the title of this book. English can, of course, refer to either language, cultural identity, geographical location, or a distinct discipline within academia. Each of these categories can be seen to overlap, although at certain moments I may prefer one area to

19   Alain Robbe-Grillet, *Snapshots and Notes towards a New Novel*, trans. by Barbara Wright (London: Calder and Boyars, 1965), first published 1956, p.51.
20   In fact Robbe-Grillet's definition of the term suggests a linkage between experimental literary form and a revolutionary politics. I discuss this in greater detail in chapter five below.
21   Sinfield, *Literature, Politics and Culture*, pp.23–38.

another. However, this also necessitates a few brief comments on the nationality of writers covered in the second part of the book. In strict national terms perhaps only two of the writers discussed could be described unproblematically as English: Alan Sillitoe and John Wain. Kingsley Amis is strictly speaking Welsh, although he tended to see himself as part of an English literary tradition. Muriel Spark has a variety of cultural influences but in national terms is Scottish, while Colin MacInnes has English and Scottish parents and was brought up in Australia. Sam Selvon, likewise, has a mixed national and cultural background. Ethnically he has Scottish, Indian and Black Caribbean ancestors, and eventually took Canadian nationality after he settled there in 1978. This complex range of ethnic and national identity shows something of the cultural heterogeneity of the literature of the 1950s and this is somewhat eclipsed by the use of 'English' in the title of this book. However, 'English' was preferred as all of the writers were resident in England during most of the 1950s and nearly all of the novels they produced are set in England. There are times in the book, however, when 'Britain' and 'British' are deemed to be more appropriate. This is, in part, responding to the spirit of the use of these terms in the context of the 1950s, however, when any of these terms is used they should not be understood as referring to fixed categories of national identity. In fact, their very fluidity says something of the profound cultural changes that were taking place during the period.

Chapter Synopses

The book is divided into two parts, the first of which is concerned with interrogating the social, theoretical, aesthetic and ideological discourses informing 1950s writing in England. The second represents analyses of individual novelists. Each part is further sub-divided into chapters.

In chapter one, I argue that the 'radical' fiction of the period is produced at the intersection of three contemporary 'crises' in contemporary socio-cultural and literary-critical debate. The first of these 'crises' can be identified in the contemporary function and role of realism as a literary mode, foregrounded through debates on the 'death of the novel'. The crisis in the position of the novel as a form of expression will be read against, and shown to interconnect with, two other discourses of crisis in fifties socio-cultural theory: first, in constructions of English national identity; and second, in socialist and Marxist theoretical discourse. This chapter will provide several historical contexts informing 1950s writing and will form a basis on which the texts discussed in the rest of the book (literary, theoretical and political) will be read.

Chapter two explores the relationship between literary form and the (re-) production of ideological and political meaning in the context of 1950s literary and aesthetic theory. The chapter opens with a discussion of the theoretical relationship between literary form and ideological meaning, drawing on the work of Jacques Derrida, Roland Barthes and Catherine Belsey in this area. I go on to historicize this discussion of theory by focussing on the relevant debates in British literary studies in the 1950s. This analysis takes into account the influence of George Orwell and John-Paul Sartre with respect to the idea of commitment in fifties writing, and addresses the most important critics involved in this area during the period including Georg Lukàcs, Ian Watt and Raymond Williams.

Chapter three is concerned with an investigation of New Left writing of the period. The main contention of this chapter is that the British New Left, despite producing a re-assessment of Marxist methodology, tended to overlook the representation of emergent marginalized groups in fifties Britain. I argue that because the New Left retained class as a privileged category of analysis, there was consequently a gap in the identification of other radical discourses in terms of youth, ethnicity and gender. To support this claim, I analyze selected texts by New Left writers that reflect these issues.

The second part of the book discusses the issues raised in part one in relation to six writers working in Britain during the period. Chapter four discusses the novelists associated with 'The Movement' and in particular, offers readings of Kingsley Amis's *Lucky Jim* and John Wain's *Hurry On Down*. The chapter argues that these novels represent a 'literature of containment' in that they represent an aggrieved, but hardly radical attitude towards the class system inherited from the pre-war period. Chapter five will look at Muriel Spark's novels *The Comforters, Robinson,* and *The Ballad of Peckham Rye* with a particular emphasis on the experimental narrative techniques she uses, and how these relate to important social and cultural concerns informing the period. Chapter six offers a reading of Alan Sillitoe's fifties fiction that focuses on his experimental approach to realism in an ideological context, and problematizes the traditional reception of Sillitoe as a 'working-class' proponent of 'gritty realism'. Chapter seven explores Colin MacInnes's *City of Spades* and *Absolute Beginners,* foregrounding issues of identity in terms of youth subcultures, the nation and 'race'. Chapter eight discusses Sam Selvon's *The Lonely Londoners,* focusing on the use of experimental narrative and linguistic techniques deployed in the novel.

In each of these chapters I assess the critical response to the texts and writers discussed, and explore the concept of radicalism in relation to the texts, drawing on theoretical work by Walter Benjamin, Roland Barthes, Gilles Deleuze and Felix Guattari, Georges Bataille, Jean Baudrillard and Jacques Derrida. I identify the deployment of specific narrative techniques and strategies in each of the novels in relation to the dissemination of ideological meaning, both in a theoretical sense and in relation to specific and historicized understandings of the relationship between form and ideology in the fifties. I also draw on theories on the articulation of cultural identities in relation to class, youth subcultures, ethnicity, gender, the nation and postcolonial theory from a variety of writers including Raymond Williams, Stuart Hall, Dick Hebdige, Alan Sinfield, Steven Connor, Anthony Easthope, Paul Gilroy, Homi Bhabha and Timothy Brennan.

My aim in each of the chapters is to identify the methods and narrative techniques by which each writer attempts to articulate the way in which prevailing social and cultural codes appear to be changing during the 1950s. My approach broadly adheres to a form of cultural materialism, which assumes an attempt to read the novels as 'texts': texts that engage with the various debates and discourses informing the period in other kinds of writing. Having said this, I regard the close attention paid to the formal aspects of the fiction as itself a species of materialist criticism.

Part One

Chapter One
The Fifties Novel in Context

The Radical Fifties Novel

One of the main aims of this book is to challenge the dominant critical reading of fifties literature as representing a period in which there was a broad rejection of experimentalism and a return to realist modes as the 'traditional' form of the English novel. This (mis-) reading of the 1950s novel is a product of both critical discourses during the period and the dominant criticism from that period to the present. For example, Rubin Rabinovitz's 1967 book *The Reaction Against Experiment* gives a detailed record of this interpretation of the English novel, citing articles and books by Graham Hough, John Wain, C.P. Snow, Stephen Spender, G.S. Fraser, William Cooper, and Francis Wyndham.[1] Bernard Bergonzi sums up this position as a legacy of the Second World War: 'The slow recovery from the trauma of war was

---

1   Rubin Rabinovitz, *The Reaction Against Experiment in the English Novel, 1950–1960* (New York and London: Columbia UP, 1967). The books and articles cited here are: Graham Hough, *Reflections on a Literary Revolution* (Washington D.C.: The Catholic University of America Press, 1960); John Wain, 'The Conflict of Forms in Contemporary English Literature', in *Essays on Literature and Ideas* (London: Macmillan and Co, 1963), pp.1–55; C.P. Snow, *Public Affairs* (London: Macmillan, 1971), and various articles listed in Rabinovitz, *The Reaction Against Experiment*, pp.196–211; Stephen Spender, *The Struggle of the Modern* (London: Hamish Hamilton, 1963); G.S. Fraser, *The Modern Writer and His World* (London: Andre Deutsch, 1964), first published 1953; William Cooper, 'Reflections on Some Aspects of the English Novel', in *International Literary Annual*, No.2, ed. by John Wain, (London: John Calder, 1959), pp.29–36; Francis Wyndham, 'Twenty-five Years of the Novel', and Philip Toynbee, 'Experiment and the Future of the Novel', both in *The Craft of Letters in England*, ed. by John Lehmann (London: Cresset Press, 1956), pp.44–73.

accompanied by insular and formally conservative kinds of writing', suggesting that it was only 'by 1960 [that] what was called the re-action against experiment seemed to be coming to an end'.[2] The writers that are most often cited as representative of this return to realism are William Cooper, C.P. Snow, Kingsley Amis, John Wain, Doris Lessing, Iris Murdoch, Olivia Manning, Alan Sillitoe, John Braine and Keith Waterhouse.

More recent criticism has questioned this reading of the 1950s novel, but rarely rejects its basic assumptions. David Lodge regards the 1950s as a period in which there was a swing back towards what he calls 'metonymic' literature (which he equates to realism) and away from the 'metaphoric' (modernism), citing 'anti-modernism' as the dominant novelistic (and poetic) form of the decade.[3] In his *The English Novel in History 1950–1995*, Steven Connor acknowledges that a reading of the fifties novel as a 'simple retreat from modernism' is 'a good deal *too* rough and ready'. However, his reasons for this observation are to problematize the kind of realism produced in the 1950s rather than refute the fact that realism remained the dominant mode of the period. He writes:

> In returning to [...] the social realist ambitions of the nineteenth-century novel, certain aspects of the post-war novel are in fact furthering the debate carried on within the novel form throughout the twentieth century, as to its own in-adequacy to account for and answer to the disturbing social forces it took as its subject.[4]

For Connor, the construction of the 1950s novel as a return to 'social realist' forms remains un-refuted. In addition, Andrzej Gasiorek, al-though attempting to challenge this dominant reading of the fifties novel, actually succeeds in re-establishing it. He begins by suggesting that the postwar novel represents a negotiation between realism and

2   Bernard Bergonzi, *Wartime and Aftermath: English Literature and its Back-ground 1939–1960* (Oxford: Oxford UP, 1993), p.207.
3   David Lodge, *The Modes of Modern Writing: Metaphor, Metonymy and the Typology of Modern Literature* (London: Edward Arnold, 1977).
4   Steven Connor, *The English Novel in History 1950–1995* (London and New York: Routledge, 1996), p.45.

experiment, but by accepting the existence of two camps of writers, the realists C.P. Snow, Kingsley Amis and William Cooper, against the experimentalists B.S. Johnson, Christine Brooke-Rose and Eva Figes, it becomes apparent that the former group achieve prominence in the 1950s, whilst the latter group are more associated with the 1960s.[5] Gasiorek goes on to challenge the deployment of a binary opposition of realism and experimentalism, but his choice of texts to represent fifties writing tends to re-establish the dominant readings of the literary production of that decade.

The selection of writers these critics choose to discuss is also indicative. Lodge, to support his theory of a 'metonymic' swing to realism in the 1950s, cites the novels of Angus Wilson, C.P. Snow, Kingsley Amis, Anthony Powell, Alan Sillitoe and Margaret Drabble.[6] Connor, in fact, does not offer much discussion of the fifties novel, except for Angus Wilson's *Anglo-Saxon Attitudes* and Colin Mac-Innes's *Absolute Beginners*, and he reads both these novels as broadly realist texts. He makes passing references to Kingsley Amis (70–1), John Braine (95/136), Lawrence Durrell (138), Doris Lessing (138–9), Olivia Manning (138), Anthony Powell (137–9), Alan Sillitoe (95), C.P. Snow (138), Muriel Spark (85) and Evelyn Waugh (138), most of whom are, in his view, producing realist texts in the 1950s (the exceptions being Durrell and Spark). Connor, however, does make reference to Samuel Beckett's *Trilogy* in relation to the philosophical issue of 'endings', and the projection of writing and reference beyond the boundaries of the text. He also discusses William Golding at length, but concentrates on his 1980 novel *Rites of Passage*, making only passing reference to Golding's experimental 1950s work. Connor omits discussion of George Lamming, Samuel Selvon, V.S. Naipaul and other 1950s Caribbean writers despite his chapter on postcolonial British writing 'Outside In', which concentrates primarily on the fiction of the 1980s and 1990s. The overall tenor of Connor's book is again to position the 1950s novel as predominantly anti-experimental and anti-modernist. Gasiorek, unlike Connor, identifies the contribu-

---

5   Andrzej Gasiorek, *Post-War British Fiction: Realism and After* (London: Edward Arnold, 1995), pp.2–3.
6   Lodge, The Modes of Modern Writing, p.47.

tion of Caribbean writers to the fifties novel, especially Naipaul and Lamming, but his list of other writers from the 1950s is lacking in terms of experimental writing. He does not discuss Golding, Spark, Durrell, MacInnes, Selvon or Beckett, preferring to concentrate on the 'late modernism' of Ivy Compton-Burnett and Henry Green, and the realist texts of Doris Lessing, John Berger and Angus Wilson. Taken together these representative critics reinforce the reading of the 1950s novel as predominantly representing a return to realism and a move away from experimentalism.[7]

However, this dominant reading of the fifties novel distorts the actuality of the range of formal experiment practised by particular writers during the period. There was in fact an alternative 'group' of novelists writing in the 1950s and early 1960s who were experimenting with the form of the novel, rather than unproblematically returning to earlier modes of realism.[8] In this category I would place Colin MacInnes, Samuel Selvon, Philip Toynbee, Iris Murdoch, Lawrence Durrell, Gerald Kersch, William Golding, Muriel Spark, Alexander Trocchi, George Lamming, and of course Samuel Beckett, who, because his novels in English are translated from the French, has been regarded primarily as a continental writer.[9] In this loose grouping of 'experimentalists' I would also argue that two authors traditionally perceived to be working in a realist aesthetic should be re-assessed as experimental writers: Doris Lessing, in her later fifties work, and Alan Sillitoe. Together, these novelists represent an alternative body of fiction that I define as 'radical' in terms of experimentation with liter-

---

7   The main dissenting voice from this approach in recent criticism is John Brannigan, *Literature, Culture and Society in Postwar England, 1945–1965* (New York: Edwin Mellen Press, 2002).

8   By referring to this range of authors as a 'group' I am not suggesting that there was a conscious collective of writers who stood in opposition to the 'contemporaries', rather that when analyzed individually certain corresponding characteristics in terms of formal experiment can be identified which link these novelists together.

9   Beckett's position as a continental writer in the fifties is, in part, produced by the dominant reading of the English novel as realist. Beckett's status as an Irish writer further complicates his position in relation to the 'English' novel of the period.

ary form. In this sense, it embraces modernist experimentation, but with a tangible difference to the 'residual' or 'late' modernism of Malcolm Lowry, Elizabeth Bowen, Ivy Compton-Burnett and Henry Green. Rather, it anticipates more conscious experimentation in the novel in the 1960s by writers such as B.S. Johnson, Christine Brooke-Rose, Eva Figes, John Fowles and Angela Carter.

It is necessary to stress, however, that within this group of experimental fifties writers there are distinctions in terms of the definition of 'radical' as defined in the introduction of this book. Although all these authors produce works that experiment with realist modes to varying degrees, not all of them combine that formal experimentation with a radical political content. For example, although Spark, Murdoch, Durrell, Golding and Toynbee are experimental in terms of literary form, they are less concerned to deploy narrative techniques strategically as part of a political or ideological project. This does not mean that their texts remain 'above' or 'outside' of ideology, rather that they are not specifically concerned with this function of narrative technique. However, their texts still reveal some of the ideological and cultural preoccupations and anxieties of fifties Britain. For example, both Muriel Spark and William Golding produce texts that articulate the break-up of traditional constructions of Englishness through encounters with marginalized voices and perspectives.[10] We shall also see in chapter five how Spark's experimental approach to writing produces a form of ideological radicalism that emerges through her use of narrative strategies and techniques.

Throughout the book I will make reference to several specific contexts during the period that inform and engage directly with the 'radical' novels and writers I have identified. In this chapter, I identify three inter-related 'crises' that help to contextualize the fiction produced during the period. Firstly, I identify a discourse of crisis in the status and function of the novel. Secondly, I discuss the perceived crisis in Britain's 'traditional' role as a dominant world power, and as a cultural and literary centre articulated through a re-assessment of the

---

10   I discuss these writers in this context in the next section.

construction of English national identity.[11] Thirdly, I examine the status and character of left-wing radical theory and discourse in the fifties often articulated in terms of a 'crisis' in communism, socialism and theoretical Marxism. Furthermore, I will show how these three crises interact, and find articulation in the radical novel of the period.

Crisis One: The End of the Novel

At the end of the first chapter of book five of Graham Greene's *The End of the Affair*, occurring about three-quarters of the way through the novel, Bendrix, the novelist-narrator of the text, writes:

> If I were writing a novel I would end it here: a novel I used to think, has to end somewhere, but I'm beginning to believe my realism has been at fault all these years, for nothing in life now ever seems to end.[12]

This moment in Greene's text operates in various ways. Firstly, it produces what Roland Barthes calls the 'reality effect' of realism through focusing on the difference between the way novels represent and order experience and the way 'real' life resists closure in any neat and ordered sense.[13] By foregrounding what happens in 'novels', Greene's text suggests to the projected reader that what they are reading stands outside, or above, the form of an 'ordinary' novel; it masks its own status as a fictional construct by alluding to some other form of writing that it pretends not to be. This narratological device is one method by which the novel produces its *vraisemblable* as Roland Barthes puts it.

11 As suggested in the introduction to this book, I am aware of the problems of associated with the terms 'England/English' and 'Britain/British', however, the often interchangeable nature of these terms in the fifties reflects the very crisis in national identity informing the period.
12 Graham Greene, *The End of the Affair* (London: Heineman, 1951).
13 Roland Barthes, *The Rustle of Language* (London: Blackwell, 1986) first published 1967, pp.141–8.

Secondly, the passage also alludes to contemporary discourses outside the text: in particular to the failure of realism to represent reality faithfully: 'my realism seems to have been at fault all these years'. Greene's problem with realism in this novel is that, as a literary form, it is equated with a rational and empirical understanding and interpretation of the world, which is seen to be inadequate to explain the 'supernatural' elements of the novel that are incorporated into Greene's treatment of Catholic faith.[14] Written in 1951, it also repeats a fifties trope in literary and cultural criticism concerning the 'end' or 'death' of the novel, and in particular the problems inherent in the assumptions and the claims made by 'conventional' realism. That realism represents a cultural expression of a philosophy of English empiricism has been identified by several critics[15], and I would argue that the rise of the trope of 'crisis' in the novel is intricately linked with a crisis in empiricism and rationalism, and which engages with other contemporaneous 'crises' in national identity and in Marxist and socialist models of history and representation.

Bernard Bergonzi has identified the emergence of a generation of literary critics concerned to identify a 'death of the novel' phenomenon in the late forties and fifties in Anglo-American criticism.[16] He cites examples of this position by Lionel Trilling, Ortega y Gasset, Alberto Moravia, Cyril Connolly and George Steiner.[17] Bergonzi refutes the extreme nature of this discourse but he does identify a particular resistance to experimentalism in English fiction:

14   This expression of Catholic faith through the disruption of conventional realism in the novel is also identified in Muriel Spark's fifties novels The Comforters (London: Macmillan, 1957), and Memento Mori (Harmondsworth: Penguin, 1961), first published 1959. The narratological expression of Catholic faith as an essentially irrational and non-empirical discourse links to the other crises identified in this book, but is beyond the scope of my main set of criteria.

15   For example, Catherine Belsey, *Critical Practice* (London and New York: Routledge, 1980); and Anthony Easthope, *Englishness and National Culture* (London and New York: Routledge, 1999).

16   Bernard Bergonzi, 'The Novel No Longer', in *The Situation of the Novel* (London: Macmillan, 1970), pp.11–34.

17   Ibid., pp.13–15.

Recent fiction is, indeed, about life, but scarcely about life in a wholly un-
conditioned way; the movement towards the genre [realism] means that experience is mediated through existing literary patterns and types. This movement is
particularly strong in English fiction; the French and many Americans may still
feel impelled to strive for novelty, but the English [...] seem to have settled for
the predictable pleasures of generic fiction. (20)

Bergonzi's reading here dilutes the 'end of the novel' discourse to
a certain extent but maintains a linear structure to literary history
through his reading of English fiction of the postwar period broadly
representing a return to older (realist) forms. It is significant that
Bergonzi, like many of the critics he discusses, implicitly assumes that
the 'novel' equates more or less with the specific form of realism, and
I would argue that the 'death of the novel' trope is more precisely
understood during the period as a death of the *realist* novel.[18]

This 'death of the novel' discourse is produced in relation to two
factors. Firstly, because of the technical innovations produced by the
experimental novel of the twenties and thirties it was suggested that
by 1950 the novel had reached an end point in terms of development.
Secondly, the arrival of other art forms, such as film and television
was perceived to have taken over the role of the realist novel to present the reader with information about everyday life in a linear form.
John Wain's essay 'The Conflict of Forms in Contemporary English
Literature', published in 1963, is a good example of both these positions.[19] In terms of the limits of experimentalism, he writes: 'the
experimental novel died with Joyce' (52). He goes on to argue that
because of the rise of radio, film and television the novel had lost its
primary function of providing documentary information to a widespread public, leaving its contemporary function as more directly
aesthetic rather than 'public': 'the novel, once its documentary under-
pinning has been kicked away, crumbles into a score of minor forms'

---

18   Gasiorek also identifies this tendency in the 'death of the novel' theories of the
      postwar period. He also suggests that the implicit linkage is produced through a
      discourse of liberal humanism; Gasiorek, *Post-War British Fiction*, pp.6–9.
19   John Wain, 'The Conflict of Forms', pp.1–55. In chapter four below, however,
      we shall see that Wain's comments on the death of experimentalism are not
      always supported in his own fiction.

(39). He concludes by stressing that the novel's 'essential development was over' (51).

Wain's argument, however (and the 'end of the novel' thesis in general) is based on two problematic assumptions. First, it assumes a linear progression of literary history, which suggests that certain literary forms rise to prominence and then retreat as a response to specific socio-cultural conditions pertaining at particular periods. This assumption is strongly held in Marxist criticism, but can also be identified behind Ian Watt's influential fifties theory and analysis of the novel.[20] Second, the 'death of the novel' thesis is implicitly based on a structure of binary opposition between 'realist' and 'experimental' writing, which assumes that the novel has to be one or the other, and that once the experimental element of the novel has been exhausted, and the realist element has been superseded by new media, then the novel no longer has scope to develop and loses its centrality as a popular cultural form. Both of these positions deny the possibility of a pluralistic model of development of the novel, by which it can continue to develop *alongside*, rather than in direct opposition to, other cultural forms. The 1950s *radical* novel is concerned to challenge these assumptions by rejecting a binary model of realism and experimentalism, and also by engaging with other contemporary cultural forms.

It is significant that the discourse that identifies crisis in the (realist) novel occurs contemporaneously with the 'crises' in English national identity and traditional forms of Marxist and socialist theory. This can be identified in the parallel structural assumptions that underpin realism, narratives of the nation and Marxist theoretical models of history and cultural production. Many post-structuralist theorists have identified specific problems with what they define as 'classic' realism and its affinity with both English empiricism and Marxist discourse.[21]

---

20   See Ian Watt, *The Rise of the Novel: Studies in Defoe, Fielding and Richardson* (London: Hogarth Press, 1987), first published 1957. See the discussion of Watt in chapter two below.

21   For example see Belsey, *Critical Practice*; Colin MacCabe, *James Joyce and the Revolution of the Word* (London: Macmillan, 1979); and Stephen Heath, *The Nouveau Roman: A Study in the Practice of Writing* (London: Elek, 1972).

However, as Andrzej Gasiorek argues, the association of realism with (English) bourgeois liberal humanism is maintained in post-structuralist models of the realist novel. Gasiorek provides a list of criteria by which post-structuralist critics have identified the structural assumptions of 'classic' realism:

> a view of language as a transparent tool through which to view an external world; reliance on a reflectionist aesthetic; a concept of (relatively) stable character; reliance on a universalizing metalanguage that establishes a 'hierarchy of discourse' and produces the 'social' as the 'natural'; closure.[22]

He goes on to stress that the critique of realism developed by these critics 'rests on thoroughly conventionalist assumptions' (ibid.). The fifties radical novel was beginning to deconstruct both the formal assumptions of realism and its reliance on 'language as a transparent tool', and the ideological frameworks that underpinned it.

Crisis Two: The (Grand) Narrative of Englishness

One of the important historical contexts informing 1950s English society, politics and culture is that of the changing construction of national identity. As Seamus Heaney has argued, the postwar period constitutes a time of self-reflection on the construction and constitution of Englishness, and although Heaney is primarily concerned with poetry (in particular Larkin, Hill and Hughes), his observations also apply to the novel.[23] Many fifties novels reveal a deep concern with the nation's changing identity, its international status and role, and the reconstruction of Englishness. This response is precipitated by various socio-cultural factors such as the end of empire, signalled most visibly by Indian independence in 1947; the continuing process

---

22 Gasiorek, *Post-War British Fiction*, p.9.
23 Seamus Heaney, 'Englands of the Mind', in *Preoccupations: Selected Prose 1968–1978* (London and Boston: Faber & Faber, 1980), pp.150–69.

of decolonization in the 1950s; the arrival of immigrant communities in Britain from the colonized and newly decolonized states; and the influence of American popular culture in Britain, perceived as a form of cultural colonization by some, but utilized by others as a challenge to traditional constructions of Englishness. Anthony Easthope's intention to undertake a 'post-colonial study of Englishness' proves fruitful in this context, especially in relation to a period in which many of the factors that have produced contemporary re-assessments of English national identity were beginning to emerge during this time, such as the pluralization of national identity in terms of ethnicity, the re-assessment of Englishness in relation to class, and the promotion of a multicultural model of the nation.[24]

The Suez Crisis of 1956 represented an emblematic episode in this reconstruction of English national identity. The failed attempt by Anthony Eden's government to resist Colonel Nasser's nationalization of the Suez Canal became a powerful symbol of Britain's diminished status as a world power in the postwar and postcolonial world. This international political crisis revealed to the public, and to the government, that Britain was no longer in a position to enforce its colonial power militarily over wayward and potentially revolutionary colonial states. The isolation of Britain and France, emphasized by the lack of support given by the United States to the Anglo-French military venture the crisis precipitated, also indicated that the age of British (and French) imperialism was coming to an end. Decolonization of the Empire evoked a sense of existential crisis in national terms as Britain's status as a major international power was undermined. As Michael Kenny argues:

> The failed Anglo-French military expedition to the Suez Canal encouraged the realisation that Britain's position in the world was fundamentally different in the post-war world; and that with the relinquishing of formal imperial responsibilities, a new national identity and self-image had yet to be forged.[25]

---

24   Anthony Easthope, *Englishness and National Culture*, p.4.
25   Michael Kenny, *The First New Left: British Intellectuals After Stalin* (London: Lawrence and Wishart, 1995), p.5.

The impact of decolonization and the immigration of black and Asian communities into the colonial 'centre' had a profound effect on the construction of English national identity. The 1950s and early 1960s was the period in which both decolonization and immigration into Britain from the colonies and ex-colonies reached its height. In England, this was evidenced first-hand with mass immigration. Between 1951 and 1961, the Caribbean population residing in England rose from 17,218 to 173,659, most of whom came from Jamaica, the highest immigration levels being reached between 1955 and 1962.[26] Immigration was not only for economic purposes but also extended to social and familial links, a process called 'chain migration'.[27] Sam Selvon represents this process well in *The Lonely Londoners*. In one scene, Tolroy (one of the black characters of the novel who is resident in London), expects to meet his mother on the boat train from Jamaica, but discovers that it is not only his mother who has made the journey to England, his Aunt Bessie, his brother Lewis, the latter's wife Agnes, and their two children have accompanied her: representing three generations of the same family.[28] This 'chain migration' meant that most of the immigrants were not 'sojourners', but were part of a larger, diasporic, cultural process by which familial and social communities were established in Britain.

This establishment of black and Asian communities gave sections of the white English population direct experience of other ethnic peoples and cultures for the first time. This process therefore replayed historic colonial encounters and power relationships in the colonial 'centre' rather than on colonized territory, and this had a profound effect on the nature of Englishness. As Jean-Paul Sartre has argued, the effects of decolonization and migration to the colonial 'centre' can be identified in both individuals and the nation in terms of the disruption and fragmentation of previously fixed models of identity:

26   Margaret Byron, *Post-War Caribbean Migration to Britain: The Unfinished Cycle* (Aldershot: Avebury, 1994), p.78.
27   J.S. MacDonald and L.D. MacDonald, 'Chain Migration: Ethnic Neighbourhood Formations and Social Networks', in *Millbank Memorial Fund Quarterly*, No.42, 1964, pp.82–97.
28   Sam Selvon, *The Lonely Londoners* (Harlow: Longman, 1985), first published in 1956, pp.29–30.

Let us look at ourselves, if we can bear to, and see what is becoming of us. First, we must face that unexpected revelation, the strip-tease of our humanism. There you can see it, quite naked, and it's not a pretty sight. It was nothing but an ideology of lies, a perfect justification for pillage; its honeyed words, its affectation of sensibility were only alibis for our aggressions [...] Today violence, blocked everywhere, comes back to us through our soldiers, comes inside and takes possession of us. Involution starts; the native recreates himself, and we, settlers and Europeans, ultras and liberals, we break up.[29]

Sartre identifies the break up of empire as a direct threat to European consciousness, a consciousness that had traditionally been constructed as stable, integrated, centred on the individual and supported by a philosophy of liberal humanism. However, through the processes of decolonization, the (white Western) individual had to re-assess his/her identity in relation to racial and national distinctions and definitions. The importation of other ethnicities into England promoted a disruption of national and individual constructions of identity, which was re-engaged in the heart of the colonizing country. As R.F. Holland argues, decolonization affected the colonial metropolis as much as it did the previously colonized periphery.[30]

This factor produces a transition in the type of racism practised in Britain in the 1950s, represented by a move from a crude biological racism, supported mainly by those who have never come into contact with other 'races', to a 'cultural' racism that foregrounds cultural practices as the scene of difference. As Paul Gilroy argues, the style and nature of the politics of racial encounters is specific to particular events and locations.[31] The violent clashes between white and black groups in Britain in 1958, (in Nottingham in August, and Notting Hill in September), represented a new kind of social unrest in England: away from class and towards racial conflict. The *Universities and Left Review*, in particular, identified this problem and responded with a special section on the relations between white youth and black sub-

---

29   Jean-Paul Sartre, 'Preface' to Frantz Fanon's *The Wretched of the Earth*, trans. by Constance Farrington (Harmondsworth: Penguin, 1967), first published in French, 1961, pp.21–3.

30   R.F. Holland, *European Decolonization 1918–1981: An Introductory Survey* (London: Macmillan, 1985), p.191.

31   Paul Gilroy, *Small Acts* (London: Serpent's Tale, 1993), p.22.

cultures in London.[32] The events in Nottingham and Notting Hill largely represented indiscriminate attacks by white youths on black individuals, but the construction in the media of these events as 'race' riots helped to fuse a specific construction of black and Asian identity. This construction of racial identity was subsequently used by the right in Britain to support their argument for a Commonwealth Immigration Act, eventually implemented in 1962, which restricted immigration rights to Britain from the colonies.[33] This policy depended on artificially constructed images of racial identity. In particular, as Paul Gilroy has argued, the black immigrant to Britain had a constructed identity that revolved around images of criminality and sexual promiscuity, identified in cultural anxieties concerning prostitution and miscegenation.[34]

Mass immigration and the presence of a black 'other' in the colonial centre acted as a constant reminder to the white population of England's colonial heritage. This had two effects. Firstly, it reminded England of her colonial victories of the past and the extent and power of the British Empire in the nineteenth century and postwar period. It did this just at the moment when the empire was seen to be fragmenting and dissolving. The presence of black individuals in Britain, therefore, acted as a reminder to the dominant culture of the loss of power and prestige in the postwar world. Secondly, it re-projected the guilt of colonial aggression and exploitation by the colonizing nation back onto the white population of that nation. The presence of a black population in Britain represented a return of repressed guilt for past colonial aggression. The impact of a black presence, therefore, worked in a dual way and produced differing reactions. On the one hand, there was the beginning of an acknowledgement of England's

32   See *Universities and Left Review*, No.5, Autumn 1958. I discuss these texts in greater detail in chapter three below
33   See Ann Dummett and Andrew Nicol, *Subjects, Citizens, Aliens and Others: Nationality and Immigration Law* (London: Weidenfeld and Nicolson, 1990), especially chapter ten: 'Secrecy and Discretion'.
34   See Paul Gilroy, *There Ain't No Black in the Union Jack: The Cultural Politics of Race and Nation* (London: Hutchinson 1987), pp.79–85. Also, see Colin MacInnes's parody of a typical newspaper article on the immigration 'problem' in *Absolute Beginners*, and my discussion of this in chapter five of this book.

postcolonial status and an attempt to re-construct national identity in relation to the impact of the colonial legacy. On the other hand, there was a continuing rejection of responsibility of guilt for colonization manifest in a return to traditional myths of 'Englishness' and the recuperation of 'authentic' English cultural practices. Examples of this ambiguous relationship with the colonial legacy can be seen in a literary context in the Movement writers' reclamation of traditional forms of English writing in poetry and the novel, and in the New Left's recuperation and celebration of traditional British working-class culture.[35]

The re-assessment of English national identity in fifties culture is revealed in much of the fiction of the period. This is articulated in the novel through a negotiation of literary forms and narrative techniques that reveal and engage with discourses of the nation. Following Benedict Anderson's definition of nations as 'imaginary communities', Paul Gilroy describes the complex construction of discourses of the nation:

> Their existence and continuity cannot simply be assumed. They are not spontaneously formed and although they sometimes appear to us as if they are natural or eternal associations, they have been constructed through elaborate cultural, ideological and political processes which culminate in the feeling of connectedness to other national subjects and in the idea of a national interest that transcends the supposedly petty divisions of class, religion, dialect or caste.[36]

According to Gilroy, constructions of national identity are produced in relation to other discourses and categories including 'race', class and gender that are negotiated in the recurrent (post)colonial encounters of a multicultural society. The construction of 'Englishness', therefore, remains 'fluid, changing, unstable and dynamic' (24), and is repeatedly re-constructed in the cultural production of both dominant and marginalized sites.

The re-construction of national identity in the fifties novel, therefore, interconnects with discourses around decolonization. Alan

35   I discuss these issues in greater detail in chapters two and three below.
36   Gilroy, *Small Acts*, p.49.

Sinfield has made a direct connection between decolonization and the crisis in literary studies in the 1950s. He argues that members of the ruling establishment and the main literary radicals at the end of the war both came from the same (upper-middle) class, and often the same families. Decolonization, therefore, was a threat to both traditions, that of empire, and of the 'great tradition' of English literature.[37] In *England Your England*, George Orwell argued that empire had involved: 'two important sub-sections of the middle class. One was the military and imperialist middle class [...] and the other the left-wing intelligentsia.'[38] In the 1950s, this process was articulated in the general conservative nature of the established literary scene. Sinfield writes: 'So writers continuing the main literary tradition [...] tended to associate decolonization with the threat to the leisured class and hence to "civilization".'[39] Sinfield is concerned to identify the socio-cultural correspondences within England's dominant class; however, this can also be seen in the experimentation with literary form in the fifties as an expression of the disruption of dominant ideologies.

Timothy Brennan develops this point when he identifies the novel as a powerful textual site for the construction of national identity.[40] He writes:

> It was the novel that historically accompanied the rise of nations by objectifying the "one, yet many" of national life, and by mimicking the structure of the nation, a clearly bordered jumble of languages and styles [...] Its manner of presentation allowed people to imagine the special community that was the nation. (49)

Although Brennan is particularly interested in the parallel rise of the novel and the modern nation state, his persuasive argument on the

---

37   Alan Sinfield, *Literature, Politics and Culture in Postwar Britain* (Oxford: Oxford UP, 1989), p.116.
38   George Orwell, 'England Your England', in *England Your England* (London: Secker and Warburg, 1953), pp.192–224, first published in 1941.
39   Sinfield, *Literature, Politics and Culture*, p.116.
40   Timothy Brennan, 'The National Longing for Form', in *Nation and Narration*, ed. by Homi K. Bhabha (London and New York: Routledge, 1990), pp.44–70.

linkage between the novel form and the public conception of the nation can also be applied to the effects on the national psyche of the process of decolonization and loss of national prestige. Homi Bhabha goes further by defining the connection between narrative form and national identity in the similar assumptions and structural models utilized by realism and a (grand) narrative of national identity. Bhabha writes: 'Such a form of temporality produces a symbolic structure of the nation as "imagined community" which, in keeping with the scale and diversity of the modern nation, works like the plot of a realist novel.'[41] If the realist novel represents the ideal literary expression of the nation, then formal experimentalism can be said to function ideologically as a disruption of that narrative of the nation. Therefore, literary form articulates the symbolic production of the nation, and experimental narrative techniques can produce contesting models of national identity.

This is supported in the fifties because of the presence of a sustained discourse by literary commentators such as Philip Larkin and William Cooper that links conventional realism and anti-experimentalism to a traditional construction of national (English) culture.[42] In the context of the 1950s, experimental writing represents an ideological and political gesture that engages with the construction of the nation. Experimental writing is conceived not only as a challenge to dominant literary forms, but ideologically as a radical strategy to challenge dominant constructions of Englishness. In addition, the return to realism represented by the Movement writers and the Angry Young Men is a way of articulating a nostalgic desire for a return to the certainties and fixed identities of traditional constructions of Englishness. Conversely, as Bhabha's argument suggests, experiment with realist

41   Homi K. Bhabha, 'DissemiNation: Time, Narrative, and the Margins of the Modern Nation', in Bhabha, *Nation and Narration*, pp.291–322, (p.308).
42   Robert Conquest, 'Introduction', to *New Lines* (London: Macmillan & Co., 1957); Philip Larkin, 'Interview' (1964) in *Twentieth Century Poetry*, ed. by Graham Martin and P.N. Furbank (Milton Keynes: Open University Press, 1975), pp.243–54; William Cooper, 'Reflections on Some Aspects of the Experimental Novel', in *International Literary Review*, No.2, ed. by John Wain (London: John Calder, 1959), pp.29–36. See also Easthope, 1999, pp.153–99.

modes suggests an anxiety with, and a re-negotiation of, dominant constructions of Englishness.[43]

The re-analysis of Englishness through experimental writing can be identified in many of the novels produced during the fifties. In addition to the writers discussed in the second part of this book, several novels of the period implicitly reflect the impact of decolonization on the national imagination. For example, William Golding's mid-fifties novels implicitly involve themes that re-assess traditional assumptions about Englishness in relation to encounters with an 'other'. The most obvious is *Lord of the Flies*, which parodies Ballantyne's colonial text *The Coral Island*.[44] The degeneration of the moral and ethical codes of the group of English school children marooned on a desert island reverses the traditional colonial narratives of British fortitude, courage, moral bravery and explicit superiority when encountering other 'races' and regions. It thereby reverses the colonial ideology of texts such as *Robinson Crusoe* by foregrounding the collapse of the ethical status and centrality of 'Englishness'. The arrival of the naval officer at the end of Golding's novel reinforces this ethical demise in national terms when he tells the marooned children: "'I should have thought that a pack of British boys – you're all British aren't you? – would have been able to put up a better show than that".'[45] Also, in Golding's *The Inheritors*, an experimental novel that attempts to represent the experience of the evolutionary progression of Neanderthal to Cro-Magnon 'man', the decision to foreground the perspective of the text on the former and to construct homo sapiens as a morally inferior species can be read historically as a text that displaces the crisis in confidence in the moral superiority of Englishness and the racial condescension implicit therein.[46] Golding's technique of foregrounding the perspective of the 'other' in terms of species is also related to contemporary cultural concerns about national loss of power and the

43   I discuss the relationship between the Movement, the Angry Young Men, and the construction of national identity in chapter four below.

44   William Golding, *The Lord of the Flies* (London: Faber & Faber, 1954).

45   Ibid., p.222.

46   William Golding, *The Inheritors* (London: Faber & Faber 1955).

increasing breakdown of the perception of England as a superior nation.[47]

In Muriel Spark's *Memento Mori*, the mysterious telephone calls to the various aged characters of the novel, which remind them of their impending death, are significantly voiced in terms of several 'others' to the traditional white, middle-class, male, adult construction of dominant Englishness.[48] Although I agree with Peter Kemp's reading of the novel that these voices represent multiple manifestations of 'Death' as a supernatural being, it is significant, in the context of the 1950s, that the 'otherness' of Death is represented, partly ironically, by marginalized others who would be recognized as central to debates on the decline of traditional constructions of the nation.[49] The voice of 'Death', therefore, which also represents the 'death' of the nation, is introduced variously as 'a common man', a 'Teddy boy', a 'foreigner', and a 'woman', representing the very marginalized groups that were perceived to be threatening the traditional construction of the nation.[50]

Angus Wilson's *Anglo-Saxon Attitudes* offers an exploration of contemporary Englishness through its presentation of a wide range of characters from different classes and backgrounds that combine the academic and commercial worlds.[51] At the heart of this novel, though, is an elaborate hoax that symbolically disrupts the certainties upon which the narrative of the nation rests. The main protagonist, the history professor Gerald Middleton, becomes increasingly aware that a major understanding of the accepted academic religious history of the British Isles has been founded upon a student prank undertaken by the son of his now dead mentor Professor Lionel Stokesay. On an

---

47   This discourse of the 'other' in evolutionary terms raises issues around the perception of black and Asian individuals. Golding's focus on the evolutionary 'other' reveals implicit anxieties and stereotypical racial discourses still dominant in fifties Britain.

48   Muriel Spark, *Memento Mori* (Harmondsworth: Penguin, 1961), first published by Macmillan in 1959.

49   Peter Kemp, *Muriel Spark* (London: Peter Elek, 1974), pp.38–48.

50   Spark, *Memento Mori*, pp.148–9, (p.153).

51   Angus Wilson, *Anglo-Saxon Attitudes* (Harmondsworth: Penguin, 1958) first published 1956.

archeological dig in the years before the First World War, on which his father has built his reputation, Gilbert Stokesay had planted a pagan fertility symbol in the grave of a seventh-century Christian bishop. Gilbert dies in the war and his secret is only revealed to Gerald through reading his letters. This plot line provides the central moral dilemma of the novel, but it is also revealing in the context of 1950s anxieties concerning Englishness. Just as the official religious history of the nation is seen to be based on a falsehood, so the grand narrative of Englishness is itself suspected of being arbitrary and fragile rather than established upon a fixed set of characteristics.

What each of these novels reveals is a concern with national identity, and those concerns are displaced imaginatively onto discourses of transition, evolution, fragility and death. This can be viewed allegorically in terms of the evolution of Englishness into a different form, and the inevitable death of a moribund image of the nation.

The link between the novel and the construction of national identity raises questions concerning the method by which cultural production and meaning in a literary text function as signifiers of the nation. One primary site of engagement between national identity and the novel is, of course, language. The linguistic style deployed in a text can comment directly or indirectly upon the status of the nation. Thus, as Ashcroft, Griffiths and Tiffin argue, the crucial function of language as a medium of power demands that postcolonial writing define itself by seizing the centre and re-placing it with a discourse fully adapted to the colonized space.[52] Experimentation with 'Standard' English, therefore, has ideological as well as formal significance and several novels of the period use this technical device as part of their ideological perspective. Because literature is a privileged site in Britain in the fifties, and one in which the English language is reproduced, it is also a site upon which the ideological function of English culture in relation to power structures and hegemony is re-negotiated.

---

52   Bill Ashcroft, Gareth Griffiths and Helen Tiffin, *The Empire Writes Back* (London and New York: Routledge, 1989), pp.38–77.

Therefore, experimentation with Standard English represents a strategy of empowerment for marginalized voices and discourses.[53]

However, it is important to identify the problems associated with representing the marginalized 'other' in the novel, a genre that has traditionally been perceived as a Western middle-class literary form.[54] 'Literature' and the 'serious' novel occupy privileged textual sites in Western cultures, probably more so in Britain in the fifties than today. Because of this privileged position the possibility of representing marginalized voices becomes problematic. Gayatri Spivak, for example, asks, 'Can the Subaltern Speak?', referring to the 'subaltern' in terms of class, ethnicity and gender.[55] Her provocative and challenging question refers to the possibility of marginalized voices being able to represent themselves in textual forms that are concerned in maintaining – politically, philosophically, structurally and ideologically – the dominant power structures. Fundamentally, she questions the possibility of producing a subaltern discourse in *literary* writing. To take the question further: assuming that the subaltern has at least the potential to 'speak' textually, what form of writing, and what specific narrative techniques and strategies, would make that expression possible?

As Andrew Gibson has argued, first-person narratives (which predominate in fifties radical fiction) are particularly conducive to the ideological function of allowing marginalized voices to speak directly

---

53   In the second part of this book I discuss the way in which the manipulation of Standard English produces ideological and political significance in the novels of MacInnes and Selvon.

54   See Ian Watt, *The Rise of the Novel*. See also Terry Lovell's critical analysis of Watt's theory: 'Capitalism and the Novel', in *Consuming Fiction* (London: Verso, 1987), pp.19–45. I discuss this in greater detail in chapter two below.

55   Gayatri Chakravorty Spivak, 'Can the Subaltern Speak?', in *Marxism and the Interpretation of Culture*, ed. by Cary Nelson and Lawrence Grossberg (Houndmills and London: Macmillan Education, 1988), pp.271–313. Although specifically concerned with the marginalized categories of class, gender and 'race', Spivak's question is also significant in relation to youth subcultures in a patriarchal society.

and openly in a textual form.[56] Following Levinas's ethics of alterity, Gibson writes:

> There is a radical distinctness [...] to the mode of narration that Genette called extradiegetic-homodiegetic [...] The narrator is also an experiencer. He or she is engaged, involved in the world narrated. Thus narration as reflection appears to supervene upon pre-reflective experience. The ethics of narrator-character or focalized narration thus entails a play of levels and dimensions.[57]

Therefore, first-person narration contains the structural and linguistic devices to allow a range of differing voices to be re-constructed textually to give the illusion that they are speaking directly. This narrative technique is particularly useful in producing empowering discourses, as the strategic manipulation of narrative voice, linguistic styles and the disruption of realist assumptions and structures can open up the ideologies implanted in a dominant national literature.

Although relevant in terms of class and youth (and as Gibson argues, gender), these strategies are particularly useful for the group of Caribbean, African and Asian writers living and working in England in the fifties, most of whom directly confront issues relating to the experiences of living within a multiracial society, of diaspora, and the postcolonial encounters of the 'periphery' and the 'centre' re-enacted in the heart of the colonizing country. Writers such as G.V. Desani, Wilson Harris, George Lamming, Sam Selvon, and V.S. Naipaul all either settle, or spend a considerable amount of time, in Britain during the 1940s, 1950s and 1960s. They produce novels that describe the experiences of the black Caribbean immigrant in their postcolonial encounters with the white English population. In addition, white English writers begin to explore issues of the colonial legacy and post-colonial encounters. For example, Colin MacInnes in *City of Spades* and *Absolute Beginners*, and Alan Sillitoe in *Saturday*

---

56   The use of first-person narration articulated in non-Standard English can be seen in several fifties works of fiction including *The Lonely Londoners*, *The Loneliness of the Long Distance Runner*, *City of Spades* and *Absolute Beginners*.

57   Andrew Gibson, *Postmodernism, Ethics and the Novel: From Leavis to Levinas* (London and New York: Routledge, 1999), p.27.

Night and Sunday Morning and, more extensively, in *A Key to the Door*, record the experiences of black/white encounters. Furthermore, several contemporary plays investigated Britain's colonial past and the impact of decolonization. For example, John Arden's *Sergeant Musgrave's Dance* displaces the colonial encounter to an unspecified period and place in the nineteenth century to explore the nature of colonial military expansion in terms of class and power relationships.[58] John Osborne's *Look Back in Anger* also identifies Britain's declining status as a world power. This is focused through the lack of a political radicalism to which the central character, Jimmy Porter, could commit: 'I suppose people of our generation aren't able to die for good causes any longer [...] There aren't any good, brave causes.'[59] British Cinema also begins to investigate and record the implications and the 'problems' associated with the emergence of a multiracial society. Films such as *The Pool of London* (1951), *The Wind of Change* (1961), *Flame in the Streets*, (1961), and most directly, *Sapphire*, (1959), all deal with the interaction of black and white communities.[60] That this range of cultural production engages with issues of ethnicity and 'race', and its impact on class, can be understood further by identifying a further 'crisis' in fifties Britain.

58   John Arden, *Sergeant Musgrave's Dance: An Un-Historical Parable* (London: Eyre Methuen, 1960).
59   John Osborne, *Look Back in Anger* (London: Faber & Faber, 1957), p.84.
60   See John Hill, *Sex, Class and Realism: British Cinema 1956–1963* (London: BFI Publishing, 1986), pp.83–90, (pp.102–03).

Crisis Three: Communism, Socialism, Marxism

The third 'crisis' that helps to contextualize English fiction in the 1950s can be seen in the contemporary theoretical debates concerning left-wing politics.[61] One outcome of these debates is the rise of the New Left in the latter half of the fifties, as a response to the perceived failure of the socialist/Marxist project in Britain after the promise of the 1945 Attlee government. The editorial of the first edition of *Universities and Left Review*, the main journal of the New Left, articulates this sense of crisis in contemporary socialism:

> What is needed therefore is the regeneration of the whole tradition of free, open, critical debate. The socialist tradition ought to be the most fruitful and the most stringent of the intellectual traditions: a tradition of thought and action, alive to the realities of our contemporary world and sensitive to the pressures of the ideals and social justice which have distinguished it in the past.[62]

The project of the *ULR*, as identified here, implicitly identifies (and positions itself as a reaction to) a sense of crisis in socialist theory and practice in two areas: the lack of openness, and the responsiveness of contemporary socialist theory to the actualities of social and cultural practice in the 1950s.[63]

There is, of course, a range of contributing contextual issues that influenced the appearance of the New Left. Domestically, this was fuelled by three factors: the successes of the Tory Party in the 1951 and 1955 elections; the politics of consensus and the advocacy of a mixed market economy in the Labour Party as a response to electoral defeat; and the persuasive trope of 'classlessness' as an observable

---

61 'Left' politics in the fifties designates a complex range of positions and group-ings including communism, socialism, liberal humanism, Labour Party re-visionism, theoretical Marxism and nihilism. This variety is itself indicative of the fragmentation of radical left politics in the fifties as opposed to the 'popular front' policies of the late thirties and forties.

62 'Editorial', in *Universities and Left Review*, No.1, Spring 1957, p.i. (Hereafter referred to as *ULR*)

63 In chapter three below I discuss the style and methodological project developed by the New Left in response to these stated aims.

effect of the 'affluent society'.[64] In the first half of the fifties, there was a visible retreat of the left in Britain in response to the electoral successes of the Tory Party.[65] The Tories had run their campaign in 1955 on the claim that Britain was no longer subject to wide class divisions and that the country was rapidly becoming a classless society.[66] The presence of an economic boom in the early fifties, allowing the majority of people in Britain to buy into a new consumer culture, supported this argument and represented a crisis in traditional socialist and Marxist models of production and the desires and aspirations of the working classes. Macmillan's claim that 'You've never had it so good' was evidenced in this consumer spending, and was represented in the popular imagination by the presence of what was defined as the 'affluent society'.[67] In the Labour Party, the response was to embark on a revision of political aims and strategies, represented by Hugh Gaitskell's leadership, and theoretically by Anthony Crosland's *The Future of Socialism*.[68]

Internationally, two events had a profound effect on the nature and future direction of the British Left: the Twentieth Party Congress of the Communist Party, in which Kruschev revealed and denounced the activities of the Stalinist regime in the USSR, and the invasion of Hungary by Soviet troops following demonstrations by Budapest

64 See Stuart Laing, *Representations of Working Class Life 1957–1964* (London: Macmillan, 1986), pp.3–30; and Chas Critcher, 'Sociology, Cultural Studies and the Post-War Working Class', in *Working Class Culture: Studies in History and Theory*, ed. by John Clarke, Chas Critcher and Richard Johnson (London: Hutchinson, 1979), pp.13–40.

65 The Tories won general elections in 1951, 1955 and 1959, increasing their majority over Labour in each election. See David Childs, *Britain Since 1945: A Political History* (London and New York: Routledge, 1997), p.309.

66 See David Widgery, *The Left in Britain: 1956–1968*, (Harmondsworth: Penguin, 1986), p.44; and Laing, *Representations of Working Class Life*, pp.3–30.

67 This contemporary trope was based on J.K. Galbraith's influential book on fifties economics, *The Affluent Society* (London: Andre Deutsch, 1958). For a discussion and critique of the 'affluent society' debate see Critcher, 'Sociology, Cultural Studies and the Post-War Working Class'.

68 Anthony Crosland, *The Future of Socialism* (London: Cape, 1956). See also Lin Chun, *The British New Left* (Edinburgh: Edinburgh UP, 1993), p.4; and Kenny, The First New Left, pp.121–9

workers and intellectuals.[69] These events precipitated an internal sense of 'crisis' within British socialism that undermined any active challenge by the radical Left to respond to potential faultlines in Britain's hegemonic power structure. The Twentieth Congress and the Hungarian Crisis precipitated, for the intellectual Left in Britain, a period of navel-gazing self-scrutiny of its theoretical foundations, which Jacques Derrida has described as the repeated 'déjà-vu' of the question 'Whither Marxism?'[70] As Clancy Sigal wrote in 1958:

> The Communist Party generously assisted in digging its own grave. It only needed Korea and the 20th Congress to finish the job. The organized movement of men of goodwill [...] crumbled [...] And when the moral failure of the Soviet Union became nakedly apparent, a very great number of people [...] had *had* it.[71]

This pervasive sense of disillusionment deflected the New Left from producing an integrated and concerted critique of dominant power structures and relationships in Britain during the period, as many of its commentators were concerned with the state of their own political movements. As Lin Chun argues, at this specific moment in the 1950s:

> Socialism had to be redefined along the lines not only of class struggle but also of other emancipatory politics, and a socialist project had to begin with a struggle against some root values, concepts and images of the social consciousness of the day.[72]

This 'redefinition' is inscribed through discourses on the nation, imperialism and the threat of revisionism.

---

69   See Peter Sedgwick, 'Introduction: Farewell, Grosvenor Square', in Widgery, *The Left in Britain*, pp.19–41.

70   Derrida has identified the historical repetition of the 'crisis' of Marxism, Jacques Derrida, *Specters of Marx The State of the Debt, the Work of Mourning, and the New International*, trans. by Peggy Kamuf (London and New York: Routledge, 1994), p.14.

71   Clancy Sigal, Clancy, 'Nihilism's Organization Man', in *Universities and Left Review*, No.4, Summer 1958, p.65.

72   Chun, *The British New Left*, p.xv.

In terms of the nation, this can be identified in the move, after 1956, towards a renewed interest in single nation socialist policies and the revival of interest in a specifically British socialist tradition. This discourse greatly informs the New Left's assessment of contemporary Marxist theory, and can also be seen in the re-drafted publication of the Communist Party of Great Britain's *The British Road to Socialism* in 1958, which sets out a specific political agenda for British socialist policy.[73] Jack Klugmann summarized the position taken in this document:

> The new draft of the *British Road to Socialism* is about to be published, and it is, precisely, an attempt, on the basis of the essential principles of Marxism-Leninism, to work out the special, specific road to socialism of Britain in the world today.[74]

This marks a reaction to the pre-1956 reliance on the Soviet Union as the guiding source for socialist movements internationally,[75] and is a direct result of the disillusionment felt amongst many intellectual Marxists in Britain due to the Hungarian Crisis.[76]

There was also an increased interest on the left in the 'imperial' question – an area in which international power frameworks were manifestly seen to be changing through the process of decolonization. For example, several articles in *Marxism Today* in the fifties identify

---

73   The Communist Party of Great Britain, *The British Road to Socialism*, second draft, (London: 1958).

74   Jack Klugmann, 'The Road to Socialism', in *Marxism Today*, Vol.2, No.2, February 1958, p.42.

75   In 1949, Harry Pollitt was stressing: 'Today the international solidarity of the working people must have as its central point the recognition of the determining role of the Soviet Union, the leader of the anti-imperialist front. Any weakening in the appreciation of this plays straight into the hands of reaction', *The Political Report to the 21st Congress of the Communist Party*, (London: Communist Party, 1949), p.10.

76   E.P. Thompson and John Saville left the Communist Party in 1956 as a protest against the Hungarian Crisis and the resistance within the Communist Party to dissenting voices. However, they continued to regard themselves as Marxists, and to pursue a re-assessment of Marxist theory. See Kenny, *The First New Left*, pp.15–23.

this process as an indication of the anticipated collapse of Western capitalism.[77] This discourse also served to deflect attention away from the apparent successes of capitalism and consumerism within the so-called 'affluent society' of fifties Britain, manifest in working-class voting for the Conservatives in the general elections of 1955 and 1959.

The response in Marxist literature to the fifties boom, and the resulting consensus politics, is partly focused on an analysis of the threat of revisionism to the Marxist project. In Britain, this is directed against the policies of the Gaitskellite Labour Party, informed as it was by the theoretical work of Anthony Crosland, Richard Crossman and John Strachey.[78] Revisionism was seen as an international threat to the basis of the whole project of socialism. In an article in *Marxism Today* of 1959, V. Gomulka sums up this threat:

> At the present stage, revisionism is the main danger for the Party [...] because of the objective association of revisionism with anti-social tendencies and bourgeois social forces [...] The danger of revisionism [...] consisted in the fact that it exerted pressure against the ideological unity of the Party from the inside.[79]

However, it becomes increasingly apparent that 'protest' in the fifties novels were exceeding the discussion of 'economic' and class issues as their primary focus. Writers such as Sillitoe, MacInnes, Selvon, Alexander Trocchi and later Doris Lessing began to question

77 There were several articles in *Marxism Today* between 1957 and 1959 on the freedom movements in colonial states as indicative of the imminent collapse of Western capitalism. For example, see: Idris Cox, 'New Factors in the Struggle Against Imperialism', in *Marxism Today*, Vol.2, No.1, January 1958, pp.5–12; I. Pothekin, 'The Formation of Nations in Africa', in *Marxism Today*, Vol.2, No.10, October 1958, pp.308–14; and B.R. Mann, 'The Fight of African Nations to Self-Determination', in *Marxism Today*, Vol.3, No.1, January 1959, pp.16–21.
78 See *New Fabian Essays*, ed. by R.H.S. Crossman (London: Turnstile Press, 1952); John Strachey, *Contemporary Capitalism* (London: Gollancz, 1956); and Crosland, *The Future of Socialism*.
79 V. Gomulka, 'The Cultural Revolution, Revisionism and the Party', in *Marxism Today*, Vol. 2, No.3, April 1959, pp.119–22.

the inconsistencies and limitations of a Marxism that privileged class as the primary form of social discrimination. Texts such as Sillitoe's *Saturday Night and Sunday Morning* and *The Loneliness of the Long Distance Runner* implicitly articulate these problems in contemporaneous Marxist and communist discourse. This is achieved through a rejection of Marxism as a practical political solution to the specific social and cultural problems encountered by the characters in the fiction. This rejection of Marxist theory extends to the neglect of other discourses of social division. For example, MacInnes's texts articulate the issues of youth and ethnicity, whilst commenting directly on the failure of Marxist theory to offer anything for the individuals within these 'minority groups'. Selvon's texts perform a similar function in terms of growing black British community in the 1950s. The treatment of Marxism and left-wing political action is conspicuous by its absence in Selvon's writing. Whilst his fiction addresses the experiential connection of class and ethnicity, anticipating the work of Stuart Hall and Paul Gilroy in this field,[80] his characters reject organized left-wing political action as a means for dealing with the specific concerns of a black British/Caribbean subculture during the period.

Because of the tendency in fifties socialist and Marxist discourses to overlook these 'other' marginalized categories of inequality, radical discourses of the period are dispersed across a range of marginalized identities. It is interesting here to consider the idea put forward by Ernesto Laclau and Chantal Mouffe, regarding the possibility of a 'chain of equivalence' between diverse radical discourses articulating the position of different marginalized groups. In *Hegemony and Socialist Strategy*, Laclau and Mouffe argue for a radical political alliance between Marxism (and its privileging of the class struggle) and a plurality of other radical discourses that include:

> the rise of new feminism, the protest movements of ethnic, national and sexual minorities, the anti-institutional ecology struggles waged by marginalized

---

80   Stuart Hall, 'Gramsci's Relevance for the Study of Race and Ethnicity' and 'New Ethnicities', in *Stuart Hall: Critical Dialogues in Cultural Studies*, ed. by David Morley and Kuan-Hsing Chen (London and New York: Routledge, 1996) pp.441–9; Paul Gilroy, *There Ain't No Black*. There will be further discussion of these issues in chapter two below.

layers of the population, the anti-nuclear movement, the atypical forms of social struggle in countries on the capitalist periphery – all these imply an extension of social conflictuality to a wide range of areas, which creates the potential, but no more than the potential, for an advance towards more free, democratic and egalitarian societies.[81]

As they intimate, this alliance remains at the level of the potential and is not realized in actual political movements, and this is certainly the case in the 1950s. However, it is also the case that Marxism as a monistic theory centred on the class struggle theoretically resists the pluralization (and perceived dissolution) of its radical agenda. As Stuart Sim has noted, discussing Laclau and Mouffe, 'post-*Marxism* is a doomed attempt to render pluralist an unplurisable, indeed actively pluralism-resistant, theory [...] One is tempted to say that Marxism is a universal theory or it is nothing'.[82] In the context of the 1950s, a chain of equivalence between the various radical discourses was impossible to construct if the totalizing theoretical approach and methodology of Marxism was to be retained.

However, there is a correspondence, articulated through the radical fiction of the period, between the various marginalized discourses, that offers the potential for a collective radical position *vis-à-vis* the dominant social and political groups. It is through the correspondence of formal and narrative strategies that this connection can be identified. Here, it is useful to introduce Derrida's comments on the operation of 'canonical' texts that can, through their writing, produce correspondences with anti-canonical theses.[83] A text that highlights a particular radical discourse from a specific minority or marginalized position can produce associations with other marginalized discourses, even when the text appears to reproduce the marginalization of the silent group. One of the problems here is that in the cold

81   Ernesto Laclau and Chantal Mouffe, *Hegemony and Socialist Strategy: Towards a Radical Democratic Politics* (London and New York: Verso, 1985), p.1.
82   *Post-Marxism: A Reader*, ed. by Stuart Sim (Edinburgh: Edinburgh UP, 1998), p.8.
83   Jacques Derrida, '"This Strange Institution Called Literature": An Interview with Jacques Derrida', in *Acts of Literature*, ed. by Derek Attridge (London and New York: Routledge, 1992), pp.33–75, (p.50).

war climate of the fifties, the position of the radical is constructed within a binary opposition of right and left-wing politics. In the 1950s, to be defined as 'radical' almost universally implied an allegiance to left-wing politics, which was tied, through its association with Marxism, to a privileging of the category of class. However, the radical fiction succeeds in disrupting dominant contemporary definitions of the 'radical' beyond issues of class to other sites of oppositional and marginalized identities. These texts thus serve to anticipate a more pluralized model of radical theory, further developed in the 1970s and 1980s, around issues of youth, subcultural theory, postcolonialism, ethnicity, gender issues and feminism.

It is important to stress, here, that the relationship between the perceived crisis in the novel and the direction of contemporary socialist analysis overlap. In fact, these two factors are connected. The correspondences between the 'grand narratives' of Marxism and literary realism are re-negotiated during the same period and reveal concomitant assumptions in the two discursive models. Both Marxism and realism assume an understanding of time and history as a linear progression. Robert Young, in particular, has shown how the model of Hegelian Marxism established by Georg Lukàcs, is reliant upon a model of history as a totalizing discourse.[84] This particular Marxist model, like most models of the realist novel, assumes a direct relationship between cause and effect as a structural criterion in its representation of historical and temporal progression. In addition, the relationship between individual figures in history, or 'characters' in a novel, and the society through which they move, is based on a balance between individual agency and the restrictions of the socio-economic aspects of a particular society (Lukàcs identifies this as the dialectic between abstract and concrete potentiality that gives realism its power).[85] Furthermore, both the realist novel and the Lukàcian Marxist model assume the possibility of an omniscient 'author', or social

84   Robert Young, 'Marxism and the Question of History', in *White Mythologies: Writing History and the West* (London and New York: Routledge, 1990), pp. 21–7.
85   See Georg Lukàcs, *The Meaning of Contemporary Realism*, trans. by John and Necke Mander, (London: Merlin Press, 1963), first published in German 1957.

critic, who can identify both society's structures and the individual's actions within that society from a position of transcendence and greater understanding, allowing for the concept of 'false consciousness' to be developed, and exemplified in the realist novel through the construction of omniscient narration that assesses and evaluates the actions of its characters. There is, then, a structural link between the methodological approaches underlying a Hegelian / Lukàcian Marxist reading of history and society and the representation through narrative techniques of time passing in the conventional realist novel. It is, therefore, more than coincidence that, in the fifties, the crisis in Marxism that initiated a re-analysis of some of its central concepts occurs concurrently with a questioning of the theoretical and philosophical assumptions of the realist novel.

It is important to stress, however, that the Lukàcian model of Marxist literary criticism is not the only one present in the 1950s. The period in fact exemplifies the plurality of Marxisms suggested by Derrida in his book *Spectres of Marx*, and it is possible to identify (at least) three distinct models or theoretical approaches during the decade that have some allegiance to a Marxist understanding of literary production.[86] For example, Julie Rivkin and Michael Ryan have identified three major strands in Marxist criticism: reflection theory; the critical examination of mass culture and literature associated with the Frankfurt School; and a structuralist Marxism.[87] Each of these strands can be identified in the fifties, both in Britain and on the continent, and at different stages of their influence. The 'reflectionist' approach was a dominant but residual form of Marxist literary theory at the beginning of the decade. This can be seen in the theoretical positions adopted by Christopher Caudwell, Jack Mitchell and Arnold Kettle, whose work was still influential in Britain during the 1950s.[88]

---

86   Derrida, *Specters of Marx*, p.13.
87   Julie Rivkin and Michael Ryan, 'Starting with Zero: Basic Marxisms', in *Literary Theory: An Anthology*, ed. by Rivkin and Ryan (Oxford: Blackwell, 1998), pp.231–42, (p.239).
88   Caudwell's 'reflectionist' Marxist literary theory was established in the thirties but was still the dominant model in the early fifties. An example of this approach can be identified in the following quotation from his 1937 book, Illusion and Reality: 'Pope's poetry, and its "reason" [...] with its polished lan-

Arnold Kettle alludes to this model in his 1951 study of the English novel: 'Great revolutions in human society change men's consciousness and revolutionize not only their social relationships but their outlook, their philosophy and their art.'[89]

The Hegelian Marxist tradition established by Lukàcs is also influential in the fifties, although he problematizes the reflectionist model by introducing distinctions between what he calls 'critical realism' and 'socialist realism'.[90] Arnold Kettle, for example, adopts Lukàcs's model in a British context in a 1961 article, which suggests its influence in Britain in the late 1950s, (Kettle's definition assumes the prevalence of the concepts he defines for some time previous to the date of the article):

> By *Socialist Realism*, in the field of literature, I assume we mean literature from the point of view of the class-conscious working class [...] By *Critical Realism* I assume we mean literature in the era of class society from a point of view which, while not fully socialist, is nevertheless sufficiently critical of the class society to reveal important truths about that society.[91]

The influence of the Frankfurt School can also be identified in Britain in the 1950s through the development of cultural materialism in the New Left. There is also the emergence of a structuralist/Marxist approach in the fifties in the work primarily of Roland Barthes in France, developed later through Louis Althusser, Pierre Macherey and Etienne Balibar in the sixties. Although these structuralist models are not identified in Britain until the later sixties, the presence of another

---

guage and metre and curt antithesis, is a reflection of the bourgeois illusion where freedom for the bourgeoisie can only be "limited" [...] Pope perfectly expresses the ideals of the bourgeois class in alliance with a bourgeoisified aristocracy in the epoch of manufacture', in *Marxists on Literature: An Anthology*, ed. by David Craig (Harmondsworth: Penguin, 1975), p.108.

89   Arnold Kettle, *An Introduction to the English Novel: Volume 1* (London: Arrow Books, 1962), first published 1951, p.32.

90   Lukàcs, *The Meaning of Contemporary Realism*, p.93.

91   Arnold Kettle, 'Dickens and the Popular Tradition', in Craig, *Marxists on Literature*, pp.214–44, (p.214). Kettle's definition here reproduces Lukàcs's definitions in *The Meaning of Contemporary Realism*, although Kettle does not refer to Lukàcs directly.

strand of Marxist thought has relevance within the overall frame of fifties Marxist thought.

The 'crisis' in Marxism during the period manifests itself in literary theory through the presence and development of multiple and fragmented models of the relationship between society, history and literary production. This also has effects on the understanding of the ideological frameworks in which the 1950s novel was produced. The radical novel of the period engaged with these issues and articulated the sense of crisis in radical political thought, the novel and national identity through an experimental approach to literary form. The novels discussed in the second part of this book anticipate some of the central concerns of post-structuralist theory in relation to a problematization of the realist form as dependent upon an untenable theory of language that suggests it is able to reflect the 'real' world transparently. The 'radical' fiction achieves this by foregrounding the 'textuality' of fiction and the technical and strategic devices by which realist modes artificially claim impartiality in both formal and ideological terms. The radical literature of the fifties, then, rather than representing a return to residual models and conventions of a philosophical and formal realism, can be described as a kind of 'pre-postmodernism' that represents an emergent form. This is developed more self-consciously during the 1960s and onwards to the present day.[92] It is with respect to these contexts that the radical 1950s novel engages with the ideological frameworks of literary form, and it is with these issues that the next chapter will be concerned.

---

92   I acknowledge the term 'pre-postmodernism' is a little clumsy and suggests a
      desire to produce a historical narrative of literary forms, a structural model that
      I reject in other parts of the book; however, I offer it here not as a fixed relation
      of cause and effect but as a 'genealogy' of influence between the positions
      within the various theories of realism, modernism and postmodernism.

Chapter Two
Form and Ideology in the Fifties Novel

The Strange Institution of 1950s Fiction

In interview, Jacques Derrida has argued that what he calls the 'strange institution' of 'literature in the West':

> is linked to the authorization to say everything, and doubtless too to the coming about of the modern idea of democracy [... But] In the end, the critico-political function of literature, in the West, remains very ambiguous. The freedom to say everything is a very powerful political weapon, but one which might immediately be neutralized as a fiction. This revolutionary power can become very conservative.[1]

Here, Derrida identifies the problematic relationship between the 'institution of literature' and its political function in Western democracy, based on the amount of freedom of expression allowed to 'literature' as a socio-cultural practice. I begin this chapter on form and ideology with this quotation because it seems to me that Derrida opens some interesting questions on the agency of individual writers to *choose* the forms in which they write. According to Derrida, literary writing is a negotiation between the 'freedom to write everything' and the restrictions put in place by the socio-political and ideological frameworks reproduced by the 'institution of literature' at any particular moment in history. Therefore, the choice to write in a particular form generates, and is ultimately restricted by, specific ideological assumptions that curtail the 'freedom' to which Derrida alludes.

---

1   Jacques Derrida, '"This Strange Institution Called Literature" An Interview with Jacques Derrida', trans. by Geoffrey Bennington and Rachel Bowlby, in *Acts of Literature*, ed. by Derek Attridge (London and New York: Routledge, 1992), pp.33–75, (pp.39–40).

The 'institution of literature' is, of course, a problematic concept in itself. If we assume that what constitutes the 'institution' is 'literary' writing, and writing about 'literary' writing, then it includes a wide variety of textual sites that combine to make up this elusive body. Novels, plays, poetry, literary reviews, literary journalism, biography, bibliography, critical and theoretical analysis of 'literary' texts and of social, cultural, political, philosophical, ethical and moral issues as they are reproduced in literature, and the whole literary-critical apparatus in terms of teaching, research and assessment criteria: all these are involved in the construction of the 'institution of literature'. All these 'sites' combine to establish a range of positions in terms of the 'function' of literature and the individual work is interpreted in relation to this ideological nexus of writing. The institution of literature, therefore, is imbued with ideological implications in its construction, propagation and reproduction. As Etienne Balibar and Pierre Macherey argue:

> literature is historically constituted in the bourgeois epoch as an ensemble of language – or rather of specific linguistic practices – inserted in a general schooling process so as to provide appropriate fictional effects, thereby reproducing bourgeois ideology as the dominant ideology.[2]

Balibar and Macherey identify the ideological processes involved in the construction of the category of literature, though I would suggest that their argument is problematic in that it presumes that there is no place outside of 'bourgeois' ideology from where a radical writing might be produced.[3]

The institution of literature must be understood in relation to its historical context; it is not a fixed model but one that changes historically, as Raymond Williams has identified: 'the crucial theoretical break is the recognition of "literature" as a specializing social and

---

2   Etienne Balibar and Pierre Macherey, 'On Literature as an Ideological Form', in *Untying the Text: A Post-Structuralist Reader*, ed. by Robert Young (London and New York: Routledge and Kegan Paul, 1981), pp.79–100, (p.84).

3   I discuss this issue in greater detail in the introduction to this book.

historical category'.[4] In addition, it is apparent that particular periods show an increased self-awareness amongst writers of the construction of the contemporaneous literary institution, its relationship with socio-cultural and political issues, and the ideological discourses and frameworks that it sets up and reproduces. The fifties represents a period of this kind, and it is necessary for the scope of this book to analyze some of the debates concerning the nature of literary production and the ideology of literary forms that were prevalent in the cultural and theoretical writing of the period. Debates on the political nature of writing in the 1950s are articulated through two related discourses: firstly, on the relationship between specific literary forms and the ideological signification of those forms; and secondly, on the relationship between the production of literature and discourses of national identity. In this chapter, I investigate some of the issues raised during the period in relation to these two areas.

The writers I analyze in the second part of this book are engaged, to varying degrees, in the debates around these issues, and part of the purpose of their fictional writing is to address them self-reflexively. All are aware of the limitations of the dominant critical and political models of literary form and ideology in the 1950s, especially in their understanding of specific literary tropes such as 'realism' and 'experimentalism', and they foreground the formal aspects of their texts in order to negotiate, scrutinize or question these models. As Roland Barthes has written (discussing specific examples in French literature of the kind of writing I am alluding to):

> [These] modes of writing, though different, are comparable, because they owe their existence to one identical process, namely the writer's consideration of the social use which he has chosen for his form, and his commitment to this choice. Placed at the centre of the problematics of literature, which cannot exist prior to it, writing is thus essentially the morality of form, the choice of that social area within which the writer elects to situate the nature of language.[5]

---

4   Raymond Williams, *Marxism and Literature* (Oxford: Oxford University Press, 1977), p.53.
5   Roland Barthes, *Writing Degree Zero*, trans. by Annette Lavers and Colin Smith (New York: Hill and Wang, 1977), first published 1953, p.15. Barthes is discussing a wide range of French writers of the first half of the twentieth-

Here, Barthes identifies literature as an engagement with the 'social use' of particular and specific modes and *forms* of writing. His reference to the 'morality of form' placed at the 'centre of the problematics of literature' identifies an ideological framework for the production and deployment of specific literary forms. According to Barthes the choice of form is dependent on the ideological significance of that choice as communicated to the reading community and, therefore, becomes one aspect of the socio-political meaning of the text. This correspondence between literary form and ideological signification is more prominent during periods when there is extensive literary and critical debate on the functionality of literary form, as is the case in the 1950s.

Now, as Andrzej Gasiorek, following Stuart Laing, has argued, there is no intrinsic, or *a priori* relationship between a particular literary form and a specific political or ideological position.[6] This is true in an abstract sense: there is nothing intrinsic about a literary form such as 'realism' or 'modernism' that *automatically* equates to an ideological position. However, it is also the case, in a material sense, that any literary text becomes engaged in, and is interpreted in relation to, the ideological framework sustained and reproduced by the literary institution on the 'occasion' of that text's writing and publication. This institution is always already in place prior to the text, and the text cannot but be understood or interpreted in relation to the institution. There is no 'place' where the formal properties of a text could be free from ideology as the ideological/form framework is reproduced and contested through (literary) historical contexts. So although there is no essential or *a priori* relationship between a particular literary form and the ideology that it supports or propounds, literary forms operate in the world as ideological *signifiers*. It also follows that any text can be read ideologically, against an ideology/form nexus or classification

century whom he identifies as differing widely in terms of 'tone, delivery, purpose, ethos and naturalness of expression', but who are comparable in their recognition of the ideological and social implications of the *form* in which they choose to write.

6   Andrzej Gasiorek, *Post-War British Fiction: Realism and After* (London: Edward Arnold, 1995), p.4.

which, following Foucault, would represent a historicized framework of an ordered system.[7] This 'order' is not fixed, even in a specific historical moment or space, but is contested by other possible 'orders' that challenge the dominant patterns of the relationship between literary form and ideology. Therefore, there is always contestation over what represents the ideology of certain literary forms at any given moment in time, and therefore, how a particular text generates its ideological significance.

For example, the ideological importance of a form such as 'classic realism' is not fixed but changes historically. As Catherine Belsey argues:

> Classic realism [...] roughly coincides chronologically with the epoch of industrial capitalism. It performs [...] the work of ideology, not only in its representation of a world of consistent subjects who are the origin of meaning, knowledge and action, but also in offering the reader, as the position from which the text is most readily intelligible, the position of subject as the origin both of understanding and of action in accordance with that understanding.[8]

Belsey, following Althusser, establishes the ideological function of classic realism as a form that masks its own nature as a constructed set of literary techniques and practices, claiming rather to be a mode of transparent and direct communication between two stable subjects: the author and the reader. She also suggests that classic realism as a literary form equates directly to a philosophical understanding of language that she defines as 'expressive realism'. Both these concepts she places as dominant modes of thought and expression during 'the epoch of industrial capitalism' (67). She identifies, therefore, specific literary forms as indicators of socio-economic conditions in a way that

---

7   Foucault argues that 'the stark fact that there exists, below the level of its spontaneous orders, things that are themselves capable of being ordered, that belong to a certain unspoken order; the fact, in short, that order exists', Michel Foucault, *The Order of Things: An Archaeology of the Human Sciences*, trans. by Alan Sheridan Smith (New York and London: Routledge, 1970), p.xx.

8   Catherine Belsey, *Critical Practice* (London and New York: Routledge, 1980), p.67.

corresponds to an Althusserian approach to ideology and narrative.[9] However, she does not acknowledge the fact that what constitutes 'classic realism', both in a formal and ideological sense, changes over the period she identifies.

She also argues that: 'Formulations of common sense positions are found most often in periods when the position in question is new and in the process of displacing an earlier position, or when it is under attack' (7). Belsey suggests that this explains the defences of 'common sensical' positions in the sixties. This also explains the often vehement defences of 'conventional' realism in the fifties by commentators such as Cooper and Wain, articulated as a response to the claims being given to 'experimentalism', both in a contemporary sense but also in relation to twenties and thirties modernism. The correspondence between the defence of 'common sense' philosophical positions and of 'conventional' realism is connected and can be related to the fractures of two specific 'grand narratives' developing in the 1950s: the Marxist or communist model of the historical dialectic, and of Englishness as a narrative of national identity, both of which, as we have seen, were in crisis in the 1950s.[10] Both these 'crises', therefore, are articulated through a re-negotiation of realism in terms of its adequacy to represent a form of social critique in literature, and in terms of its expression of a historicized narrative of national identity.

The 1950s was a decade in which these issues were articulated through a specific debate concerning the relationship between literary forms and ideology, by which individual novels were valued and judged. The 'institution of literature' during the period established certain constructions and understandings of literary forms that were felt to signify specific ideological and political assumptions. Therefore, concepts such as 'conventional', 'critical' and 'socialist' realism, experimentalism, modernism, naturalism, and the documentary novel, all carried explicit ideological significance that were identified by

9   See Louis Althusser, 'Ideology and Ideological State Apparatuses', in *Lenin and Philosophy and Other Essays*, trans. by Ben Brewster (London: New Left Books, 1971), pp.122–73.
10   I discuss these two 'crises' in greater detail in chapter one above.

writers, critics and an informed interpretative community. At the beginning of the fifties, there was a general assumption, reproduced in contemporary literary and critical debate, that a politically self-conscious and motivated literature was most productively articulated through the realist form, whilst 'modernism' or 'experimentalism' represented an apolitical and overly aestheticized writing that signified a politically conservative or even reactionary ideology. The mandarin pronouncements of T.S. Eliot and the right-wing political sensibilities of Yeats and Pound from an earlier generation of modernist writers gave extra credence to this interpretation of the ideology of modernism as conservative or reactionary.[11] Realism, on the other hand, was acknowledged as the primary form for producing a literature of social critique through association with the literary and critical work of thirties writers such as Orwell, Isherwood and Greenwood, and given a theoretical framework in the work of Georg Lukàcs. However, as the decade moved on, it became increasingly apparent to certain writers that this form/ideology model was untenable and, in fact, detrimental to the production of a committed literature. Conventional, and even socialist, realism was, by the end of the 1950s, beginning to lose its privileged position as the primary literary form for a literature of social critique.

This 'crisis' in the ideological function of realism was attended by a growing discontent amongst 'committed' writers with the aesthetic quality of novels identified as 'socialist realism', and, as suggested earlier, was intricately bound up with the crisis in Marxist and socialist politics. The debate was fuelled by two other factors concerning form and the socio-political function of the novel. Firstly, the identification, made most powerfully in the 1950s by Ian Watt, that the novel, and in particular the realist novel, far from being a form that was associated with a radical or socialist project, was in fact more closely related to the dominant political outlook and sensibilities of

11 See Cairns Craig, *Yeats, Eliot, Pound and the Politics of Poetry* (London and Canberra: Croom Helm, 1982); and Lawrence Rainey, 'The Cultural Economy of Modernism', and Sara Blair, 'Modernism and the Politics of Culture', both in *The Cambridge Companion to Modernism*, ed. by Michael Levenson (Cambridge: Cambridge UP, 1999), pp.33–69; pp.157–73.

the middle classes.[12] This argument problematized the role of realism as a form that could produce a radical critique of Western society, and rather posited it as representative of the aspirations and tastes of the dominant middle classes. Secondly, the retrieval of realism by the novelists associated with the Movement of the early fifties (Amis, Wain, Cooper) as a form specifically related to an English tradition, suggested that this form was implicated in a discourse of national identity, which ultimately allied it to a reproduction, rather than a critique, of dominant English socio-cultural ideologies.

Keep it Real: The Ideological Heritage of Literary Realism

As identified in the previous section, the 1950s represents a period in which there was increased debate over the ideological role and function of the realist novel. Two figures, in particular, were informing this debate: Jean-Paul Sartre and George Orwell.

In the 1940s, Sartre had argued that one of the primary impulses behind writing should be to engage in the social and political environment in which the writer found him or herself. In *What is Literature?*, he writes: 'The "committed" writer knows that words are action. He knows that to reveal is to change and that one can reveal only by planning to change'.[13] This project or agenda for a committed literature became a powerful influence in fifties writing especially for novelists who regarded themselves as politically on the left, for example Doris Lessing, Alan Sillitoe and John Berger. The debate on commitment in fact extended beyond the novel to several forms of aesthetic production. In the late 1950s, *Universities and Left Review*, ran a series of articles on the concept of 'commitment' and its practice

12   Ian Watt, 'Realism and the Novel Form' and 'The Reading Public and the Rise of the Novel', in *The Rise of the Novel: Studies in Defoe, Richardson and Fielding* (London: Hogarth Press, 1987), first published 1957, pp.9–59.

13   Jean-Paul Sartre, *What is Literature?*, trans. by Bernard Frechtman (London: Methuen & Co., 1967) first published in English translation in 1950, p.13.

across various forms of cultural production. This series included articles by the film critic Lindsay Anderson, art critic Peter de Franscia, as well as cultural commentators and academics such as Michael Armstrong, John Mander, Stuart Hall and E.P. Thompson.[14] Although few mention him by name, all these British critics were essentially responding to Sartre's *What is Literature?* in a contemporary context. This involved the attempt to inscribe an obligation for the post-war artist and writer to become or remain politically motivated through their aesthetic production. Sartre's argument in *What is Literature?* had implicit assumptions about the representational function of literature in committed writing. Sartre argues that 'since words are transparent' critics should not attack committed writers for foregrounding political and ideological concerns in their writing:

> In prose the aesthetic pleasure is pure only if it is thrown into the bargain [...] If contamination of a certain kind of prose by poetry had not confused the ideas of our critics, would they dream of attacking us on the matter of form, when we have never spoken of anything but content?[15]

Here, Sartre suggests that commitment is an issue for the 'content' of literature rather than its 'form', but in doing so, and in disparaging the 'contamination' of prose by poetry, he is implicitly constructing a model in which realist assumptions about language are allied to a committed literature, and 'experimental' writing or 'modernism' is regarded as an aesthetic distraction from commitment. Virtually all of the British commentators on commitment and the arts identified above make the assumption that 'realism' was the primary form for a com-

---

14 Doris Lessing, 'The Small Personal Voice', in *Declaration*, ed. by Tom Maschler (London: MacGibbon and Key, 1957), pp.13–27; John Mander, *The Writer and Commitment* (London: Secker and Warburg, 1961); Lindsay Anderson, 'Commitment in Cinema Criticism', in *Universities and Left Review* (hereafter, *URL)* 1, pp.44–8; Peter de Franscia, 'Commitment in Art Criticism', in *ULR* 1, pp.49–51; Michael Armstrong, 'Commitment in Criticism', in *ULR* 2, pp.65–6; E.P. Thompson, 'Commitment in Politics', in *ULR* 6, pp.50–6; *ULR* 4 included a whole section on 'Commitment' including discussion by Stuart Hall, Raymond Williams, John Berger and Paddy Whannel, in *ULR* 4, Summer, 1958.
15 Sartre, *What is Literature?*, p.15.

mitted aesthetics. For most of the critics on the left, therefore, Sartre's concept of an *engagé* literature was produced formally through recourse to the reproduction of a realist aesthetic.

In a British context, George Orwell was the primary influence at the beginning of the fifties in terms of the production of politically committed writing, especially amongst the Movement writers and the 'Angry Young Men'. Although he was dead by the beginning of the decade, Orwell's influence was very important for the 1950s novel. As Anthony Hartley wrote in 1963: 'The "no-nonsense" air of an entire generation comes from Orwell', and Blake Morrison argues that, 'George Orwell's novels ... provide[d] the precedent which they [the Movement] required.'[16] Orwell's influence on fifties writing has three main facets: his production of a politically committed literature; his advocacy of an accessible writing style that suggests affiliation to realism in the novel through his use of a mode allied to documentary;[17] and the construction of Orwell as an archetypal English writer.

The connection between Orwell's political commitment and realism as the best form to produce such a writing is stressed by Raymond Williams: 'He [Orwell] chose content before form, experience before words; [...] he became the socially conscious writer of the Thirties rather than the aesthetic writer of the Twenties.'[18] Williams identifies the link between Orwell's ideological project for the novel, and the emphasis on content over form, which, in the context in which Williams was writing, suggests an advocacy of realism over the aestheticism of modernist writing. Williams's comments also reinforce the assumption that conventional realism was associated with a literature of political commitment, whereas modernism (the 'aesthetic' writing of the twenties) signified an apolitical aestheticism. This aspect of Orwell's writing was also identified by Kingsley Amis, who in his *Socialism and the Intellectuals*, writes:

16   Anthony Hartley, *A State of England* (London: Hutchinson, 1963), p.47; Blake Morrison, *The Movement: English Poetry and Fiction of the 1950s* (London and New York: Methuen, 1980), p.73.
17   For example, in works such as *Down and Out in Paris and London* (Harmondsworth: Penguin, 1940), and *The Road to Wigan Pier* (London: Gollancz, 1937).
18   Raymond Williams, *Orwell* (Glasgow: Collins/Fontana, 1971), p.32.

70

Of all the writers who appeal to the post-war intelligentsia, he [Orwell] is far and away the most potent [...] No modern writer has his air of passionately believing what he has to say and of being passionately determined to say it as forcefully and simply as possible.[19]

Behind this evaluation of Orwell lie assumptions about the ideology of specific literary forms that are as revealing about Amis as they are of Orwell. When Amis celebrates Orwell's aim to write 'as forcefully and simply as possible', it shows assumptions about the status of Orwell's realism and its direct relationship with his committed political discourse ('passionately believing').[20] As Blake Morrison argues: 'This [Orwell's quietism] is the formula adopted by Amis and Wain.'[21]

Another factor that connects Orwell to fifties writers is his position within the English tradition. Raymond Williams, for example, has written: 'Much of Orwell's writing about England is so close and detailed, his emphasis on ordinary English virtues so persistent, that he is now often seen as the archetypal Englishman, the most native and English of writers.'[22] Williams, whilst acknowledging the artificiality of this interpretation, nevertheless accepts the power of this construction of Orwell in relation to national identity. The influence of Orwell was evoked by the Movement writers, in particular, as part of the (re)construction of a specifically English literary tradition. The combination of political, formal and national discourses, celebrated by the Movement, and influential throughout the 1950s, finds a key point of axis in Orwell's writing. Anthony Easthope has identified the linkage between an English philosophical tradition of empiricism and the assumptions of a realist form in Orwell's writing. Easthope argues that

19   Kingsley Amis, *Socialism and the Intellectuals*, Fabian Tract No.304 (London: The Fabian Society, 1957), p.8.
20   Amis's reading of Orwell is problematic considering the latter's use of non-realist forms such as allegory and the futuristic novel in his last two novels: *Animal Farm: A Fairy Story* (Harmondsworth: Penguin, 1945), and *Nineteen-Eighty-Four* (Harmondsworth: Penguin, 1949). Orwell's experiment with form can also be identified in his early novel: *The Clergyman's Daughter* (London: Gollancz, 1935).
21   Morrison, *The Movement*, p.94.
22   Williams, *Orwell*, p.16.

this tension between English empiricism and a 'foreign' modernism is incorporated into the narrative structure of Orwell's final novel *Nineteen-Eighty-Four*, which again establishes a context of national identity for specific literary forms.[23]

Together, Sartre and Orwell represent a connection between 'commitment' and the realist novel that proved to be a powerful discourse in fifties literary and cultural criticism. Doris Lessing, for example, stresses the function and power of 'great' realism to produce a committed literature:

> For me the highest point of literature was the novel of the nineteenth century, the work of Tolstoy, Stendhal, Dostoevsky, Balzac, Turgenev, Chekhov: the work of the great realists. I define realism as art which springs so vigorously and naturally from a strongly-held, though not necessarily intellectually-defined, view of life that it absorbs symbolism.[24]

Although Lessing identifies the 'great realists' as part of a European, rather than an English tradition, she advocates realism as the primary form of a committed literature: 'This is what I mean when I say that literature should be committed. It is these qualities that I demand, and which I believe spring from being committed; for one cannot be committed without belief' (15). Commitment and realism are thus integrally connected for Lessing, and to a certain extent the political agenda determines the form in which it was to be communicated.[25] In Barthes's terms, realism carried with it a 'morality of form' that limited the aesthetic choice of the committed writer. Alan Sillitoe also acknowledges an allegiance to realism in his 1968 preface to *Saturday Night and Sunday Morning*, when he emphasizes the 'sweat of writing clearly and truthfully, the work of trying to portray ordinary people as I knew them, and in such a way that they would recognize

23 Anthony Easthope, *Englishness and National Culture* (London and New York: Routledge, 1999), pp.156–9.

24 Lessing, 'The Small Personal Voice', pp.11–27.

25 It is significant that Lessing, writing here in 1957, is about to go through a process of re-assessing this assumed connection between form and ideology which ultimately results in *The Golden Notebook*, an 'experimental' novel which remains 'committed', though problematizing that concept as a parallel move to the problematization of form in the novel.

themselves'.[26] This kind of justification of experiential evidence is produced as a value-laden apology for the form of the novel and assumes certain ideological relationships between form and content; namely, that the kind of realism Sillitoe deploys in the novel records real life people and actions in a fictional form, thereby establishing both its 'authenticity' and its committedness. That Sillitoe's novel in fact questions and re-assesses these assumptions is an indication both of the power of the form and ideology framework that was dominant during the fifties, and the problems Sillitoe's writing highlights in relation to it.

However, as Belsey argues, the defence of a particular form usually assumes extra force at the moment when it is challenged, and this helps to explain the relationship between realism and 'experimental' writing in the 1950s.[27] Alongside the advocacy of a realist form for the committed novel there was a parallel attack on experimentalism in the novel that was identified as representing an ideology of apoliticism, and thus equated to an implicit acceptance of dominant political and social frameworks and power relationships. For example, John Wain suggested that 'the experimental novel died with Joyce'[28], and C.P. Snow argued that the experimental novel:

> effectively cut out precisely those aspects of the novel where a living tradition can be handed on. Reflection had to be sacrificed; so did moral awareness; so did the investigatory intelligence. That was altogether too big a price to pay, and hence the 'experimental' novel [...] died from starvation, because its intake of human stuff was so low.[29]

26   Alan Sillitoe, 'Introduction' to New Edition of *Saturday Night and Sunday Morning* (London and New York: W.H. Allen, 1973), p.8. It is significant to add here that in an earlier introduction to the novel Sillitoe problematizes the relationship between the 'real' and 'fictional' elements of the text: 'In taking up the book now I am often unable to pick out the background, take it to pieces and disentangle fact from fiction. It seems the choicest blend of truth and lies', Alan Sillitoe, 'Introduction' to *Saturday Night and Sunday Morning* (London: Longmans, Green and Co., 1968), p.xii.

27   Belsey, *Critical Practice*, p.7.

28   John Wain, *Essays on Literature and Ideas* (London: Macmillan, 1963), p.50.

29   C.P. Snow, 'New Trends in First Novels', in *Sunday Times*, 27 December 1953, p.3.

Here, Snow makes the case that the disconnection between the 'experimental' novel and the social framework upon which the novel traditionally established itself resulted in the impossibility in the modernist novel of producing any 'moral' or political comment. William Cooper went further by suggesting that the experimental novel was anti-intellectual:

> The impulse behind much Experimental Writing is an attack from the inside on intellect in general, made by intellectuals so decadent that they no longer mind if intellect persists – in fact some of them sound as if they would be happier if it didn't.[30]

Cooper also describes these 'intellectuals' to be the 'ripest of meat for authoritarianism and then totalitarianism' (33). Cooper presents his argument against experimentalism by stressing the ideological significance of the approach. Experimental writers are thereby equated with a decadent intellectualism that, according to Cooper, has tendencies towards a totalitarian politics. Cooper's argument in this article on French experimental writing, although based on a mis-understanding of Alain Robbe-Grillet's technique in *The Voyeur*, represented a powerful attack on literary experimentalism that received support amongst many fifties writers including Kingsley Amis, Angus Wilson and C.P. Snow.[31]

This framework of literary form and ideology was given a more theoretical basis in the work of the Hungarian Marxist critic, Georg Lukàcs. Lukàcs argued that what he defined as 'critical' realism represented the primary literary form in the establishment of a politically engaged literature:

> Great realism [...] does not portray an immediately obvious aspect of reality but one which is permanent and objectively more significant, namely man in the whole range of his relations to the real world, above all those which outlast mere fashion. Over and above that, it captures tendencies of development that

30 William Cooper, 'Reflections on Some Aspects of the Experimental Novel', in *International Literary Review*, No.2, ed. by John Wain (London: John Calder, 1959), pp.29–36, (p.36).

31 See Rubin Rabinovitz, *The Reaction Against Experimentalism in the English Novel, 1950–1960* (New York and London: Columbia University Press, 1967).

only exist incipiently and so have not yet had the opportunity to unfold their entire human and social potential. To discern and give shape to such underground trends is the great historical mission of the true literary avant-garde.[32]

For Lukàcs, the (great) realist text achieved a balanced dialectic between what he identified as the 'abstract' and 'concrete' 'potentiality' of the individual subject in relation to the world in which he/she found him/herself. Through the interaction of characters within the representational world of a realist novel a balance was established between the abstract desires of the individual and the concrete restrictions upon those desires that produced an implicit political and ideological reading of society. His parallel criticism of the modernist novel was based on the imbalance between these two poles in favour of 'abstract potentiality'. Lukàcs argued that in modernist texts the over-subjectivism, or the foregrounding of ontological rather than social concerns, resulted in the 'fading away' of the 'concrete' world, leaving only the abstract imaginings of the character that could never be grounded in a lived reality, (23–4). Whilst it was the 'literature of realism' that 'must demonstrate both the concrete and abstract potentiality of human beings', it was modernism that failed in this attempt. For Lukàcs, this reveals the ideological implications of the form itself:

> The problem, once again, is ideological [...] The rejection of narrative objectivity, the surrender to subjectivity, may take the form of Joyce's stream of consciousness, or of Musil's 'active passivity' [...] or of Gide's *action gratuite* [...] If the distinction between abstract and concrete potentiality vanishes [...] human personality must necessarily disintegrate. (23–5)

According to Lukàcs's model, modernist writers are susceptible to modern society's *appearance* of fragmentation and reflect this through the portrayal of disconnected, alienated and overly subjective narratives. Critical realist writers, on the other hand, are able to transcend the subjectivity of individual characters and to observe the

---

32   Georg Lukàcs, *The Meaning of Contemporary Realism*, trans. by John and Necke Mander (London: Merlin Books, 1963), first published in German, 1957, p.48.

social and political frameworks that determine individual character's actions.

Lukàcs's model is fraught with problems. For example, he is unconvincing in his privileging of the critical realist novel as a mode that can transcend its moment of production. To accept this is to go against one of the central tenets of Marxist literary criticism: that the ideology of the text is dependent upon the economic base in place at the moment of its construction, a theory that Lukàcs accepts at other moments in his discussion. This inconsistency is overlooked, relying rather on a neo-romanticized image of realism as a privileged form that has the ability to transcend socio-political conditions. Ironically, his theory with regard to the realist novel is imbued with the very 'bourgeois' ideologies that he claims 'great' realism serves to challenge. Nevertheless, his position corresponds with the dominant understanding of the relationship between literary form and ideology, as evidenced in writers such as Lessing, Wain and Cooper.[33] His model therefore corresponds to the discussions of literary form in a wide range of fifties writers, including those who were grouped together under the headings of the Movement and the Angry Young Men.

Also in the 1950s, and from a different critical tradition, Ian Watt was arguing that the novel, and the realist novel in particular, could be identified as a cultural expression of the rise of the middle classes. Watt's theory identified the parallel trajectory of the rise of the middle classes and the importance of what he calls formal realism as a cultural expression of the ideologies of that group, culminating in the pre-eminence of the form in the middle of the nineteenth century. As with Lukàcs, Watt's argument identifies a direct relation between aesthetic form and socio-economic conditions and power structures. The advances in printing technology, the creation of a mass market and the development of a cultural taste for narratives of financial and moral progression in the period make his a powerful theory that was

---

33   There is no evidence that these writers were acquainted directly with Lukàcs's work, but they correspond in a contextual 'structure of feeling' concerning these issues in the 1950s.

accepted by the majority of literary critics in the late fifties.[34] As Terry Lovell has written: 'There is near universal consensus among Marxist and non-Marxist theorists of literature that the novel is a bourgeois form, closely linked in its rise with the development of capitalism [...] The *locus classicus* of this thesis is Ian Watt's book [*The Rise of the Novel*].'[35]

However, Watt's theory represented a problematic for committed writers who identified realism as the primary literary form for a politically engaged writing that supported both socialist and communist ideas. If the realist novel was the traditional form of the middle classes, how could it also represent the form of a future socialist literature as Lukàcs was arguing, and was already being claimed in the Soviet Union through the Union of Soviet Writers led by Zhdanov.[36] Raymond Williams, in 'Realism and the Contemporary Novel', attempted to address this problem by introducing distinctions in realism between 'bourgeois' and 'socialist' variants.[37] Although deploying similar techniques and assumptions to Lukàcs about the relationship between writing and 'reality', Williams argued that bourgeois realism and socialist realism had different ideological functions. The former

---

34 Although there were subsequent critiques of Watt's interpretations of individual novels, for example see Dorothy van Ghent's *The English Novel: Form and Function* (New York: Harper and Row, 1961); and Terry Lovell, 'Capitalism and the Novel', in *Consuming Fiction* (London: Verso, 1987), pp.19–45.

35 Lovell, 1987, p.19.

36 Zhdanov was head of the Union of Soviet Writers, which claimed that because the U.S.S.R. had officially achieved socialism, then the writing produced in the Soviet Union could be defined as truly socialist literature, a position which was problematic for many socialist writers in the West. For discussion of fifties socialist realism in Britain see Raymond Williams, 'Realism and the Contemporary Novel', in *The Long Revolution* (London: Chatto and Windus, 1961), pp.274–89; 'After Socialist Realism', in Gasiorek, *Post-War British Fiction*, pp.71–96 (Gasiorek discusses the influence of socialist realism on John Berger and Doris Lessing in particular); Doris Lessing offers a fascinating account of her visit to the Soviet Union in the 1950s as a guest of the Union of Soviet Writers, Lessing, *Walking in the Shade: Part Two of My Autobiography, 1949–1962* (London: Harper Collins, 1997) 52–80. See also Morrison, 1980, pp.34–5.

37 Raymond Williams, 'Realism and the Contemporary Novel', in *The Long Revolution* (London: Chatto & Windus, 1961), pp.274–89.

enacted the desires and ambitions of the individualistic middle classes through narratives of social progression, whilst the latter attempted to articulate an empowering and revolutionary project for working-class activism through narratives of collectivized social struggle. Williams developed this argument to call for a return to realism for the contemporary committed novel, as the most productive form in which an integrated and holistic view of society could be produced. From this representation of a holistic society a political project of commitment could be generated:

> literature is committed to the detail of known experience, and any valuable social change would be the same kind of practical and responsible discipline [...] In the highest realism, society is seen in fundamentally personal terms, and persons, through relationships, in fundamentally social terms. The integration is controlling, yet of course it is not to be achieved by an act of will. If it comes at all, it is a creative discovery, and can perhaps only be recorded within the structure and substance of the realist novel. (287)

However, despite Williams's attempt to re-define a contemporary committed project for the realist novel, the status of socialist realism as the literary evocation of a revolutionary politics proved problematic for many fifties writers. As Doris Lessing writes:

> To say, in 1957, that one believes artists should be committed, is to arouse hostility and distrust because of the quantities of bad novels [...] produced under the banner of committedness; [...] The reaction is so powerful [...] that one has only to stand up on a public platform and say one still believes in the class analysis of society and therefore of art, in short that one is a Marxist, for nine-tenths of the audience immediately to assume that one believes novels should be simple tracts about factories or strikes or economic injustice. [38]

Here, Lessing identifies a central problem in terms of the form in which a committed writer could articulate a socialist critique of Western capitalism. She accepts the continued need for a 'committed' literature, but questions the form in which that literature had previously been produced. The 'social tracts' she refers to relate to socialist realist novels, and, as she intimates, many were beginning to regard

38   Lessing, 'The Small Personal Voice', p.13.

the ideological and formal restrictions of this literary mode with suspicion. The constraints of both socialist and critical realism (as defined in Lukàcs's work and appropriated by Zhdanov) were beginning to open up anxieties amongst committed writers who were concerned about the adequacy of these forms to produce a contemporary and successful radical literature in a British context. In addition, the correspondence of the realist form with the dominant ideology of the middle classes raised contradictions in terms of form and ideology that the radical writers felt it necessary to treat with scepticism.

It is this concern with form that is informing the approach to narrative technique adopted by the writers discussed in the second part of this book. Before moving on to the novelists, however, I want to explore the impact of another important area of cultural writing in the 1950s: the theories and analyses developed by the British New Left.

Chapter Three
The Early New Left: Class Revision

The Early New Left: Contexts, Contents and Contests

One of the main contentions of this book is that the radical fiction of the 1950s attempted to articulate empowering discourses for marginalized groups that were not being adequately represented in contemporary intellectual and theoretical discourses. The British New Left emerged as the main location for radical intellectual writing in the late fifties and to fully engage with the radical fiction of the period it is necessary to explore the way in which marginalized voices were being represented in the corpus of texts produced by this group. The New Left were responding to contemporary 'structures of feeling'[1] that intersected with, and corresponded to, similar impulses in the radical fiction, but the theoretical models developed by the New Left produced textual (mis-) representations and silences with regard to emergent and marginalized identities in Britain in terms of class, youth, 'race', ethnicity and gender.

Paul Gilroy suggests that 'thinking about identity' was a key linking characteristic in much of the early New Left and British Cultural Studies work produced in the fifties and sixties. As he writes:

---

1   Here I refer to Raymond Williams's definition of a holistic 'structures of feeling' underlying a specific (national) culture at any moment in history. Raymond Williams, *The Long Revolution* (London: Chatto and Windus, 1961), pp.64–88. Although Williams's concept is problematic in its unitary and holistic form, which excludes a multiple sense of 'structures' rather than 'structure', it is still a useful concept in identifying an elusive and unquantifiable awareness of the cultural and social make-up of a specific historical 'moment'. See also my discussion of Williams's concept in chapter one.

It may be that an interest in identity and its political workings in a variety of different social and historical sites provided a point of intersection between divergent intellectual interests from which a self-conscious cultural studies was gradually born.[2]

This 'thinking about identity', he goes on to suggest, is the key impulse behind the three central texts of the emerging New Left, Richard Hoggart's *The Uses of Literacy*, Raymond Williams's *The Long Revolution* and Edward Thompson's *The Making of the English Working-class*.[3] Gilroy identifies the impulse to represent a particular sense of identity, centred on the English working classes, which informs all of these texts, and he goes on to identify the underlying process of reconstructing national identity evident in these works. The core work of the New Left should, therefore, be understood as a series of texts that articulated contemporary anxieties about the nature of identity, both in terms of class and the nation, and which were responding to specific changes in social, political and cultural relationships. These include debates concerning 'classlessness'; the 'affluent society'; the 'crisis' in left-wing politics articulated in terms of communism, socialism and Marxism; and the impact on the nation's 'imagined community' by the processes of decolonization and the immigration of black cultures and communities from Britain's former colonies.[4]

Following Gilroy, I aim to make two related points. Firstly, the theoretical models developed by the New Left produced misrepresentations and silences in relation to the specific concerns of certain marginalized groups in Britain. This is because, as Gilroy argues, the New Left was primarily concerned with a unitary conception of Brit-

2   Paul Gilroy, 'British Cultural Studies and the Pitfalls of Identity', in *Black British Cultural Studies: A Reader*, ed. by Houston A Baker, Jr., Manthia Diawara and Ruth Lindborg (Chicago and London: University of Chicago Press, 1996), pp.223–39 (p.231).
3   Ibid., p.234. Richard Hoggart, *The Uses of Literacy* (Harmondsworth: Penguin, 1958), first published 1957; Williams, 1961); E.P. Thompson, *The Making of the English Working-class* (Harmondsworth: Penguin, 1968), first published 1963.
4   I am using Benedict Anderson's phrase here to represent the construction of national identity as an 'imagined community', Benedict Anderson, *Imagined Communities* (London: Verso and New Left Books, 1983).

ish national identity, grounded as it was on a re-assessment and re-analysis of working-class culture: 'The boundaries of the nation formed the essential parameters in which these conflicts took shape.'[5] In particular, the New Left's representations of youth subcultures and the impact of emerging 'immigrant' communities were affected by its primary focus on the articulation of a distinct 'imagined community' of the English working classes. Furthermore, the New Left's theoretical models obscured differences and inequalities in relation to gender, with the result that dominant representations of gender identities were reproduced rather than challenged.

Secondly, the lack of emphasis on identifying and representing alternative marginalized identities in early New Left discourse was caused by an over-emphasis on class as a category of analysis. As Gilroy argues:

> The subtle and thoughtful concern with class and its dynamics yielded slowly and only partially to different agendas set by countercultural movements and oppositional practices that constituted new social actors and consequently new political identities.[6]

Despite the New Left's attempt to re-assess and re-negotiate the traditional methodologies and approaches of Marxism, it maintained a central reliance on the Marxist privileging of class in its analysis of power relationships within society. In fact 'class' was the category on which the debate around the inconsistencies of Marxist analysis was articulated. The debates on 'revisionism', the 'affluent society' and 'classlessness' provided the basis for the re-assessment and re-negotiation of Marxist theoretical models; but the fact that class retained its primary status as a category of analysis resulted in the tendency to overlook 'other' categories of identity.

The combination of various historical contexts, as discussed in chapter one above, contributed to the substance and theoretical frameworks developed by the early New Left. The Suez Crisis and the

---

5   Gilroy, 'British Cultural Studies and the Pitfalls of Identity', p.234.
6   Ibid., p.232.

Hungarian rebellion were particularly important events in this context. As Stuart Hall has written:

> 'Hungary' and 'Suez' were thus 'liminal', boundary-marking experiences. They symbolized the break-up of the political Ice Age [...] Its [The New Left] rise signified for people on the left in my generation the end of the tyranny, the imposed silences and political impasses, of the Cold War in politics, and the possibility of a break-through into a new socialist project.[7]

These events acted as a catalyst for an already discontented attitude towards the contemporary direction of socialist strategies in Britain. E.P. Thompson, writing about the history of left-wing struggle over the decades between the 1930s and the 1950s, commented that: 'Those who [...] are still committed to politics, are often committed with glassy-eyed submission.'[8] Williams, going further in identifying the contemporary crisis of socialism, argued: 'The main challenge to capitalism was socialism, but this has almost wholly lost any contemporary meaning.'[9] In response to this perceived crisis in the state of socialism, Williams and Hall, in particular, felt there was a need to reinvigorate and re-negotiate the theoretical models on which contemporary socialism in Britain was based.[10] The underlying aim, as Stuart Hall suggested, was to 'make socialists' rather than 'building another socialist sect'.[11] It was felt by Hall and Williams that this should be

7   Stuart Hall, 'The "First" New Left: Life and Times', in *Out of Apathy: Voices of the New Left 30 Years On*, ed. by The Oxford University Socialist Discussion Group (London and New York: Verso, 1989), pp.11–38 (p.13).

8   E.P. Thompson, 'Commitment in Politics', in *Universities and Left Review*, No.6, Spring 1959, p.50–5.

9   Williams, *The Long Revolution*, p.301.

10   It is important to note that this project was approached differently by various members of the early New Left ranging from E.P. Thompson's continuation of a broadly conventional Marxist approach to the historical study of working-class political movements, to Stuart Hall's re-assessment of some of the basic models of Marxism, to Raymond Williams's attempt to produce an alternative vocabulary and approach for socio-cultural analysis, to Richard Hoggart's post-Leavisite approach to the study of contemporary working-class culture and society.

11   Stuart Hall, 'The Big Swipe', in *Universities and Left Review*, No.7, Autumn 1959, p.52.

achieved through a re-evaluation of the methodology and approach of 'traditional' Marxist interpretations of society and culture by responding to the specifically 'new' cultural and social phenomena. As Hall pointed out: 'Clearly, there has been a major shift in the patterns of social life.'[12] For Hall, this involved responding to localized social, cultural, political and economic conditions rather than deploying an abstracted analytical Marxist theory imposed from above. The need for an experiential approach that identified these specific and localized social practices necessitated, according to Hall and Williams, a re-formulation and re-negotiation of the approaches of a social theory developed from the previous generation of Marxist critics. As Hall has since written: 'the New Left always regarded Marxism as a problem, as trouble, as danger, not as solution [...] the first British New Left emerged in 1956 at the moment of the disintegration of an entire historical/political project'.[13]

In response to the crisis in socialism, the New Left attempted to shift the theoretical terrain from economic issues to the study of *cultural* frameworks. If there was strong evidence that Britain was becoming a more 'classless' society economically, it could be argued that, culturally, there were still deep divisions between the classes. It was upon this recognition of a class structure understood in cultural terms that the New Left could ensure the continuation of a socialist politics. One important issue here was the traditional base/super-structure model in Marxist theory and how it related to cultural production. Williams stresses that in Marx the base/superstructure model is 'definite' but 'no more than an analogy',[14] emphasizing the contemporary 'vulgarization' of the complexity of Marx's original writing on the issue. Hall also contested the contemporary reliance in Marxist theory on the base/superstructure model, arguing that it was necessary to 'break the "economic base" down into constituent fac-

---

12 Stuart Hall, 'A Sense of Classlessness', in *Universities and Left Review*, No.5, Autumn 1958, p.26.
13 Stuart Hall, 'Cultural Studies and its Legacies', in *Cultural Studies*, ed. by Lawrence Grossberg, Cary Nelson and Paula A. Treichler (London and New York: Routledge, 1992), pp.277–94 (p.279).
14 Ibid.

tors, permitting a much freer play in our interpretation between "base" and "superstructure" [...] This is necessary because we are concerned with a changing pattern of life, attitudes and values.'[15] According to Hall, this would expand upon 'vulgar-Marxist interpretations' of art and culture as manifestations of the 'ideological superstructure'. He writes:

> The model of 'base and superstructure' is – or ought to be – at the heart of every 'rethinking' and 'revisionist' controversy. It seems clear to me [...] that the simplistic economic-determinist reading of this formula has now to be discarded.[16]

Here, Hall is anticipating later developments in Marxist theory based on the 'relative autonomy' of cultural practices in relation to economic conditions associated in the sixties with Louis Althusser.[17] This can be seen as a strategic move for a group of socialist theorists who were attempting to construct a persuasive discourse of social critique in a period when there was strong empirical evidence that capitalism seemed to be working economically, not only for the middle classes, but also for the working classes.

15   Hall, 'A Sense of Classlessness', p.27.
16   Ibid., p.27
17   Louis Althusser, 'Ideology and Ideological State Apparatuses', in *Lenin and Philosophy: and Other Essays*, 2nd. edn., trans. by Ben Brewster (London: New Left Books, 1977). See also the engagement with Althusserian post-Marxist theory by the New Left in the sixties and seventies, by Williams, Hall and Terry Eagleton in particular. See Williams, *Marxism and Literature* (Oxford: Oxford University Press, 1977); Hall, 'A Critical Survey of the Theoretical and Practical Achievements of the Last Ten Years', in *Literature, Society and the Sociology of Literature*, ed. by F. Barker and others (Essex: University of Essex, 1977), pp.1–7; Terry Eagleton, *Criticism and Ideology* (London: Verso, 1976).

Class, Culture and Community in New Left Discourse

The debate on the nature and direction of a contemporary socialist politics was often articulated through the issue of 'classlessness'. As Chas Critcher identifies:

> It is only an apparent paradox that the serious study of working-class culture should emerge just at the moment when it was being loudly proclaimed that the working class had ceased to exist. The discovery of working-class culture was a *response* to this argument.[18]

The 'serious study' Critcher refers to is the range of sociological studies of working-class life and culture produced in the 1950s. These included several articles in *Encounter* and *The Spectator*, such as T.R. Fyvel's 'The Stones of Harlow: Reflections on Subtopia', Wayland Young's 'Return to Wigan Pier', and two articles on class by Charles Curran.[19] In addition, 'The Institute of Community Studies' produced research reports on working-class life from 1957 onwards, including Young and Wilmot's influential study, *Family and Kinship in East London*.[20] This increase in the sociological study of working-class culture was, as Critcher argues, in response to contemporary discourses of classlessness, that were undermining the theoretical ground on which socialist political activity had traditionally been based.

From within the New Left, Stuart Hall attempted to theorize the debate on classlessness in a 1958 article in the New Left journal, *Universities and Left Review*.[21] Here, Hall argued that a contemporary

---

18 Chas Critcher, 'Sociology, Cultural Studies and the Post-War Working-class', in *Working-class Culture: Studies in History and Theory*, ed. by John Clarke, Chas Critcher and Richard Johnson (London: Hutchinson, 1979), pp.13–40 (p.16).

19 T.R. Fyvel, 'The Stones of Harlow: Reflections on Subtopia', in *Encounter*, June 1956, p.15. Wayland Young, 'Return to Wigan Pier', in *Encounter*, June 1956, p.5. Charles Curran, 'The New Estate in Great Britain', in *The Spectator*, Jan. 1956, p.72. I discuss these texts further in chapter six below.

20 M. Young and P. Wilmot, *Family and Kinship in East London* (London: Routledge and Kegan Paul, 1957).

21 Stuart Hall, 'A Sense of Classlessness'.

shift in the mode of production in contemporary society had fundamentally altered the relations of production between the classes. He argued that technological advances meant that the worker no longer felt alienated from the product s/he produced because a level of sophistication and skill was required. According to Hall, this shift had altered the models for analyzing class and class struggle in contemporary society. Hall was subsequently attacked from within the New Left, by E.P. Thompson and Raphael Samuel, for his 'revisionist' position.[22] Thompson and Samuel's position was more conventionally Marxist and they were suspicious of any attempt to identify new socio-economic frameworks in contemporary society that threatened to undermine the model of a class-based society that they felt to be essential in maintaining a discourse of class struggle. But, in fact, Hall was not suggesting that a new 'classless' society had emerged as a result of new economic conditions, rather that 'classlessness' was a superficial appearance of the new modes of production. He was concerned to stress that there were still deep divisions between the classes, and focusing on cultural rather than economic phenomena could bring these to light more productively. What is apparent in the ensuing exchange in the pages of *ULR* is that despite the attempt by Hall to re-negotiate Marxist theoretical models, the ground of the debate consistently returned to issues of class.

Hall's article also highlights problems in the critical vocabulary of traditional Marxist analysis. He suggests that conventional Marxist theoretical vocabulary was often restricted in its overall aim by the very language it used. It is useful at this stage to deploy Steven Connor's concept of the 'addressivity' of textual discourse.[23] Connor

22   In reply to Hall's article Thompson and Samuel attempted to historicize Hall's claims and to show that the contemporary focus on style, new technological and market practices were not in fact new, but could also be identified in Victorian society, thereby implicitly arguing that traditional Marxist approaches were still the most relevant form of social critique. See Hall (1958; 1959); E.P. Thompson, 'Commitment in Politics'; Raphael Samuel, 'Class and Classlessness', in *Universities and Left Review*, No.6, Spring 1959, pp.44–50.

23   See Steven Connor, *The English Novel in History: 1950–1995* (London and New York: Routledge, 1996), pp.8–13. I return to Connor's model in part two

argues that a text constructs a projected addressee through the ideological assumptions of the structure and language it deploys. Hall identified that the critical method and vocabulary deployed by fifties Marxist discourse was being reproduced in some New Left analyses, and it produced a discourse that failed to 'address' the primary groups from which it was attempting to gain political support. This observation was again located primarily in terms of class. Hall argued that the discourse produced by contemporary socialist analysis alienated its primary target by re-objectifying the working class as a 'subject' of analysis by an external cultural analyst. This resulted in the distancing of the object of analysis from the discourse, which, of course, was problematic for a socialist discourse that was attempting to 'make socialists' from *all* classes in society, and primarily from the working classes.[24]

Hall later approached this problem in terms of Gramsci's concept of the 'organic intellectual'.[25] Gramsci argued that the duty of the socialist and revolutionary intellectual was twofold. Firstly: to be one step ahead of the theories propounded by dominant society and thereby represent a theoretical avant-garde; and secondly: to communicate that theoretical position to the revolutionary group who would ultimately provide the actual force of revolution. The organic intellectual, therefore, needed to reproduce and communicate his/her theoretical

of this book when discussing the narrative techniques deployed by Sillitoe, MacInnes and Selvon.

24   Stuart Hall, 'The Big Swipe', in *Universities and Left Review*, No.7, Autumn 1959, pp.50–2 (p.52). Thompson adds a further dimension to this issue by claiming both an 'anti-working-class' element in contemporary working-class analysis (alluding to Hall), and with an opposite, but equally detrimental approach that he describes as 'romanticizing' the working class. He notes this latter approach particularly in Hoggart's construction of older working-class culture: 'To romanticise the working-class, or to abstract from it a doctrinaire emblem of evergreen militancy, is as much a betrayal of living working people as are the attitudes which I have termed "anti-working-class".', Thompson, 'Commitment in Politics', p.52.

25   Hall discusses the importance of Gramsci's notion of the 'organic intellectual' for understanding the failure of the early New Left to appeal to a broad support amongst the working class as well as the intellectual middle class, Hall, 'Cultural Studies and its Legacies', p.281.

findings in a form, and using a vocabulary, that would be understood at all levels of society.[26] The early New Left were attempting to produce a more accessible theoretical discourse on class, but the objectification, distancing and homogenizing of the working classes in traditional Marxist approaches was often re-articulated and re-adopted by some early New Left analyses.[27]

It is apparent that there was a range of methodological approaches and theoretical models being produced in the late 1950s both inside and outside the New Left that attempted to represent working-class society and culture. The sociological approaches of 'The Institute of Community Studies' contrasted with the theoretical discussions adopted by Hall and the stress on political class struggle pursued by Thompson. These differing approaches inevitably produced different representations of working-class life. It is within this context of differing, and often contesting, forms and methodological approaches of working-class analysis that Richard Hoggart's *The Uses of Literacy* was produced. Hoggart's overall project was to record the cultural practices and communal values of a traditional English working-class culture and to identify an emergent working class that he felt to be challenging those cultural values. His representation of the working class was, therefore, informed by a project of resistance to the effects of newer forms of social, economic and cultural frameworks on the older working class. He was concerned to produce a critique of the consumerist Americanization of English culture based on cheap sensationalism, which, alluding to Matthew Arnold, he described as 'shiny barbarism'.[28] He defined the new society as anti-

---

26   Antonio Gramsci, '[The Intellectuals]', in *A Gramsci Reader: Selected Writings 1916–1935*, ed. by David Forgacs (London: Lawrence and Wishart, 1988), pp. 301–11.

27   E.P. Thompson identifies this problematic in terms of tone in New Left writing especially in what he sees as the younger generation of New Left writers. Thompson writes: 'These attitudes seem to me to stem from an ambiguity as to the place of the working-class in the struggle to create a socialist society: a tendency to view working people as the *subjects* of history, as pliant *recipients* of the imprint of the mass media, as *victims* of alienation, as *data* for socio-logical enquiry', Thompson, 'Commitment in Politics', p.51.

28   Hoggart, *The Uses of Literacy*, p.193.

intellectual, 'highbrow-hating' (183), and the move to consumerism of the new culture as representing a 'limitless "progressivism" of things' (172). He also stressed the move from a sense of community in traditional working-class culture to a pleasure seeking individualism: 'The temptations, especially as they appear in mass-publications, are towards a gratification of the self and towards what may be called a "hedonistic-group-individualism".' (173). Hoggart argued that this resulted in the imprecise use of moral definitions such as 'freedom', and 'tolerance':

> the new manners include a variety of 'democratic' tones of voice and are decided by the urge for gaiety and slickness at all costs; the main assumptions are over-weaning egalitarianism, freedom, tolerance, progress, hedonism, and the cult of youth. (241)

Hoggart also focused on the role of the mass media in the creation of this new society, describing most mass entertainment as 'full of a corrupt brightness, of improper appeals and moral evasions' (340), perpetuated by 'those who provide the entertainment' (331). According to Hoggart, this new culture promoted a *sense* of classlessness, although it masked actual economic distinctions between rich and poor. He sums up his argument with the belief that: 'We are becoming culturally classless' (342), an observation that appears more threatening to Hoggart than the existence of an *economic* classlessness.

Hoggart's approach combines autobiography, quasi-fictional forms and critical analysis, and represents an attempt on his part to include the subject of analysis within the frame of the critical discourse produced. His approach is initially defined against what he perceives as traditional sociological or anthropological approaches to the study of working-class life. He achieves this by foregrounding a distinction in perspective in terms of an internal/external opposition between a 'visitor', who would focus upon the 'understandably depressing' working-class environment, and the 'insider' who is attuned to the positive aspects of community and solidarity represented by the 'neighbourhood'.[29] Hoggart develops this binary opposite of inclusion and exclusion through a discourse that places him as a kind of narrator-observer who is able to represent the 'imaginative' culture of the working class to an external addressee.

However, the theoretical limitations of Hoggart's approach can be identified in his tendency to overlook other categories of marginalized identity. Hoggart bases his analysis on the construction of the cohesive social unit of the 'neighbourhood', which for him represents the true nature of working-class culture and community. Because of his concern to resist newer forms of working-class cultural practices, most notably amongst working-class youth, he produces an essentially nostalgic construction of older working-class culture. His discourse identifies the processes by which white working-class culture defines itself in relation to a series of other marginalized and excluded identities. He, therefore, refers to the creation of an intimate community through a series of negations in terms of identity with the exclusion of, for example: 'those who have a daughter who went wrong', the 'housewife' who is a 'fusspot and scours her window-ledges and steps twice a week', and the 'young woman [who] had her black child after the annual visit of the circus' (60). These definitions reveal the theoretical limitations of Hoggart's model as the categories of 'race' and gender remain outside of the scope of his analysis, partly because they might threaten to undermine the cohesive model of working-class identity he is trying to produce.

Raymond Williams engaged in the debate on the representation of the working class through a critique of the traditional Marxist understanding of class in relation to the creation of an artificial distinction between the individual and society, a distinction that he regarded as historically contextualized and dependent on a range of 'superstructural' factors, rather than primarily dependent on economic conditions. According to Williams, Marxist approaches construct an artificial and problematic model of the 'masses' (or the proletariat), and subsequently read 'class' as an abstraction.[30] This resulted in an

29   Hoggart articulates this opposition in the working-class vernacular terms and concepts of 'them and us', ibid., pp.72–101.
30   Williams, *The Long Revolution*, p.72.

alienation of the contemporary working class from the discursive practice of Marxist theory. Williams replaces the Marxist concepts of 'class', the 'proletariat', 'alienation' and 'false consciousness' with a set of alternative concepts for analysing contemporary (British) working-class culture and society. He introduces the concepts of 'structures of feeling', 'community', 'a whole way of life' and 'solidarity', which attempt to articulate a holistic understanding of society and a collective group consciousness within working-class culture based on experiential, empirical and 'organic' evidence rather than the abstractions of 'vulgar' Marxism.[31] In *The Long Revolution*, Williams stresses the importance of 'community' as a moral necessity in the organization of society, defining it as an imperative cohesive force which was being eroded by the individualism of consumer capitalism: 'Unless we achieve some realistic sense of community, our true standard of living will continue to be distorted' (299).

The Long Revolution represents a crucial moment in the early New Left's agenda of re-assessing the traditional Marxist project. Within Williams's model is contained the possibility of marking what Stuart Hall later calls the two 'interruptions' of British Cultural Studies: feminism and 'race'.[32] However, Williams's discourse does not stress these 'interruptions' because to do so would undermine his attempt to develop a methodology for reading culture in terms of 'a whole way of life' and 'structures of feeling': concepts that attempt to unify, rather than pluralize, the reading of cultural practices within the boundaries of the working class in national terms.[33] Williams's attempt to identify a *generational* structure to cultural development through emergent cultures remains resistant to distinctions of youth, 'race' and gender within the working classes (or 'working people' as

31 Williams was producing an 'independent' and alternative model of socialist critique throughout the 1950s that culminated in his two seminal texts *Culture and Society*, and *The Long Revolution*. The fact that this alternative discourse was taken up by the New Left after 1956 is another indication of the crisis of contemporary socialist and Marxist theory as perceived by the intellectual left in Britain. See in particular his discussion of these alternative concepts in Williams, *The Long Revolution*, pp.46–9.

32 Hall, 'Cultural Studies and its Legacies', p.282.

33 Williams, *The Long Revolution*, pp.64–88.

Williams refers to them).[34] To identify these other categories *within* his model of community would open up the potential of structurally undermining the very foundations upon which the model was built.

The concepts of 'neighbourhood', 'a whole way of life', 'structures of feeling', 'community', and 'solidarity' introduced, or reassessed, by Williams and Hoggart offer an alternative range of theoretical concepts to the Marxist vocabulary of 'proletariat', 'false consciousness', 'alienation' 'agency' and 'mode of production', and they represent an alternative model of class, based on cultural rather than economic factors. Hoggart and Williams deploy these concepts as part of a project to celebrate the positive characteristics of a traditional working-class culture, as a way of re-engaging politically active socialists with a core of common values for which socialism could fight to retain. They were responding to the emergence of a new consumer and individualist culture that was felt to be threatening these core values. Paul Gilroy's perceptive reading of the early New Left writings as discourses in identity becomes crucial here.[35] Williams and Hoggart, in particular, were attempting to recover an older diminishing working-class culture based on community and solidarity. Hoggart articulates this through his celebration of 'neighbourhood', which he argues was a strong element in the binding collective identity of older working-class life.[36] This sense of neighbourhood, he suggests, was being replaced in the new working-class culture by a loose 'group sense' which he calls a 'callow democratic egalitarianism' based on 'ramified forms of individualism'.[37]

Stuart Hall engages with this issue of representation by identifying the formal and linguistic distinctions between New Left and Marxist discourses and the articulation of an oppositional politics in imaginative literature. In a critique of John Mander's book *The Writer and Commitment*, he writes:

34   This represents Williams's initial position on what he later defines as dominant, emergent and residual cultures identifiable during a particular period of a nation's cultural history. See Raymond Williams, *Problems in Materialism and Culture* (London: Verso, 1980), pp.37–45.
35   Gilroy, 'British Cultural Studies and the Pitfalls of Identity', p.231.
36   Hoggart, *The Uses of Literacy*, pp.58–68.
37   Ibid., pp.178–9.

we need the theory of literature which no critic has attempted to provide [...] I believe that [...] we are constantly being offered, in literature, and more generally, in our culture, ways of seeing, definitions and meanings, which are not available in any other way.[38]

Here, Hall regards literature as providing a different range of technical and linguistic approaches, denied to contemporary models of sociological study, which were potentially more successful in the representation, empowerment and production of a political consciousness amongst working-class people.

This concern was articulated particularly in the radical fiction of the period. Fiction allowed a range of formal techniques and strategies by which the representation of marginalized identities could be produced without alienating the marginalized subject that discourse.[39] The number of novelists connected to the New Left reveals this phenomenon. Michael Kenny lists several writers who were attached to the New Left, either officially as members of New Left groups, or indirectly through producing articles for the New Left journals: John Osborne, Dennis Potter, Shelagh Delaney, Doris Lessing, John Braine, Kenneth Tynan, and Alan Sillitoe.[40] The issue of working-class representation is also revealed by the number of 1950s novels specifically concerned with showing the contemporary British working class. As well as the traditional range of 'Angry' novelists dealing with this issue (Sillitoe, Braine, Williams, Waterhouse)[41], the number of 'middle-class' writers who produced novels set in British working-class environments reveals the importance of the issue for late fifties culture. Novels in this category would include Muriel Spark's *The*

38   Stuart Hall, 'Commitment Dilemma', in *New Left Review*, No.10, July/August, 1961, pp.67–9 (p.69).
39   I will develop this point about form and representation in greater detail in the following chapters.
40   Michael Kenny, *The First New Left: British Intellectuals After Stalin* (London: Lawrence and Wishart, 1995), p.99.
41   In chapter four below I discuss the issues raised in this chapter in relation to Alan Sillitoe's writing in the late fifties. John Braine, *Room at the Top* (Harmondsworth: Penguin, 1959), first published 1957; Raymond Williams, *Border Country* (London: Chatto and Windus, 1960); Keith Waterhouse, *Billy Liar* (London: Michael Joseph, 1959).

Ballad of Peckham Rye, Clancy Sigal's *Weekend in Dinlock*, John Berger's *A Painter for Our Time*, Gerald Kersch's *Fowlers End*, and, in particular, Doris Lessing's semi-autobiographical, *In Pursuit of the English*, which foregrounds the problems in locating and defining the English 'working class' for the externalized, middle-class, post-colonial writer.[42] It is significant, however, that the writers who were concerned to identify specific radical discourses related to youth and 'race' are excluded from Kenny's list of New Left writers, in partic-ular, Colin MacInnes, Alexander Trocchi, Sam Selvon and George Lamming. This factor reveals the distance between the New Left and the marginalized groups of teenage youth cultures and the new black British communities that are beginning to be represented in the radical fiction.

'Barbarians in Wonderland': New Left Readings of 1950s Youth Subcultures[43]

One of the significant preoccupations of fifties culture was the rise and nature of new forms and social categories identified as 'youth' and/or the 'teenager'. This phenomenon was identified across a range of forms and became a principal site for imaginative cultural pro-duction and a category of analysis for sociological and cultural com-mentary. The economic conditions prevailing in 1950s Britain were conducive to the rise of a distinct subcultural group of adolescents and young adults who had free capital due to increased employment opportunities, without having the financial commitments required by

---

42   Muriel Spark, *The Ballad of Peckham Rye* (London: Macmillan, 1960); Clancy Sigal, *Weekend in Dinlock* (London: Secker and Warburg, 1960), although this book is more a social investigation than a novel it deploys many formal char-acteristics usually found in fiction; John Berger, *The Foot of Clive* (London: Methuen, 1962); Gerald Kersch, *Fowlers End* (London: Heineman, 1958); Doris Lessing, *In Pursuit of the English* (London: MacGibbon and Kee, 1960.

43   The quotation is taken from Hoggart, *The Uses of Literacy*, p.193.

family and children.[44] The importation of American popular cultural forms in music, fashion, film and fiction, directed specifically towards this new subculture, offered British youth a site of escape from the traditional career and development trajectories expected and experienced by dominant and 'parent' culture. Musical forms such as jazz, skiffle and rock'n'roll; films such as *On the Waterfront, The Wild One, Rebel Without a Cause, Blackboard Jungle* and *Rock Around the Clock*; new fashion styles that represented an increased emphasis on youth to express itself through visual symbols; and fiction, in particular J.D. Salinger's *Catcher in the Rye* and the influence on certain youth subcultures of American Beat writers such as Jack Kerouac, Allan Ginsberg and William Burroughs, all offered varying, but connected and imported cultural sites for the expression of the specific concerns and anxieties of British youth.[45] These cultural forms offered texts of potentially radical resistance for British youth; resistance both to dominant culture and to the working-class subordinate, or 'parent', culture.[46] However, the construction of, and reaction to, the phenomenon of 'youth' culture varied across different textual sites. The mainstream media tended to view youth subcultures as indicative of a general moral malaise focusing on images of violence, excess and sexual promiscuity. Much was made of the Teddy Boys subculture and the aura of urban violence that surrounded it, fuelled by reports in the press of specific instances of violent clashes, for example, at the release of the film *Rock Around the Clock* in film theatres up and

44 Between 1951 and 1963 wages rose by 72%, whilst prices rose by only 45%, see Robert Hewison, *Too Much: Art and Society in the Sixties 1960–75* (London: Methuen, 1986), p.6.

45 See Alan Sinfield 's discussion of the importance of these youth cultural forms in the 1950s as sites for radical British youth, 'Making a Scene', Alan Sinfield, *Literature, Politics and Culture in Postwar Britain* (Oxford: Basil Blackwell, 1989) pp.152–81.

46 Here, I am using Sinfield's model of dominant, subordinate and radical distinctions within a specific historical culture (Ibid., p.34), and allying it with the distinctions developed in much New Left writing on working-class youth subcultures between 'youth' and 'parent' cultures (for example, in Phil Cohen, 'Sub-Cultural Conflict and Working-class Community', in *The Subcultures Reader*, ed. by Ken Gelder and Sarah Thornton (London and New York: Routledge, 1997), pp.90–9.

down the country.[47] In Britain, the association of youth with Americanized popular forms and with 'black' culture helped to focus mainstream 'adult' reaction on to the 'immoral' and 'foreign' influences and practices that contemporary youth culture was thought to represent.

Before analyzing the response to youth by the New Left, it is necessary to summarize the kind of radicalism that youth subcultural lifestyle and cultural practice offered. 'Youth' as a distinct social category represents a heterogeneous range of cultural practices and productions that includes music, fashion styles, inter-group relationships, cultural 'spaces' and literature. In the 1950s, these practices and products involved the appropriation of different layers of signification in terms of visual and aural culture as well as distinct codes of practice and physical spaces, such as coffee bars, record and clothes shops, jazz clubs and dance halls. These marginalized spaces represented the sites where a variety of youth subcultures could form and interact with each other. Although the New Left tended to focus on Ted and 'teenage' subcultures, fifties 'youth' can be located across a wide range of subcultural identities. I will discuss these in greater detail in the next section, but a list of the variety of youth subcultures will here demonstrate the heterogeneity of the phenomenon. Apart from the Teds and 'teenagers', there were distinct subcultural groups who followed jazz, including 'trad' and 'mod' variants, both with distinct subcultural identities.[48] CND, despite its cross-generational support, also contained a specific youth following within its ranks and offered an alternative form of youth subcultural identity. There was also a rising subcultural youth element in the art schools, represented by British Pop Art and the 'Independent Group', a movement developed in the 1950s by a group of working-class artists and art students such as Richard Hamilton, Peter Blake, Eduardo Paolozzi and David Hockney as a response to the specific cultural influences impacting on them and

---

47 See Sinfield, *Literature, Politics and Culture*, pp.153–4.
48 MacInnes offers a description of the distinct cultural differences and forms of identity produced by these subcultures in *Absolute Beginners*, Colin MacInnes (Harmondsworth: Penguin, 1964), first published in 1959, pp.70–1.

conceived in opposition to the 'dominant' and 'elitist' art world.[49] It could also be argued that the 'scholarship boys', those children of working-class parents who had gained government grants to pursue a university education, constituted a form of youth subcultural identity, albeit one that stressed the isolation of the individual young scholar.[50] All these sites offered the potential for radical discourses and cultural forms in relation to dominant and parent culture: from the utopian egalitarianism and anti-prejudicial environment of the jazz clubs to the articulation of distinct and radical fashion styles as expressions of a rejection of mainstream culture; from the anti-intellectual and anti-hierarchical incorporation of high and popular cultural forms represented by Pop Art to the engagement with American Beat writing as a rejection of traditional and capitalist forms and codes of behaviour. In addition, the emphasis on sexual liberation, across youth subcultures, was associated with an undirected project to radically challenge the

49 See Hewison, *Too Much*, pp.186–91. Also the fifties art schools saw the interaction of various popular cultural forms which developed into a distinct British popular forms in the sixties with people such as John Lennon, Paul MacCartney, Mick Jagger and Pete Townshend.
50 Within this loose subcultural group, which represented a transition between classes through education, could be included Kingsley Amis, John Holloway, Donald Davie, D.J. Enright and Tony Harrison. Raymond Williams and Richard Hoggart represent a slightly older generation of this phenomenon, although they do not recognize it in terms of a specific youth 'subculture' in their writing. Also, considering the ages of the editorial team of *Universities and Left Review*, all in their early-to-mid-twenties, this constitutes a kind of subcultural youth group, one that was not recognized as such in their writing. The 'scholarship boy' is represented more fully in fiction and drama, for example in key texts such as John Wain's *Hurry On Down*, and John Osborne's *Look Back in Anger*, both of which deal with individuals from working, or lower-middle-class, backgrounds who face disillusionment and alienation once educated through the university system. See also Ken Worpole's 'Scholarship Boy' in *The Bloodaxe Critical Anthologies 1: Tony Harrison*, ed. by Neil Astley (Newcastle: Bloodaxe, 1991), pp.61–74; Brian Jackson and Dennis Marsden, *Education and the Working-class* (Harmondsworth: Penguin, 1966), first published 1962; and Frances Stevens, *The New Inheritors* (London: Hutchinson Educational, 1970).

moral and ethical codes and patterns of behaviour of the preceding generation.[51]

However, the New Left tended to overlook this aspect of youth culture, despite the importance of 'youth' identified in the range and amount of writing it dedicated to the topic.[52] This focus on youth was, in fact, part of a project of regenerating socialism by appealing to, and attempting to politicize, a new generation of activists. The analyses of youth subcultures, though, tended to be based not on formal or aesthetic representations, but on socio-economic issues of consumption, class and cultural practices. Therefore, rather than identifying potentially radical sites, the New Left's readings of youth ranged from a dismissal of distinctions between 'youth' and 'parent' culture as anything more than a perennial generational difference, to the concept of youth as a new 'problem' needed to be addressed. Much New Left analysis of youth subcultures follows what Kevin Davey has identified as the combination of 'Western Marxist critique of mass culture' and

51 Lynne Segal identifies the subversive aspects of the sexual revolution. Although she identifies the sixties as the main decade in which this sexual radicalism appeared, it can also be identified in 1950s discourses on youth subcultures. Segal, though, informs her analysis with identification of the gender politics involved in this sexual 'liberation', Lynne Segal, *Straight Sex: The Politics of Pleasure* (London: Virago, 1994).

52 The range of texts concerned with the issue of 'youth' culture in the 1950s and early 1960s include Hoggart, *The Uses of Literacy*, Williams, *The Long Revolution*, and a particularly interesting set of articles in *Universities and Left Review*, Vol. 4 in the summer of 1958 entitled 'The Face of Youth' by Michael Kullman, Derek Allcorn and Clancy Sigal, 'Nihilism's Organizational Man', *Universities and Left Review*, 6, Summer, 1958, pp.51–65. Stuart Hall's article 'Absolute Beginnings' is also interesting in this context, *Universities and Left Review*, No.7, Autumn, 1959, pp.17–25. Later texts concerned with this issue produced by New Left and CCCS writers include Stuart Hall and Paddy Whannel, *The Popular Arts* (London: Pantheon, 1964); Phil Cohen, 'Subcultural Conflict and Working-Class Community'; *Resistance Through Rituals*, ed. by Stuart Hall and others (London: Hutchinson, 1976); Peter Laurie, *The Teenage Revolution*: (London: Anthony Blond, 1965); Kenneth Leech, *Youthquake: The Growth of a Counter Culture Through Two Decades* (London: Sheldon Press, 1973); there are also several articles specifically on fifties youth culture in Colin MacInnes's *England, Half English* (London: Chatto and Windus, 1986).

'establishment defenders of distinction', both of which undermine the importance of youth cultural *forms*.[53] Youth subcultures were interpreted either as examples of the process of 'false consciousness' that reproduced the consumerism of 'late capitalism', or as a growing cultural malaise caused by the massification of culture, and described rhetorically in pseudo-medical tropes of transgression, delinquency, and hysteria. Typically, they were read as symptomatic of something else: whether it be the Americanization of British culture, or the reproduction, in a different generation, of traditional class structures. This approach remained dominant in New Left analyses of youth until the late seventies, with the publication of Dick Hebdige's *Subcultures: The Meaning of Style*.[54] In retrospect, Hebdige's focus on the formal and stylistic aspects of youth subcultures, through his utilization of semiotic methodologies influenced by Roland Barthes, offers a critique of the New Left's (post-)Marxist methodologies that rejected the possibility of interpreting youth subcultures as potential sites for a radical resistance to dominant power structures.

Gary Clarke summarizes the critique of the New Left approach to youth subcultures implicit in Hebdige's work.[55] He argues that the dominant approach deployed by the New Left and the later Centre for Contemporary Cultural Studies[56] is problematic for several related reasons. Firstly, that the approach isolates the 'deviant' elements of youth subcultures and then homogenizes that 'deviant' group to represent an indicative reading of the working class as a whole. Secondly, he argues that the reading of youth thus produced is 'essentialist and

---

53   Kevin Davey, *English Imaginaries* (London: Lawrence and Wishart, 1999), p.81.
54   Dick Hebdige, *Subcultures: The Meaning of Style* (London and New York: Routledge, 1979). Paul Willis's work in the late 1970s also attempted to re-articulate the methods of analysis developed by the New Left's analysis of youth subcultures.
55   Gary Clarke, 'Defending Ski-Jumpers: A Critique of Theories of Youth Subcultures', in Gelder, *The Subcultures Reader*, pp.175–80.
56   The Centre for Contemporary Cultural Studies was set up in Birmingham in 1964 under the directorship of Richard Hoggart until 1969, and then under Stuart Hall from 1968 to 1979. For a more thorough history of the Centre see the introduction to Stuart Hall (et.al.), *Culture, Media and Language: Working Papers in Cultural Studies, 1972–79* (London: Routledge, 1980), pp.7–11.

non-contradictory'.[57] He goes on to stress that the methodology of British New Left analyses (particularly in *Resistance Through Rituals*[58]) tended to homogenize youth and subcultures in terms of class. Unlike the image of youth being constructed in the radical fiction, the majority of early New Left analyses were concerned to offer a reading of youth culture as a 'reflection' or cultural expression of the dominant ideology of contemporary capitalism. This process had two main aspects. Firstly, youth subcultures were perceived as threatening to older working-class cultures, rather than to dominant cultural frameworks; and secondly, the potential of subcultural practices to generate a discourse of radicalism was overlooked.

The first of these approaches is exemplified by Hoggart's analysis of the 'Teddy Boys' in *The Uses of Literacy*. His reading centres on the detrimental effects on British youth of Americanization and the resulting deterioration of 'organic' working-class culture. He describes the teenagers in the 'milk bars' as 'less intelligent than the average, and therefore even more exposed to the debilitating mass-trends of the day' (249). Hoggart's perspective constructs a critical reading of youth subculture as exemplifying the process of 'massification'. He is equivocal in terms of the causes of this characteristic of the Ted subculture as he is not sure whether to apportion blame to the youthful individuals themselves for rejecting older working-class culture, or to the appealing superficiality of Americanized culture to which these groups were (mistakenly, in his view) attracted. As Dominic Strinati argues, Hoggart's text proposed the idea that: '"genuine" working-class community [was] in the process of being dissolved into cultural oblivion by mass culture and Americanization'.[59] Hoggart goes on to develop his reading of contemporary youth as politically, socially and culturally apathetic, stimulated only on a surface level by shallow consumer products that are designed to

57   Clarke, 'Defending Ski-Jumpers', p.176.
58   *Resistance Through Rituals: Youth Subcultures in Post-War Britain*, ed. by Stuart Hall and Tony Jefferson (London and New York: Routledge, 1993), first published 1975. This later collection of analyses of youth is based on methodological principles established by the New Left.
59   Dominic Strinati, *An Introduction to Theories of Popular Culture* (London and New York: Routledge, 1995), p.31.

appeal to their limited powers of critical judgement. In a section from *The Uses of Literacy* entitled 'The Juke Box Boys', Hoggart produces a lengthy description of the new phenomenon of British youth. In describing the culture of the milk bars he writes:

> this is all a thin and pallid sort of dissipation, a sort of spiritual dry-rot amid the odour of boiled milk. Many of the customers – their clothes, their hair-styles, their facial expressions all indicate – are living to a large extent in a myth-world compounded of a few simple elements which they take to be those of American life. (248)

Hoggart's observation of youth culture is part of his agenda of celebrating traditional working-class culture. His interpretation of youth is based on his project to, as Hebdige observes 'preserv[e] the "texture" of working-class life against the bland allure of post-war affluence – television, high wages, and consumerism'.[60] Furthermore, the presence of alternative youth subcultures threatened the New Left project of constructing a new socialist and culturalist politics of proletarian solidarity and homogeneity.

The potential radicalism of youth was diluted in New Left writing by stressing their transitory nature. Hoggart, for one, views youth subcultures as generational aberrations in the process of socialization. He argues that rebellious working-class youth eventually succumbs to older working-class patterns of life after a brief rebellious stage.[61]

60   Dick Hebdige, *Hiding in the Light: On Images and Things* (London and New York: Routledge, 1988), p.51. A similar approach is adopted in Michael Kullman's *Universities and Left Review* article of 1958, which stressed the cultural paucity of youth culture, regarding pop forms such as Rock and Roll as indicative of entertainment for the mis-educated. Michael Kullman, 'The Anti-Culture Born of Despair', in *Universities and Left Review*, No.4, Summer 1958, pp.51–4. Kullman records the preponderance of what he calls 'anti-culture' in popular youth cultures to be the result of the early segregation of British youth in education because of the eleven-plus examination. His definition of working-class youth subculture as 'anti-culture' indicates a particular construction of what 'culture' means based on older models of high and low culture.

61   Hoggart, *The Uses of Literacy*, p.152. This has been the dominant reading of Sillitoe's *Saturday Night and Sunday Morning* in terms of Arthur Seaton's eventual socialization and acceptance of his 'parent' culture through his marriage to Doreen for example, see Stanley S. Atherton, *Alan Sillitoe: A Critical*

This is also the position held by Williams. In *The Long Revolution*, he writes: 'it is commonplace in some societies for adolescents to move through the stages of rebel, exile or vagrant before becoming members or servants'.[62] The early New Left, therefore, was engaged in a discourse that reduced the potential of youth subcultures to produce a resistance to dominant culture, preferring to identify a straightforward generational conflict that was self-resolving in that the youth culture dissipates as its members reach adulthood.[63]

The reason for this stance in Williams and Hoggart is that they interpreted youth subculture as a reflection of new forms of capitalist economy, which they considered were integral factors in the creation of a new market specifically aimed at youth and which saturated that new market with capitalist ideologies of individualism and commodity fetishism. In the 1950s, 'youth' and 'the teenager', as cultural phenomena, were intricately tied up with discourses around the Americanization of British culture and, therefore, added to the New Left's distrust of these forms of challenge to dominant British society.[64] As a

Assessment (London: W.H. Allen, 1979), pp.114–15. I offer an alternative reading of the end of this novel in chapter six below.

62   Williams, *The Long Revolution*, p.93.

63   Derek Allcorn also reads youth subcultures as transitory cultures created during, but isolated in, a fairly brief adolescent period. Derek Allcorn, 'The Unnoticed Generation', in *Universities and Left Review*, No.4, Summer 1958, pp.54–8. Allcorn's analysis is interesting in that it identifies radical non-hierarchical structures and an economic egalitarianism within the subcultural group he analyses. His method of identifying three distinct factors, i) economic and political, ii) ideological and cultural, and iii) social relations, is clearly within the limits of the approach deployed by the CCCS studies. The reasons for the egalitarianism in youth subcultures, he suggests, is partly related to a reaction to the hierarchical power structures inherent in school, and in the factory and office environments that the adolescents were moving into, and also a general equality of wealth within the groups. This potential for a radical form of social organization is restricted to within the group, but it is an observation that is lacking in Hoggart and Williams.

64   Williams writes on the Americanization of British culture: 'the failure of democratic culture in Britain, by the restriction of education both absolutely and along class lines, has left a vacuum which pseudo-Americanism seems to be rapidly filling', Raymond Williams, 'Television in Britain', in *Journal of Social Issues*, 18, 2, 1962, pp.6–15 (p.9).

result, the New Left's attempt to access youth as a source for a rein-vigorated socialism was undermined by the implicit prejudices against the Americanized forms in which British youth subcultures were ar-ticulating themselves. As Peter Sedgwick writes:

> the brilliance with which the cultural anthropologists of the New Left reported on the folkways of the young was in the end hopeless: the only section of young people among whom the movement made any progress was its own further-educated juniors.[65]

The reason for this failure to create strong 'youth' support in the New Left can be explained through analysis of the textual *forms* and critical vocabulary in which the debate was generated. In fact, both Hoggart and Hall acknowledged the inadequacy of available method-ologies of cultural analysis in the fifties for dealing with the sub-cultural representations of youth. In discussing pop songs, Hoggart writes: 'The songs seem to get more deeply under the emotional skin than the stories. Or the problem may be chiefly that I lack, in dealing with songs, the critical equipment I am accustomed to use on the printed word.'[66] Here, Hoggart identified the difficulty in discussing popular songs precisely because he did not feel he had the analytical tools or critical vocabulary to analyze their effects adequately. He is left with the imprecise description of the communicative power of them 'get[ing] ... under the emotional skin'. He recognized that the form of analysis he was deploying failed to represent the important function of the pop songs as a bonding element in the structure and internal cohesiveness of youth subcultures. In *The Popular Arts*, Hall and Whannel identified the same problem in analysing pop music:

> In what terms is it possible to establish even rough standards of judgement about this kind of music? [...] If we are unable to comment on its quality and to make meaningful distinctions, it is largely because we lack a vocabulary of criticism for dealing with the lighter and more transient qualities which are part of a culture of leisure. We need that vocabulary very much indeed now.[67]

65   Peter Sedgwick, 'The New Left', in *The Left in Britain: 1956–1968*, ed. by David Widgery (Harmondsworth: Penguin, 1976), pp.131–53 (pp.140–1).

66   Hoggart, *The Uses of Literacy*, p.224.

67   Hall and Whannell, *The Popular Arts*, pp.294–5.

The need for a new 'vocabulary of criticism' is imperative because of the limitations in New Left discourse to represent certain aspects of youth subcultures.

There were, however, two New Left articles in the 1950s that began to open up the analysis of youth subcultures. Significantly, both of these articles engaged with fictional representations of youth subcultures, and focused on the formal and stylistic properties of subcultural production rather than attempting a purely analytical approach to the socio-economic factors *behind* them. These are Clancy Sigal's article in *Universities and Left Review 4*, 'Nihilism's Organizational Man', and Stuart Hall's review of Colin MacInnes's *Absolute Beginners*.[68]

Sigal's article combines a review of Jack Kerouac's *On the Road* and a critique of Norman Mailer's celebratory article on the Beat Generation, 'The White Negro', both of which Sigal uses to develop a general critique of 'Hipster' culture. Although concerned specifically with an American phenomenon, he stresses the connections with a British context of teenagers and Teddy Boys. His critique is representative of New Left attitudes in that it is grounded on the inadequacy of youth subculture, despite its claims of radicalism, to represent a workable project or model for political change. He bases his critique on two points. Firstly, he identifies the nihilistic attitude of 'Hip' culture that rejects organized political action, but is articulated as the unstructured radicalism of the 'juvenile delinquent': 'He [the Hipster] [...] is crudely unlettered, politically illiterate, culturally frigid, unread and unRed' (60). Secondly, Sigal argues that Hip's appropriation of black and jazz culture is more concerned to project white middle-class fantasies of rebelliousness on to black identity than it is to ameliorate the actual social conditions under which many black, Hispanic and native Indian groups found themselves: 'Though sympathizing with the underdog, he [the Hipster] is not a social fighter' (60). This critique corresponds to New Left attitudes to 1950s youth subcultures as it applies the models of (post)-Marxist, culturalist and class-based approaches that identify the inherent defeatism in Beat culture as part

68   Sigal, 'Nihilism's Organizational Man'; Stuart Hall, 'Absolute Beginnings', in *Universities and Left Review*, No.7, Autumn 1959, pp.17–25.

of a process of internalizing the 'dialectical extension[s] of the self-same attitudes and values' of mainstream American culture (63).

However, Sigal's article is interesting in that it attempts a pastiche of the style and form of Beat writing, and in doing so fore-grounds the formal experiments of writers such as Kerouac, Burroughs and Ginsberg.[69] The article stands out in the pages of the *Universities and Left Review* as it disrupts the 'conventional' mode of address established in the rest of the journal and by extension in New Left writing generally:

> I repeat: us. Us, fragmented, mirrors, conforming with a high vengeance to the values we only nibble at, making a mad mansion out of the capitalist ethic we think we can use for timbering our frail little moral shanties. He is beat, beat down, unutterably confused, isolated in a sea of imposed togetherness, fighting in the only way he knows how, sometimes in the only way open to him, against that contemporary body of thought which makes morally legitimate the pressures of a rudderless, alienated society against the individual. Exhausted, Hip is, before he begins, in a world he never made. (59)

Sigal deploys this pastiche of Kerouac's style in an attempt to under-mine the claims of Beat radicalism, but paradoxically succeeds in foregrounding the very nature of that formal radicalism through the disruption of 'conventional' New Left discourse. However, because of the specific concerns of the New Left's mode of cultural politics, Sigal is not concerned to acknowledge the *stylistic*, and, as Mailer argues, the political, philosophical and ethical, radicalism that the Beat's experimentation with form represents.

Hall's article on Colin MacInnes's *Absolute Beginners* is part of a review of several contemporary works on youth (including E.R. Braithwaite's *To Sir With Love*),[70] which exemplifies, to a certain

---

69   Jack Kerouac, William Burroughs and Allan Ginsberg are regarded as the three primary writers in the group known as 'Beat' writers who emerged in America in the 1950s. See *The Penguin Book of the Beats*, ed. by Ann Charters (Harmondsworth: Penguin, 1992).

70   Braithwaite's book is an account of a black teacher working in an east end 'progressive' school that, although being an autobiographical account, reads more like a documentary novel. In relation to the next section of this chapter, it is interesting to note that Hall in discussing this text chooses to concentrate on

extent, some of the traditional New Left interpretations of youth subcultures. In the first two sections of the article, he identifies socio-economic causes in the 'superstructural' elements of working-class education that result in young people compensat[ing] for their frustrations by an escape into the womb-world of mass entertainments' (21), which he regards as 'a creation by the commercial world', and to which 'young people are the most culturally exposed' (20). Following Hoggart, Hall identifies a lack of agency here in the relationship between individual teenagers and the cultural products they consume and that form a framework of exploitation:

> In response to the cultural exploitation [...] many teenagers erect cultural barriers themselves: so that their leisure world absorbs and consumes all the emotional vitality and the fantasy and imaginative projections of adolescence, and becomes a wholly self-enclosed universe. (20)

However, in the final section of this article, Hall's emphasis moves from a socio-economic framework to a discussion of the cultural, formal and aesthetic representations of youth subcultures. This move allows him to trace potentially radical characteristics of youth that he considers are represented most clearly in MacInnes's novel. He begins by identifying the existence of a new form of teenage subculture: 'In London, at any rate, we are witnessing a "quiet" revolution within the teenage revolution itself' (23). He describes this new subculture as:

> A fast-talking, smooth-running, hustling generation with an ad-lib gift of the gab, quick sensitivities and responses [...] They are city birds [...] remarkably self-possessed [...] They despise the masses [...] They seem culturally exploited rather than socially deprived. (23)

He describes this emergent form of youth culture in different terms than the New Left critiques of youth subculture by Hoggart and other

the socio-economic and class issues raised by the book, rather than the racial prejudices, encounters and tensions which is the book's primary subject matter. E.R. Braithwaite, *To Sir, With Love* (London: Four Square, 1962), first published 1959.

108

New Left writers such as Michael Kullman and Derek Allcorn.[71] Hall identifies a form of youth subculture that does not easily fit with the New Left's homogenized construction of working-class youth, most often represented by the Teds. This 'new' subculture corresponds more to that described by MacInnes in *Absolute Beginners*, one which associates with jazz music and culture, which celebrates a romanticized association with black identity, and perhaps is more prevalent amongst middle, rather than working-class youth: 'the very smart young men and women of the metropolitan jazz clubs' (23). The radicalism of this form of youth subculture therefore represents for Hall an ideologically different phenomenon in terms of the New Left's reading of class and youth. It is significant that Hall can associate more positively with this kind of youth subculture, precisely because it challenges a middle-class rather than working-class parent culture, and therefore, represents more of a potential challenge to dominant ideologies.

It also re-addresses the terms and models in which youth is analyzed. In the last section of the article, Hall is concerned with the 'cultural' impact of youth rather than its position in terms of economic conditions. This allows him to suggest a potentially 'revolutionary' element in youth subcultures as a cultural, rather than a *political* or class-based phenomenon, associating youth with a cultural avant-garde, rather than a socialist politics based on economics 'in the last instance'.[72] It is significant, therefore, that the response to youth subcultures alters specifically when the category of analysis changes from the socio-economic to the cultural. This move allows Hall to reintroduce the political with a changed emphasis on the role of youth: 'It would not be the first revolution which came out of social deprivation, nor the first Utopia with absolute beginnings' (25). This shift in emphasis anticipates the later readings of youth subcultures produced by

71   Michael Kullman, 'The Anti-Culture Born of Despair', in *Universities and Left Review*, No.4, 1958, pp.51–4; Derek Allcorn, 'The Unnoticed Generation', in *Universities and Left Review*, No.4, 1958, pp.54–8
72   I refer to this Althusserian reliance on the economic, despite the relative autonomy of cultural development, as an indication of the particular type of 'post-Marxism' being developed by the New Left at this time, Althusser, 'Ideology and Ideological State Apparatuses', pp.121–73.

Dick Hebdige, who is predominantly concerned with their stylistic manifestations rather than a restricting focus on the socio-economic conditions that produce them.[73]

It is important to stress that the emphasis placed in this article on style and cultural production is achieved through analysis of a *fictional* representation. Although Hall is keen to emphasise the 'authenticity', 'committed' and 'social documentary' form of MacInnes's novel, all of which are value-laden for Hall, he stresses the success of *Absolute Beginners* as a 'novel rather than a piece of inspired journalism' (24). This article shows that when a perceptive New Left critic such as Hall rejected the main analytical approaches favoured by the New Left, and focused rather on the fictional representation of youth subcultures, the conclusions reached about youth are altered, and he suggests that the articulation of youth through fictional forms facilitates this alternative reading: 'Perhaps Mr. MacInnes has done this generation more justice than others who have written about the same subject' (25).

Hall, with Paddy Whannel, develops this cultural reading of youth in *The Popular Arts* in 1964.[74] In this ground-breaking book they concentrate more closely on the aesthetic representations of youth culture rather than on socio-economic preconditions, and again the representation of youth is articulated in relation to a different emphasis. They refer to teenage culture in terms of 'symbols and meanings' that represent 'an *authentic* response [... to] a society in transition' (273 – my italics). Here, the sense of youth subculture 'reflecting' an inherent false consciousness has gone and been replaced by a focus on the cultural production of youth as an 'authentic' response. The shift to a reading of style and culture again allows Hall to suggest the radical potential of youth:

> Sometimes this response can be seen in direct terms – kinds of radical political energy with certain clear-cut symbolic targets (the threat of nuclear weapons, political apathy [...] 'the Establishment'). Sometimes, the response takes the form of a radical shift in social habits – for example, the slow but certain revolution in sexual morality among young people. (273)

73   Hebdige, *Subcultures*.
74   Hall and Whannel, *The Popular Arts*, pp.273–4.

The 'radical' is identified here in terms of social and political connections, but the emphasis is on the cultural manifestations of this radicalism in terms of *form* and style:

> In these and other ways the younger generation have acted as a creative minority, pioneering ahead of the puritan restraints so deeply built into English bourgeois morality, towards a code of behaviour in our view more humane and civilized. Much of the active participation of the younger generation in their own sub-culture has this flavour about it – a spontaneous and generative response to a frequently bewildering and confused social situation. In these conditions the problems of the young seem important largely because they are symptomatic of the society as a whole. (273–4)

Here, the positive evaluation of youth subculture is predicated on a changed definition of the 'radical', as Hall's emphasis is on the cultural and stylistic rather than the political or economic. Youth is still a 'problem', but one that is a representation of the problems involved within the whole of society, and therefore, from a socialist position, of capitalism as the dominant mode of production. Rather than youth being defined as a reflection of the cultural effects of contemporary social and economic conditions, it becomes representative of a position from which a critique of those conditions may be developed. It is also significant that Hall reads the potential radicalism of youth in terms of the nation. Youth is read as a site of resistance and challenge to "English" sensibilities and moralities, identifying the impact of 'youth' on the dominant construction of national identity.[75]

75   I return to this issue of youth and national identity in the chapter on Colin MacInnes below.

The Sounds of Silence:
'Race' and Gender in early New Left Writing

The 1958 article by Derek Allcorn in *Universities and Left Review* mentioned in the previous section in many ways exemplifies the dominant approach to analyzing youth subcultures in early New Left discourse. However, Allcorn makes a perceptive observation concerning the cohesive internal structure of youth groups. Within these groups, he argues:

> The notion of equality tends to be merged with that of identity, at the expense of equivalence, leading often to an intolerant and intemperate rejection of values, ideas, and innovations outside the immediate range of their everyday experience and occasionally to a brutal disregard of the human dignity of individuals.[76]

Allcorn identifies the cohesive nature of white working-class male subcultures as based on exclusionary and discriminatory principles. He specifically stresses the exclusion of women in the male subcultures, suggesting socio-economic reasons for this: 'Given the present sharp division of labour between the sexes in our society, and particularly in the working class, it is impossible to admit girls to a male peer-group as equal members and they are excluded.'[77] However, a significant gap in Allcorn's analytical social categories is the exclusion of the emergent black communities in 1950s Britain. His text reveals not only the exclusion of black identities from British subcultural identity, but also the exclusion of 'race' as a category of analysis. In this section, I discuss the relationship between youth and immigrant black subcultures in the fifties, the absence of an awareness of 'race' as a distinct issue, and the silences surrounding issues of gender in early New Left discourse.

The exclusionary structure of white working-class youth subcultures in the 1950s, as identified by Allcorn, is related to Hebdige's

---

76   Allcorn, 'The Unnoticed Generation', p.58
77   Ibid., p.57.

argument concerning the lack of awareness amongst British youth of the American origins of their appropriated subcultural icons. Focusing specifically on the manifestation of this in Ted culture, Hebdige writes: 'And when the Teddy Boys, far from welcoming the newly arrived coloured immigrants, began actively taking up arms against them, they were impervious to any sense of contradiction.'[78] The emergent British teenage jazz culture, though, which was largely anti-pathetic to the Teds, openly celebrated identification with black culture as a specific British response to the same tendency in American Hipster and Beat culture. Clancy Sigal's article, as discussed above, explores this cultural intersection of youth subculture and black identity. However, Sigal's article also identifies the lack of concern in Beat culture with actual 'race' relations (in Britain or America), arguing that it represents only the development of a distinctive racial metaphorics which served to romanticize and exoticize racial difference by linking it to the construction of the (white) youth rebel.[79] As Sigal explains: 'He [Hip ...] reveres oppressed minorities (the more primitive the better) as the coolest, goes to Negroes and Mexicans for redemption and heart's ease but seldom numbers his dark-skinned brothers as personal travelling companions.'[80] Here, Sigal emphasises the propensity for the white Hipster to appropriate black cultures in the articulation of a rebel identity. Following Mailer's definition of the hipster as a 'white negro', Sigal shows how the youth culture of white middle-class America attempted to challenge (or at least shock) dominant culture by allying itself to the most repressed groups. As Hebdige suggests:

> a whole mythology of the Black Man and his Culture was being developed by sympathetic liberal observers [...] Here the Negro was blowing free [...] He

78   Hebdige, *Subcultures*, p.51.
79   Sigal, 'Nihilism's Organizational Man'. Sigal identifies the Beat writers' prpen-sity to exoticize the 'minority' racial characteristics of American Negroes and Mexicans, which can be seen as an example of what Edward Said describes as the practice of 'Orientalizing' different racial cultures, by constructing them in opposition to white Western culture. See Edward Said, *Orientalism: Western Conceptions of the Orient* (Harmondsworth: Penguin, 1985).
80   Sigal, 'Nihilism's Organizational Man', p.60.

escaped the emasculation and the bounded existential possibilities which middle-class life offered [...] The Black Man, mistily observed through the self-consciously topical prose of Norman Mailer or the breathless panegyrics of Jack Kerouac [...] could serve for white youth as the model of freedom-in-bondage.[81]

However, the importation of this American youth subcultural style was problematized in its exportation to Britain in terms of emergent racial encounters between black immigrant communities from the Commonwealth and young white subcultural groups. The radicalism of youth through association with black cultural identity, proclaimed by American subcultures, was problematized on the streets of Britain through actual racial encounters and confrontations.

The New Left's response to this was to concentrate on the evidence of xenophobia and racial violence exhibited in Ted culture, which was identified as indicative of similar attitudes in the working-class parent culture. In its nostalgic and homogenizing construction of working-class youth subcultures, the New Left tended to overlook the promotion of racial equality and the celebration of racial 'otherness' evidenced in alternative jazz and teenage subcultures. For example, Hoggart in *The Uses of Literacy*, in a chapter significantly entitled 'Them and Us', discusses the phenomenon in older working-class communities of constructing an artificial 'other', which resulted in the exclusion of individuals and groups whose cultural interests challenged the collective identity of working-class culture. Hoggart evaluates this phenomenon in positive terms as part of a process of empowerment for the working class. However, this construction of an 'us' as a collective identity was based not only on class but also on geographical and racial distinctions. Hoggart's discourse, therefore, is not concerned to show an equivalence between the marginalized groups of white working-class youth and the emerging black and Asian communities.[82]

81 Hebdige, *Subcultures*, pp.47–8.
82 It may be argued that Hoggart's investigation of working-class culture is based on a small area of Leeds, which may not have had a large black population in the 1950s, yet the silence in terms of racial distinctions still seems to me to be significant in a text which purports to address working-class culture. As noted

Where racial issues and black culture do occasionally enter New Left discourse in the 1950s, there are significant 'textual' responses betraying assumptions both in the language and the mode of address. For example, Hoggart discusses the love of the 'East' in older working-class culture:

> It loves the East, because the east is exotic and elaborate. Perfumes should come from the Orient [...] The cinemas [... give] themselves names vaguely Eastern [...] Eastern potentates are dearly loved [in popular magazine stories].[83]

Here, Hoggart recognizes a vague association between the 'othering' of Eastern (colonial) identities and the working-class identification of itself with an unrepresented culture, but he does not develop his analysis of this phenomenon in terms of corresponding power relationships between class and 'race' and the processes of 'othering' and 'orientalism' involved therein.[84] Also, the 'oriental' is kept at a distance in Hoggart's imagination, as the presence of actual Asian communities in Leeds in the 1950s is not identified. There are very brief references to racism in the working class which he calls, 'an intricate network not of ideas but of prejudices' (94), but he does not feel it is his responsibility or within the scope of his analysis to investigate the underlying causes of this kind of prejudice. In effect, Hoggart does not acknowledge 'race' as a relevant social category in his representation of 1950s working-class culture.

This absence is also a feature of *The Long Revolution*. In this text, Williams discusses the process of constructing one's identity through a series of identifications; 'nationality, class, and *so on*' (my italics).[85] The 'so on' here reveals a significant gap in his discourse. Within the 'so on' are included distinctions of identity such as ethnicity, gender, age and sexuality, but he does not directly articulate these 'other' social categories. In discussing the tension and conflict

above, Paul Gilroy identifies the absence of 'race' as an analytic category in Hoggart's text, Gilroy, 'British Cultural Studies and the Pitfalls of Identity', p.236.

83 Hoggart, *The Uses of Literacy*, p.143.
84 Said, *Orientalism*.
85 Williams, *The Long Revolution*, p.76.

between groups in society, he restricts his analysis of 'common-interest' groups to: 'family [...] village [...] trade union [...] social class', stressing that all these groups are eventually subsumed in the wider discourse of 'society': 'A group may be a convenient mark on the scale, but it is only a mark, and the fact of continuity, over the whole scale, is fundamental' (84). His call for a holistic study of a particular culture in terms of 'patterns of thought' and 'structures of feeling' tends to mask the distinctions within a 'culture' in relation to 'race', so that it becomes unclear whether black individuals are to be included or excluded from 'English' working-class culture.

An indication of the ambivalence towards distinct black identity by the early New Left can be seen in the fifth issue of *Universities and Left Review*.[86] This begins with an editorial stressing the theme of the issue to be 'culture and community', which the editors felt to be a theme of crucial importance as it had not been discussed 'for many years' (3). This theme is articulated theoretically through Williams's approach to studying culture holistically:

> We have come to it ourselves only in the course of trying to push past the limits of specialised problems, in the attempt to find some vantage point from which to make a deep criticism, not merely of some institutions, but of a whole culture – a way of life, under capitalism. (3)

Given this attempt to represent the 'whole culture', the following article in the journal, entitled 'The Habit of Violence' (on the Notting Hill 'race' riots of 1958) provides interesting reading.[87] This article reproduces essays written by several fifteen-year-old girls (obviously white and working class, although this is not made explicit), who give their (racist) opinions on the presence of the black community in London during this period. The article goes on to discuss the racist attitudes inherent within these documents, and attempts to trace some of the possible causes for these attitudes. These include unemployment, poverty, the lack of community life, residual colonial attitudes being replayed in contemporary youth, and the lack of ambition and

86   *Universities and Left Review*, No.5, Autumn 1958.
87   'The Habit of Writing', in ibid., p.4.

prospects for white working-class youth. It is commendable that the New Left attempted to address these problems here, but the method deployed raises particular issues in relation to representation. Not only are there no black 'documents' or voices from the Notting Hill area provided, but the discourse of the article itself is addressed precisely to the white population. The discussion excludes the black population who are the main victims of the 'race' riots, and focuses more attention on the lack of moral frameworks that the riots exemplify in the white youth. The riots themselves are represented as a side effect of the more crucial issue: the neglect (in terms of education and economic factors) of white working-class youth by the state: 'This is the kind of failure of values – or the failure to project values into our relationships with the other people – for which the community itself, and all others like it, should feel a personal responsibility'. (3) Black British individuals are relegated here to the phrase 'other people', which stands in dubious relationship to the text's definition of 'community'. The 'personal responsibility' it presumes is directed towards the white population only.[88]

The presence of Stuart Hall on the editorial board of *ULR* makes the silence concerning black issues strange. Stuart Hall, as a black academic working in Britain at the time, would have been sensitive to, one would have thought, particular issues of 'race' in relation to socialist discourse, but it is not until much later in his career that he begins to write about, and formulate specific theoretical models for dealing with racial issues in conjunction with his continued socialist concerns.[89] Where Hall does mention other racial groups in the fifties, he tends to mask his own identity. In 'A Sense of Classlessness', he writes:

---

88   This silence on specific issues of ethnicity is also heightened in the article that follows the one discussed in *Universities and Left Review*, No.5, Charles Taylor's 'Alienation and Community', which nowhere discusses the 'alienation' of black communities living in Britain at this time.

89   Hall's first article on ethnicity is not published until 1970: 'Black Britons' in *Community*, 1 (pp.2–3). His later work on this subject of course was ground breaking in its development of a critical methodology for discussing black issues in literary and cultural studies.

Solid as the old working-class communities were, they were often, of necessity, defensive or aggressive towards other communities, other national and racial groups, towards the 'queer' fellow and the 'odd man out', towards the 'scholarship' boy or even, sometimes, the militant. This is not a matter of praise or blame. It is a matter of the economic and social system within which an industrial proletariat, with its own values and attitudes, grew.[90]

Hall's apology here for violence against other 'races' and minority groups by elements of the working class is part of a discourse of acceptance of working-class culture because of its socio-economic history. This masking of racial issues by Hall is again part of the New Left approach, which privileged class analysis above other marginalized discourses. It is not that Hall *failed* to establish a 'chain of equivalence' between ethnicity and class issues at this juncture, but rather that the theoretical models, methodological approach and critical vocabulary of the early New Left did not persuade him to critically or theoretically pursue that connection.[91]

This absence, it seems, is structurally integrated within the range of methodological approaches the early New Left developed. Despite the attempt to challenge certain aspects of Marxist theory by elements of the New Left, the reliance on class as the main category of analysis produced a discourse that tended to overlook specific issues related to 'race' and ethnicity. As Paul Gilroy argues:

> New types of class relations are being shaped and reproduced in the novel economic conditions we inhabit. The scale of these changes, which can be glimpsed through the pertinence of populist politics of 'race' and nation, is such that it calls the vocabulary and analytic frameworks of class analysis into question.[92]

90 Hall, 'A Sense of Classlessness', p.27
91 Again I am referring here to Laclau and Mouffe's concept of a 'chain of equivalence' between different radical discourses; Ernesto Laclau and Chantelle Mouffe, *Hegemony and Socialist Strategy: Towards a Radical Democratic Politics* (London and New York: Verso, 1985) pp.1–5.
92 Paul Gilroy, *There Ain't No Black in the Union Jack: The Cultural Politics of Race and Nation* (London: Hutchison, 1987), p.34.

This is a structural aspect of both Western Marxist and New Left socialist discourse that, in the fifties, undermined the possibility of a chain of equivalence being identified between the specific concerns of the white working class and the emergent, black immigrant communities. The gap left by intellectual and theoretical discourse in Britain in the 1950s in relation to issues of 'race' is filled more representatively in fiction by a new group of writers from the Caribbean, including George Lamming, Sam Selvon, Derek Walcott, V.S. Naipaul and E.R. Braithwaite, all of whom attempted to represent specific issues relating to black and Asian minorities through fictional forms. These writers engage with 'English' literature in varying ways, and to different levels of experimentation, but the process of challenging the dominance of white writers in the 'English' institution of literature is addressed by all of them. In addition to this group of Caribbean writers working in Britain in the 1950s, white novelists such as Alan Sillitoe, Colin MacInnes, Doris Lessing and Lynn Reid Banks (especially MacInnes) also attempted to represent the concerns of black British individuals in their fiction.[93]

The absence of a discourse sensitive to the issue of 'race' in early New Left discourse is paralleled in the representation of the socio-economic and political concerns related to the position and experience of women in the 1950s. There has, of course, been much debate on the theoretical relationship between Marxism and feminism, especially from the seventies onwards. As Heidi Hartmann states: 'while Marxist analysis provides essential insight into the laws of historical development, and those of capital in particular, the categories of Marxism are sex-blind'.[94] Lynne Segal has suggested the causes for this in her

---

93   See the discussion of Silitoe and MacInnes in chapters six and seven, respectively, below. Doris Lessing, *The Grass is Singing* (London: Michal Joseph, 1950); Lynne Reid Banks, *The L-Shaped Room* (London: Chatto and Windus, 1960).

94   Hartmann, Heidi, 'The Unhappy Marriage of Marxism and Feminism: Towards a More Progressive Union', in Lydia Sargent (ed.), *The Unhappy Marriage of Marxism and Feminism: A Debate on Class and Patriarchy* (London and Sydney: Pluto Press, 1981), pp.1–41 (p.2).

essay 'Look Back in Anger: Men in the Fifties'.[95] Following Jean MacCrindle's comment that there was a 'pathological absence of women, silencing of women, in those days',[96] Segal attempts to explain this lack of representation. She identifies the myth of sexual equality that pervaded both dominant ideology and the New Left discourses, as one of the reasons for this 'silence'. She goes on to suggest that the attempted 'domestication' of men after the war, and a new emphasis on the mother/child bond, was deployed ideologically by the left as examples of the dominant ideology attempting to emasculate the political power of the (male) working class. This results, for Segal, in many of the 'Angry' texts of the period displaying a misogyny that was confused with class antagonism: 'What was really happening in so many of these novels was that class hostility was suppressed and twisted into new forms of sexual hostility' (82). She goes on to argue that a new method of social critique was needed that recorded not only the inequalities between the classes in British society, but the inequalities at all class levels between genders.[97]

The silence with regard to women's issues in the early New Left can be seen as a combination of actual practices within the organization and the critical vocabulary, methodology and language inherent in patriarchal political frameworks.[98] This 'double silencing' of women's representation – by both dominant practices and culture, *and* the language and form in which New Left social critique was operat-

95   Lynne Segal, 'Look Back in Anger: Men in the Fifties', in *Male Order: Unwrapping Masculinity*, ed. by Rowena Chapman and J. Rutherford (London: Lawrence and Wishart, 1988), pp.68–96.

96   Jean MacCrindle's comments were made during a talk given at the *Out of Apathy Conference*, 14th November 1987, see The Oxford University Socialist Discussion Group, 1989, p.105.

97   This theoretical issue is taken up by Lydia Sargent. She asks the question: 'How can women understand their particular oppression in a way that can confront the narrowness of Marxist terminology?', Sargent, *The Unhappy Marriage of Marxism and Feminism*, p.xx.

98   The New Left failed to acknowledge the work done by Simone de Beauvoir on the patriarchal structure of Western language which posited woman as the 'Other'. Simone de Beauvoir, *The Second Sex* (New York: Bantam Books, 1961), p.178.

ing helps to explain the failure of fifties intellectual writing on the left to identify or address these gender inequalities in British society.

This 'double silencing' of women's marginalized discourse can be exemplified in key New Left texts. In *The Uses of Literacy*, gender roles in working-class life are accepted by Hoggart without any investigation of the economic and cultural inequalities on which they are formed. For example, he writes:

> There are differences of grade between occupants [in a single street]; this family is doing well because the husband is a skilled man and there is a big order in at the works; the wife here is a good manager and very houseproud, whereas the opposite one is slattern. (21)

Hoggart traces minute class distinctions, here, whilst significantly remaining blind to the seemingly more obvious gender distinctions. There follows a longer section on the traditional roles of the 'father' and 'mother' in working-class culture, which again accepts rather than questions the dominant constructions of masculinity and femininity and the gender inequalities revealed by his definitions.[99]

Raymond Williams, in an interview with *New Left Review* in 1979, attempts to respond to the issue of the 'silence' on women's politics in *The Long Revolution*. He does this by trying to place gender issues within a wider economic and class-focused context, yet he makes this revealing answer to the challenge that he should have considered women as a distinct 'minority' group in terms of representation:

> It was not however that I was not thinking of them [women ...] These are the kinds of contradiction within the very real process of liberation that I would have tried to analyse. I wish I had done so in *The Long Revolution*, and I also wish I understood what prevented me from doing so, because it wasn't that I wasn't thinking about the question.[100]

---

99   See the section in Hoggart's *The Uses of Literacy* entitled 'Mother' and 'Father', pp.41–58.

100   Raymond Williams, *Politics and Letters: Interviews with the New Left Review* (London: New Left Books, 1979), pp.148–9.

It is significant that Williams admits that he failed to address the socio-economic position of women in *The Long Revolution*, as he was 'thinking about them', but perhaps more significant is that he does not know why this focus was excluded, as with the benefit of hindsight, he acknowledges it to be of central importance to his whole project. It would seem to be the case that the historical models of analysis, the critical vocabulary and the methodological approach necessary to articulate gender inequalities were not available in the theoretical discourse predominant in the early New Left.

This is also evident in the early New Left's analysis of youth subcultures. As Angela MacRobbie and Gillian Barber argue in their critique of New Left male-centred studies of subcultures: 'Very little seems to have been written about the role of girls in youth subcultural groupings. They are absent from the classic subcultural ethnographic studies, the pop histories, the personal accounts and the journalistic surveys of the field'.[101] MacRobbie and Barber identify the silences in early New Left and CCCS discourse concerning gender distinctions, and although they also maintain the 'centrality of class' (113) as a focus in their methodology, their essay begins to open up a discourse connecting youth subcultures, gender and class. However, the fact that this discourse is not initiated until the mid-seventies retrospectively foregrounds the lack of such an approach in the 1950s.

As Lynne Segal argues, this silencing of women's representation by the New Left was more than an oversight.[102] There was, in fact, a specific antagonism between representations of working-class culture represented through a socialist politics, and the marginalized position of women. Segal suggests that through the process of positing the domestication of men and the over-emphasis on the maternal bond in dominant culture, women were metaphorically designated as colluding against a radical discourse based on the emancipation of the working-class male. As Ken Worpole argues, the 'masculinization' of popular American culture was adopted by many writers as a stylized

101 Angela MacRobbie and Jenny Barber, 'Girls and Subcultures', in Gelder, *The Subcultures Reader*, pp.112–20 (p.112).
102 Segal, 'Look Back in Anger: Men in the Fifties'.

representation of contemporary English working-class experience.[103] American constructions of 'masculinity' were, thereby, appropriated as a strategy of empowerment by some working-class writers as a challenge to the perceived effeminacy of middle-class English culture. This strategy, however, formed an oppositional relationship between radical discourses of class and the marginalized and subordinate position of women in British society, which, potentially at least, offered a site for a combined radical politics. Therefore, the misogyny within 'Angry' writing of the period resulted in a fracture in the 'chain of equivalence' of two potentially radical discourses. It was only in the seventies that a concerted effort to theorize the possibility of a combined Marxist and feminist political agenda based on the equality of the two categories was developed.[104]

It is apparent, then, that as with issues of 'race', there was no available methodological or theoretical vocabulary in the 1950s for the representation of the marginalized voice of women either in mainstream cultural discourse or in New Left organizations and writing. The fiction of the period offers an alternative representation of these issues in fifties culture. There has been a reaction (understandably) against some of the 'Angry' writing of the period by feminist critics on the left. In particular, Lynne Segal identifies Sillitoe's *Saturday Night and Sunday Morning* as an example of the explicit misogyny revealed in 'Angry' texts. The danger, though, with Segal's approach is that Sillitoe's texts (as with other Angry writers), because of their presentation of misogynistic central characters, are themselves becoming silenced by a more gender-conscious contemporary discourse. However, positing Sillitoe as a misogynist writer to be avoided by a radically informed feminist literary critique over-simplifies the matter. In fact Sillitoe's texts provide fertile ground for the analysis of

---

103 Ken Worpole, *Dockers and Detectives: Popular Reading and Popular Writing* (London: Verso, 1983), pp.29–48.
104 For example, in the theoretical work on Marxism (socialism) and feminism by Sheila Rowbotham, *Women, Resistance and Revolution* (New York: Vintage, 1974); Heidi Hartmann, 'The Unhappy Marriage of Marxism and Feminism'; Iris Young, 'Beyond the Unhappy Marriage: A Critique of Dual Systems Theory', in Sargent, *The Unhappy Marriage of Marxism and Feminism*, pp. 43–69.

the intersections of dominant ideology, a class-conscious oppositional voice, and a radical gender-informed discourse. The texts themselves, although produced through a masculine narrative perspective, offer a crucial insight into the experience of working-class women in the 1950s.

In conclusion, it is apparent that the New Left's re-negotiation and re-articulation of socialist and Marxist methodologies tended to overlook the marginalized and emergent radical discourses of youth, ethnicity and gender. This is a result of the privileging of class as a category of analysis in New Left writing. However, investigation of this writing has shown that there are different levels of representation of marginalized groups. In terms of class and youth, many in the New Left recognized that emergent social, economic and cultural frameworks had produced new models of identity that needed the development of new critical methods and analytical models to deal with them. In terms of ethnicity and gender however, the theoretical models and analytical frameworks developed by the early New Left revealed limitations in the identification of these other marginalized categories. There was a *double* silence produced here: not only was there no theoretical or critical vocabulary to articulate these concerns adequately, but often they were not even recognized as socio-cultural categories in their own right as distinct from class and youth.

Part Two

Chapter Four
Anger Management: Kingsley Amis and John Wain

A Literature of Containment

In the early 1950s, the group of writers that came to be known as the Movement promised to produce a radical form of literature that aimed to shake up the old entrenched class values of the pre-war years.[1] At the time, certain critics emphasized the link between these new writers and the social revolution that was taking place in England. John Holloway, for example, was writing in 1956 that:

> The Poetry of the 1930s may have been left-wing but it was profoundly upper-class [...] Behind it stood [...] literary Bohemia or Bloomsbury [...] The recent social revolution, gentle though real, in England, has changed this. The typical Movement writer's childhood background appears to be lower-middle-class and suburban (often staunchly non-conformist, often in the industrial or semi-industrial Midlands or North of England).[2]

Holloway suggests that the Movement was part of a broad social revolution and that it was motivated by the injustices reproduced in the contemporary class system. The main bone of contention was that despite the 1945 Labour Government's aims to make Britain a true meritocracy, the entrenched class demarcations proved more durable than expected. Most of the writers associated with the Movement

---

1   The Movement was first referred to as a recognized literary group in an article entitled 'In the Movement', in the *Spectator* in October, 1954. (It appeared anonymously, but was later known to be written by J.D. Scott. For a discussion of the construction of the Movement as a distinct literary group see Blake Morrison, *The Movement: English Poetry and Fiction of the 1950s* (Oxford: Oxford University Press, 1980), pp.1–9.

2   John Holloway, 'New Lines in English Poetry', in *Hudson Review*, No.9, 1956, pp.592–7.

(Philip Larkin, Kingsley Amis, John Wain, Donald Davie, and Holloway himself)[3] came from lower-middle-class backgrounds, and although all had benefited from the scholarship system, they still felt discriminated against once they tried to make careers after university. The arrival of the Angry Young Men in the later 1950s (John Osborne, John Braine, Alan Sillitoe, Stan Barstow, Colin Wilson) appeared to extend this rebellion against the class-based values of the dominant English establishment.[4]

However, to describe the Movement (or most of the Angry writing for that matter) in terms of a 'revolution' in English writing is unjustified, both in terms of the ideological positions adopted by its main practitioners, and the formal techniques and styles they tended to use. In fact, the Movement represents a retracing or retrieval of an English literary heritage rather than a radically new outlook. John Brannigan has gone so far as to describe this group of writers as representative of a 'new conservatism', which, despite being antagonistic to upper- and upper-middle-class attitudes, still retained a broadly conservative attitude towards English society. Brannigan writes: 'The class war raging in the pages of 1950s literature in England was mostly a war between two opposing conservative visions, not between conservatism and socialism.'[5] Brannigan makes a fair point, although,

3   Blake Morrison includes within the Movement most of the writers who appeared in Robert Conquest's *New Lines* (London: Macmillan, 1956) – those named above plus D.J. Enright, Robert Conquest, and Elizabeth Jennings – and with the addition of Thom Gunn who was not included in that volume, Morrison, *The Movement*, pp.2–3.

4   Movement writers such as Amis and Wain were included, in retrospect, into the 'Angry' group after its creation by literary journalists in 1956, mainly as a direct response to John Osborne's play, *Look Back in Anger*, and Colin Wilson's philosophical and existentialist book, *The Outsider*. John Osborne, *Look Back in Anger* (London: Faber & Faber, 1956); Colin Wilson, *The Outsider* (London: Pan, 1978), first published 1956. For a discussion of the media's role in the construction of the 'Angry Young Man' see Harry Ritchie, *Success Stories* (London and Boston: Faber & Faber, 1988); Robert Hewison, *In Anger: Culture in the Cold War, 1945–60* (London: Weidenfeld and Nicolson, 1981), pp.129–59.

5   John Brannigan, *Literature, Culture and Society in Postwar England, 1945–1965* (New York: Edward Mellen Press, 2002), p.28

as we shall see in chapter six, Sillitoe is a special case, and even in the canonical Movement texts covered in this chapter, Kingsley Amis's *Lucky Jim* and John Wain's *Hurry On Down*, there is an element of radicalism that sometimes cuts through the broadly conservative positions the texts adopt.[6]

One of the things that make these texts appear conservative is the use of a mode of narrative that can be broadly described as conventional realism. This 'return' to realism was often articulated as a rejection of the experimental modernism of Joyce, Woolf, Eliot, Pound and Yeats who could thereby be repositioned as a 'foreign' diversion from the 'grand narrative' of English literary history. Larkin, for example, stated that his influences in the novel included Barbara Pym, Dickens, Trollope, George Moore, Isherwood, Maugham and Waugh, thus placing himself firmly within a tradition of English realists.[7] Conventional realism was, therefore, constructed and 'chosen', in the Barthesian sense, by most of the Movement writers as a formal device that carried specific ideological assumptions about nation and class, and this celebration of realism supported the political and ideological ground upon which the Movement constructed itself. However, as we saw in chapter two, there was a complex relationship between literary form and ideological outlook in the 1950s. In one sense, the return to realism represented a way of challenging the perceived effete and abstruse elitism of the dominant literary institution of the previous decades. On the other hand, realism, as often used in the form it was by Movement writers, represented a conservative (with a small 'c') provincialism and a return to a traditional English literary tradition – one that rejected modernist experimentation.[8] As Seamus Heaney has

6   Kingsley Amis's *Lucky Jim* (Harmondsworth: Penguin, 1961) first published 1964; John Wain's *Hurry On Down* (Harmondsworth: Penguin, 1960) first published 1953.

7   Philip Larkin, *Required Writing: Miscellaneous Pieces 1955–1982* (London: Faber & Faber, 1983) p.53 and p.64. Although Larkin's two novels *Jill* (1946) and *A Girl in Winter* (1947) were published in the forties, they were extremely influential in the style and mode of the Movement novels of the fifties.

8   Blake Morrison, for example, identifies the 'little Englandism' of the Movement in relation to two issues. Firstly, the post-war socio-political climate that he suggests brought in a period of 'insularity' in response to Britain's diminish-

said of Larkin: 'He is a poet, indeed, of composed and tempered English nationalism, and his voice is the not untrue, not unkind voice of post-war England.'[9] This 'voice' extends to Larkin's fiction and to most of the Movement novelists that saw him as their most important immediate influence. Behind this return to realism lies a belief in the rational and common sense attitudes of English empiricism. Anthony Easthope, for one, has identified in the Movement the 'unmistakable demand for a return to the English empiricist scenario'.[10] Easthope develops this reading of the Movement in terms of a discourse of national identity that established a formal/ideological link between Englishness, realism and empiricism, and through negation, posited modernism as a foreign intervention in the great tradition of English philosophical and aesthetic production. Easthope writes: 'Modernism and empiricism are radically incompatible', suggesting, by extrapolation, that modernism is also 'un-English' (178). The construction of national identity in Movement and Angry writing, therefore, often appeared as a celebration of a nostalgic and insular construction of Englishness through the re-appropriation of realist modes.

Rather than a radical new form of writing, the Movement novels can be seen as direct descendants of their eighteenth and nineteenth-century ancestors. The same form of social critique that foregrounds inconsistencies within the dominant system, without advocating an overturning of that system, can also be identified in a long line of realistic English writing from Defoe, Richardson and Fielding to Gaskell, Dickens and Hardy. The re-articulation of the realist mode in

ing international status caused by the break up of empire and the rise of the Soviet Union and the USA as the two major powers of the new world order after 1945. Secondly, that because the majority of Movement writers came from lower-middle-class backgrounds they rejected the cosmopolitanism of the literary upper-middle-classes which they regarded as representing unfair privilege. This resulted in the celebration of an English provincialism that focused on the industrial landscapes of the Midlands and Northern England. Morrison, *The Movement*, pp.53–66.

9   Seamus Heaney, 'Englands of the Mind', in *Preoccupations* (London: Faber & Faber, 1980), p.167.

10   Anthony Easthope, *Englishness and National Culture* (London: Routledge, 1999), p.183.

the fifties reveals the Movement writers' allegiance to an ideological heritage of the novel form, as identified by Ian Watt, as a bourgeois philosophy of the moral and financial progression of the individual within a social framework and not to the alternative claims for 'socialist' or 'critical' realism that had been made in the thirties (and would be later re-claimed by writers such as Georg Lukàcs and Raymond Willliams[11]). Ultimately, the Movement, and most Angry novels re-inscribe the ethics, morality and ideology of dominant English society, despite their main protagonists challenging their relative position within that structure.[12] They articulate the desire for the individual to rise through the hierarchical system, and their resentment and anger is not generated by the system itself but by the restrictions placed on individuals due to their class background. As Frederick R. Karl writes:

> Primarily, the protagonists of these novelists are not really angry. They are, however, disgruntled – with themselves, with their social status, with their work, with their colleagues, with the shabbiness of daily life, with their frustrated aspirations for self-fulfilment, with the competitive spirit, with the inaccessibility of women and drink, with all the small activities whose pursuit takes up their depleted energies.[13]

Jonathan Dollimore has put forward the theory that certain literary texts function ideologically to contain potentially revolutionary ideas by supplying a relatively safe cultural site by which they may be expressed.[14] Dollimore is primarily concerned with Renaissance liter-

---

11 Lukàcs's writing from the 1930s, 40s and 50s was not readily available in English translation in the 1950s. Williams's main ideas on the different ideological contexts for realism appear in his *Culture and Society 1780–1950* (London: Hogarth, 1987) first published 1957, and *The Long Revolution* (London: Chatto and Windus, 1961). See the discussion of these writers in chapter two above.

12 In this respect Braine's novel is similar to Amis's and Wain's; John Braine's *Room at the Top* (Harmondsworth: Penguin, 1959), first published 1957.

13 Frederick R. Karl, *A Reader's Guide to the Contemporary English Novel* (New York: Octagon Press, 1972), p.221

14 Jonathan Dollimore, 'Introduction: Shakespeare, Cultural Materialism and the New Criticism', in *Political Shakespeare: Essays in Cultural Materialism*, ed. by Jonathan Dollimore and Alan Sinfield, Second Edition (Manchester: Manchester University Press, 1994), pp.2–17, (pp.10–15).

ature, but his theory also proves useful when considering the ideological effects produced in Movement and Angry fiction. The fifties,
as we have been stressing, was a period in which profound social and
cultural shifts were taking place in England, and some of these
changes were potentially revolutionary. The Movement and Angry
novels represent a 'containment' of the more radical ideas that were
circulating, allowing a space for the articulation of grievances and
injustices within the system, but in a form that was ultimately appropriated by the prevailing ideology. Rather than signalling a radical
literature, they occupied a subordinate position, one that challenged
the distribution of power *within* the dominant socio-cultural and economic frameworks and hierarchies, but did not challenge the criteria
upon which those frameworks were philosophically and politically
based. The writing produced by the Movement, and most of the
Angries, can be described, therefore, as a literature of containment.[15]
As Blake Morrison argues:

> What emerges in the work of the Movement [...] is an uneasy combination of
> class consciousness and acceptance of class division; an acute awareness of
> privilege, but an eventual submission to the structure which makes it possible
> [...] the Movement offered only a token rebellion, and did not attempt to change
> the social structure which made cultural 'elitism' possible.[16]

Both Amis and Wain are working within the realistic tradition,
and, ideologically speaking, represent broadly this form of contained
literature – although close analysis of the texts, especially *Hurry On*

15 There are certain novels of the period, however, that represent a more radical
form of ideological expression in that they reject outright the bourgeois desire
to ascend the hierarchical social structure. Elements of this can be identified in
the fiction of Alan Sillitoe, Colin MacInnes and Sam Selvon (as we shall see in
subsequent chapters), and also in Alexander Trocchi and Keith Waterhouse.
Sillitoe's and Trocchi's fiction, in particular, introduces characters who do not
aspire to rise out of the working-class environment in which they are placed,
but produce a radical critique of the capitalist system through rejecting its
moral, political and economic systems. 15 See Alexander Trocchi, *Young Adam*
(Edinburgh: Rebel Inc., 1996), first published 1954; and Keith Waterhouse,
Billy Liar (London: Michael Joseph, 1959).
16 Morrison, *The Movement*, 74.

Down, complicates the issue. Although *Hurry On Down* was published a year earlier than *Lucky Jim*, I have decided to look at Amis's novel first, mainly because it has come to represent the paradigmatic Movement novel. This has to a certain extent affected the reading of *Hurry On Down* as the attitudes and formal techniques adopted in the later novel have been assumed to compare directly with the earlier. This is not the case, but it seems right to address the most famous of the Movement novels first.

Kingsley Amis, *Lucky Jim*

Kingley Amis's *Lucky Jim* was published in 1954, and immediately gained certain notoriety as representing, in its main protagonist, the new social and cultural group that we have been referring to. Jim Dixon, the novel's hero, is an example of a scholarship boy, a fictional representation of one of the first crop to have had benefited from the Education reforms of Clement Attlee's 1945 government. When asked about his education, Dixon says that he went to 'local grammar school' (215), the 'local' here distinguishing him from the Public School system that still predominantly accounted for the education of most of the Oxbridge graduates in the years following the Second World War. Dixon is, therefore, part of this new generation of educated men from lower-middle-class backgrounds who found that when they attempted to make their way in the world were hampered by their social background. This is one reason why Amis was so readily taken up as an Angry Young Man in the later 1950s.[17] Dixon comments bitterly at one point on his lower-middle-class lack of privilege: 'Why hadn't he himself had parents whose money so far exceeded their sense as to install their son in London. The very thought of it was a torment. If he'd had that chance, things would be very different for him now' (178). Dixon became almost talismanic

---

17   Although he always rejected the tag, the hero of *Lucky Jim* is not too different, in class terms, from John Osborne's Jimmy Porter in *Look Back in Anger*.

for this group of disgruntled would-be parvenus, which can be seen in the immediate reaction he generated amongst more established literary figures. Somerset Maugham, for example, described his type as 'scum' who did 'not go to university to acquire culture, but to get a job and when they have got one, scamp it. They have no manners and are woefully unable to deal with any social predicament [...] They are mean, malicious and envious'.[18] Although Maugham does not name Jim Dixon outright, he clearly has him in mind, which shows the importance of the novel as an example of what he felt to be representative of dangerous new social forces.[19]

As the novel opens, Dixon is a struggling lecturer, on a fixed term contract, in the History Department of a provincial university. His position as a subordinate in this environment is established in his relationship with his immediate professional superior, Professor Welch. This relationship allows Amis to dramatize a broader social context by which Dixon, as a member of the emergent social group has to legitimise his place within the establishment, and thereby justify his raised class status. By emphasizing Dixon's lack of a privileged background, the novel is clear to show that he represents the 'new man' of the post war period. This can be seen in an early description of him in comparison with Welch:

> To look at, but not only to look at, they resembled some kind of variety act: Welch tall and weedy, with limp whitening hair, Dixon on the short side, fair and round-faced, with an unusual breadth of shoulder that had never been accompanied by any special physical strength or skill. (8)

Although Dixon has never used his strength, the suggestion is that he has the potential force to overcome the 'tall and weedy' Welch. This

18   Somerset Maugham, 'Books of the Year – I', in *Sunday Times*, 25 December 1955. There is an irony here in that the book that Maugham seems to have most directly in sight with this criticism won the Somerset Maugham Award in the same year.

19   For more on Maugham's article see Gavin Keulks, *Father and Son: Kingsley Amis, Martin Amis, and the British Novel Since 1950* (Madison, Wisconsin: University of Wisconsin Press, 2003), pp.106–8; and John McDermott, *Kingsley Amis: An English Moralist* (London: Macmillan, 1989), pp.26–8.

suggests an almost Darwinian emphasis on the physical aspects of the two. Welch's 'kind' are seen to be at the point of extinction, about to be replaced by the new breed of man as represented by Dixon, although at this early stage of the novel, the latter is not aware of his potential superiority and spends much of his time trying to adapt to Welch's environment. In Raymond Williams's terms, Dixon can be seen to represent the emergent culture of the period whilst Welch, although currently part of the dominant, is soon to become the residual.[20]

Welch is, of course, part of an older generation, so it could be argued that this distinction between him and Dixon is more generational than class-based. In this sense, Dixon's real enemy is Bertrand, Welch's son, who represents the possibility of the continuation of Welch's culture into the present (and future). Bertrand is the younger representative of the currently dominant culture, therefore, more of a direct competitor to Dixon. The antagonism between the two represents the struggle between different class factions, and it is useful to see them as more than individual characters, as representative of competing ideologies, a symbolic relationship that reveals the manoeuvring for position of two groups within the broad range of the middle classes in England in the early 1950s.

The ideological contest the novel explores is often articulated in cultural terms and, in particular, in Dixon's attack on the culture of the middle and upper middle classes. This is directed at two targets: one, the phoney nature of the established cultural circles to which the Welches belong; and two, the poverty of contemporary academic work as represented by his Welch senior. The second of these is dramatized through Dixon's initial attempts to be accepted within the academic community by getting an article published in an academic journal. This article becomes a motif in the novel and tracks his changing attitudes towards academia. Initially, the article is shown to be a necessary step in Dixon gaining an academic post, but this aspect of it outweighs any actual intellectual merit that it might have. The

20   Raymond Williams, *Problems in Materialism and Culture* (London: Verso, 1980). In this book, Williams identifies the relationship between dominant, residual and emergent forms of culture; see in particular pp.37–45.

article becomes a means of advancement, not of knowledge, but of Dixon's career. This is satirically made evident by the title, '*The Economic Influence of the Developments in Shipbuilding Techniques, 1450–1485*' (15), a topic in which Dixon (and no-one else it seems) has any real interest. The article also functions to show that at the opening of the novel he is prepared to play the academic game despite his increasing disillusionment with academia, or at least the kind of academia that Welch represents. On Welch's advice, Dixon sends his article off to L.S. Caton, the editor of a 'new historical review' (14). The fact that Dixon is pleased when he hears that Caton intends to publish the article (30) is subsequently undercut when, towards the end of the novel, he discovers that Caton has translated it into Italian and passed it off as his own:

> There could be no doubt about it; this article was either a close paraphrase or a translation of Dixon's own original article. At a loss for faces, he drew in his breath to swear, then cackled hysterically instead. So that was how people got chairs was it? Chairs of that sort, anyway. Oh well, it didn't matter now. (229)

Dixon's reaction to discovering the theft of his 'research' shows that by this stage, he is about to reject the system to which both Welch and Caton belong. The article, then, acts as a motif in what John McDermott describes as Dixon's 'coming to be his own man'.[21]

One of the other ways in which the novel engages with contemporary social and cultural debates is through its representation of Englishness. Amis uses the national context as a way of negotiating a position for the emergent group that Dixon represents, and he does this by challenging the foreign (and more specifically European) influences that are part of the Welches's effete culture. For Dixon, and Amis, there is an attempt to reclaim Englishness as part of a masculine, Anglo-Saxon, lower-middle-class authenticity. Dixon represents traditional Englishness, or at least a version of it that had been recently articulated by George Orwell.[22] He is down to earth, realistic and antagonistic to all forms of affectation and falsity. He has an

21   John McDermott, *Kingsley Amis*, p.65.
22   See George Orwell, 'England Your England', in *England Your England* (London: Secker and Warburg, 1953), pp.192–224, first published 1941.

empirical and anti-theoretical approach to life, and values common sense, as can be seen in his motto: 'nice things are better than nasty things' (140; 242). In this sense, Dixon and Amis are characteristic of a particular trend in Movement writing, as John Brannigan notes, one that was influenced by the 'dominance of the logical positivism and empiricism in philosophical circles in England'.[23]

The emphasis on Englishness can be seen in the entertainment provided at the party given at Welch's home to which Dixon is invited. At this party Dixon is coerced into taking part in two cultural set pieces that Welch has organized: the performance of a play by Jean Anouilh and the singing of some old English madrigals, both of which are seen as examples of the Welches's inauthentic, affected and effete cultural practice. At one point Margaret (Dixon's work colleague and potential love interest) mocks Dixon's attempt to involve himself (albeit reluctantly) in the Professor's penchant for European culture:

> 'You were wonderful in the Madrigals. Your best performance yet.'
> 'Don't remind me please.'
> 'Even better than your rendering of the Anouilh tough. Your accent made it sound so frightfully sinister. What was it? "*La rigolade, c'est autre chose*"? Very powerful, I thought.'
> Dixon screamed softly from a tightened throat. 'Stop it I can't bear it. Why couldn't they have chosen an English play?' (44)

Dixon's response indicates his innate Englishness. The fact that the Welches have chosen an Anouilh play shows not only the foreignness of their pretentious culture to Dixon, but also Anouilh figures as a signifier of modernism. Dixon and Amis are both clearly inimical to modernist literature and culture, which is represented as elitist foppery in contrast to the form of English realism in which the novel is operates.[24]

23   See Brannigan's discussion of the influence of the philosophical ideas of A.J. Ayer on the Movement writers: Brannigan, *Literature, Culture and Society in Postwar England*, pp.38–9.

24   Amis's novel generally adheres to a realist mode of writing, with an 'omniscient' narrator, a clear hierarchy of discourses, a linear plot structure, a logical framework of cause and effect, and recognizable characters and events that take place in a realistic setting. The novel, in fact, has been described as being in the

It is not only European modernism that Dixon attacks as representative of the Welches's culture, it is also the penchant for older
myths of Englishness as represented by the 'madrigals'. These represent a residual culture that stands in opposition to the authenticity of
Dixon's 'new' Englishness. This can also be seen in another motif
running through the novel: the lecture on 'Merrie England' he is re-
quested by Welch to give for the Open College Week. That the title is
imposed upon him by Welch marks the attempt by the professor to put
Dixon in his place by referring to an age that, mythically more than in
actuality, represents a time in which more rigid and clear-cut class
lines were drawn, a time when parvenus of Dixon's stamp would not
have been tolerated. As with the academic article, Dixon begins by
acquiescing to the onerous task of writing this speech, despite him
clearly having very little interest or knowledge in his subject. The talk
becomes one of the tests he has to pass in order to be allowed to join
the privileged set to which he initially aspires. However, Dixon gradually succeeds in subverting the discourses and ideologies embedded
in the idea of 'Merrie England'. He does this privately at first in the
articulation of his attitudes and mockery of Welch's subject, and then
more publicly in the delivery of the eventual talk. In private, this
subversion is most clearly seen when Dixon is writing or thinking
about the talk; in the following passage he is rehearsing it:

> What, finally, is the practical application of all this? Can anything be done to
> halt, or even to hinder, the process I have described? I say to you tonight that
> something can be done by each one of us here tonight. Each one of us can
> resolve to do something, every day, to resist the application of manufactured
> standards, to protest against the ugly articles of furniture and table-ware, to
> speak out against sham architecture, to resist the importation into more and
> more public places of loudspeakers relaying the light programme, to say one
> word against the Yellow press, against the best-seller, against the theatre-organ,
> to say one word for the instinctive culture of the integrated village-type

picaresque tradition, with Henry Fielding most often being cited as a model. On
this latter point see Angela Hague, 'Picaresque /structure and the Angry Young
Novel', *Twentieth Century Literature*, 32, No.2 (1986) pp.209–20; John
McDermott comments on Amis's position 'within a recognizable English comic
tradition' citing Fielding as a specific influence, McDermott, *Literature, Culture and Society in Postwar England*, pp.63–4.

138

community. In that way we shall be saying a word, however small in its individual effect, for our native tradition, for our common heritage, in short for what we once had may, some day, have again – 'Merrie England'. (204–5)

In this passage Dixon is mimicking the style and address that he knows Welch will approve. The haughty and pretentious use of rhetorical questions and modes of address ('I say to you tonight') are reminiscent of a pre-war political discourse (one thinks here of Chamberlain's declaration of war speech). The recourse to a homogenous collective group – 'each one of us here tonight'; 'integrated village-type community'; and 'our common heritage' – is also recognized by the reader as inimical to his true feelings; such a collective group would need to include both Dixon and the Welches, and this is clearly seen as unworkable. In adopting Welch's sentiment and style he finds himself falsely positioned against his actual beliefs: that the modern world should be active in shaking up the older myths of Englishness, and that the emergent culture, of which he himself is part, should be celebrated, rather than feared. However, the speech also shows the ambivalence of Dixon's (and Amis's) position. The features that Dixon chooses as examples of the effect of the new cultural framework, the 'manufactured standards', the 'ugly-articles of furniture', the 'loudspeakers relaying the Light Programme', the 'bestseller' are indicative of the negative aspects of the emergent culture of which Dixon is as suspicious as Welch. This speech shows an uncertainty about cultural life in 1950s Britain, the recognition that the old order has to be shifted, but anxiety concerning the type of cultural poverty that might replace it.[25]

Dixon's self-consciousness of the compromised position in which he is placed is shown in his reaction to his own rhetoric (or rather the rhetoric that he has borrowed from Welch). After the passage quoted above the text continues: 'With a long jabbering belch, Dixon got up from the chair where he'd been writing this and did his ape imitation all around the room' (205). Here, Dixon not only under-

---

25   This passage is similar in tone to Larkin's admonishment of contemporary consumer culture in poems such as 'The Large Cool Store' and 'Here', Philip Larkin, *Collected Poems* (London: Faber & Faber, 1988), pp.135–7.

cuts the sentiments of what he has just been writing, but shows the effect it is having on him, that he is metaphorically being turned into a performing monkey by his compliance with a set of ideas in which he clearly does not believe. The mimicry he is forced to adopt does not allow him to gain any sense of power or self-confidence, it merely confirms his subaltern position to Welch.

Any resistance to Welch remains, at this stage, private and, therefore, impotent. Dixon recognizes his false position, but it is not until the final talk that this is articulated as a public affront to Welch's ideology. At the actual Open College Day talk, Dixon, because of having a series of courage-providing tipples, eventually reaches the platform in a state of drunkenness. He begins his speech 'using Welch's manner of address' and 'a number of favourite Welch tags' (223). However, this mimicked language begins to sound foreign in his mouth: 'he began to trip up on one or two phrases, to hesitate, and to repeat words (223). As Dixon continues his talk, he begins to lose more and more control of his borrowed mode of address:

> Gradually, but not as gradually as it seemed to some parts of his brain, he began to infuse his tones with a sarcastic, wounding bitterness [...] Almost unconsciously he began to adopt an unnameable foreign accent and to read faster and faster, his head spinning. As if in a dream he heard Welch stirring, then whispering, then talking at his side. He began punctuating his discourse with smothered snorts of derision. He read on, spitting out the syllables like curses, leaving mispronunciations, omissions, spoonerisms uncorrected. (226)

The mimicry in the talk becomes so exaggerated that it begins to break down, and is revealed for what it is. As Dixon becomes more and more aware of the falsity of his position, the language in which he has been forced to speak begins to split open leaving 'mispronunciations, omissions, spoonerisms uncorrected'. The function of language to communicate is itself challenged by Dixon's lack of belief in the message he has been forced to convey. He is, of course, drunk, but the drunkenness figures here as a vehicle for the release of his true feelings as well as a challenge to the conventions and codes of behaviour acceptable to the society to which he has, up until this point, been grudgingly willing to buy into. The scene acts as a Carnivalesque mockery of authority: 'The Principal rose to his feet, opening and shutting his mouth, but without any quieting effect' (226). The figures of authority, here, are rendered impotent by Dixon's transgressive behaviour and for one moment the power relationships are inverted: 'Below him the local worthies were staring at him with frozen astonishment and protest' (226). Michie later describes Dixon's speech as going down 'like a bomb' (231). This moment allows Dixon to throw off the interpellation of him as a subaltern and to speak his true feelings in his 'own' voice:

> 'What, finally, is the practical application of all this?' Dixon said in his normal voice [...] 'Listen and I'll tell you. The point about Merrie England is that it was about the most un-Merrie period in our history. It's only the home made pottery crowd, the organic husbandry crowd, the recorder player crowd, the Esperanto'. (227)

Here, Dixon supplants the homogenous vision of Englishness with a truer account of a range of self-interested subgroups within the nation. He also debunks the myth of old England as a harmonious socially-stratified country, implicitly challenging those who would claim a return to that mythical system of social order as part of a conservative attack on the emergent society and culture of the 1950s.

This image of fifties England as made up of competing class cultures is also evident in the use of language and dialogue in the novel. Amis presents the reader with a range of registers and accents that help to establish a 'hierarchy of discourses' by which the reader is supposed to judge individual characters.[26] Dixon's speech, when he is not mimicking other characters, represents the normal way of speaking and places him closest to the novel's moral centre. This 'norm' is a form of Standard English with a slight northern accent to represent Dixon's geographical background (31). Amis presents us with a range of language styles, many of which deviate from this norm, and it is useful in this context to consider Mikhail Bakhtin's theory of heteroglossia: how differing language styles can be used in a novel to indicate the ideological framework in which characters interact socially. The main register of deviation from Standard English is given to

26   Catherine Belsey, *Critical Practice* (London and New York: Routledge, 1980), pp.70–2.

upper-class characters. This can be seen most prominently in the way Bertrand Welch speaks:

> 'And I happen to like the arts, you sam.'
> The last word, a version of 'see', was Bertrand's own coinage. It arose as follows: the vowel sounds became distorted into a short 'a', as if he were going to say 'sat'. This brought his lips some way apart, and the effect of their rapid closure was to end the syllable with a light but audible 'm'. (51)

This mockery of Bertrand's way of speaking marks out his difference from the language norm of the text, and shows Bertrand to be similarly distanced from its ethical centre. Language, therefore, is used to support the representation of the ideological confrontation between Dixon and Bertrand. Dixon comically attempts to mimic this deviation from Standard English when he makes his fake phone call to Bertrand's mother: '"Hallaher, have yaw a Miss Kellerhen steng with yaw plizz?"' (190). This mockery of upper-class speech serves, in ideological terms, to distance this group from the mainstream of British society in the 1950s and thus challenge their continued influence.

This does not mean, however, that Dixon shares an easy alliance with the working classes. Alongside the mockery of upper-class speech patterns, *Lucky Jim* follows a tradition in the English novel of representing working-class speech as non-Standard. This serves to show the distance between this group and Dixon. For example, the speech of a taxi driver, bus conductor and waiter is represented to mark out their socio-economic position within society. Dixon again deploys mimicry in the representation of this second alternative to the language norm of the text in the letter he writes to his adversarial colleague, Evan Johns, which is supposed to come from a working-class admirer of Johns's fiancé, a character Dixon calls Joe Higgins: *'She is a desent girl and I wo'nt have you filing her head with a lot of art and music, she is too good for that, and I am going to mary her which is more than your sort ever do'* (153). Dixon marks out the class background of 'Joe Higgins' through the use of stock phrases and misspellings, and serves to establish a distance between Dixon and working-class culture. This class differentiation retains a model of society based on a hierarchical structure, and ideologically speaking, argues for the advance of a new group *within* British society rather than a radical overturning of its basic frameworks. The manipulation of speech, therefore, produces an ideological framework of language that produces a discourse of containment rather than revolution, and an argument for the re-positioning of power *within*, rather than *against* the system.

This point is corroborated through attention to the treatment of socialism in the novel. Amis's move from being sympathic towards a broadly left wing position in the 1950s to an avowed supporter of Thatcherism in the 1980s is well documented, however, as John Brannigan has argued, the political messages that emerge from *Lucky Jim* already suggest this later move to the right. Brannigan has a case when he suggests that the novel reveals more of a 'new conservatism' than any socialist sentiment; nevertheless the anarchic resistance of its central characters to the framework of class privilege makes it a more complex novel to address in terms of ideology. Amis's own relationship to socialism in the 1950s is itself complex and often contradictory. In a 1957 pamphlet published by the Fabian Society entitled *Socialism and the Intellectuals*, Amis stresses his left-wing sympathies and states that 'unless something very unexpected happens I shall vote Labour to the end of my days'.[27] However, in the same article he also attacks the 'political romanticism' of many of the intellectuals on the left. For him, the romanticization of politics in the 1930s was acceptable given the international circumstances, but could lead to inaccurate and sometime dangerous analyses of political realities, especially if that romanticism continued into the present. He goes on to stress his own belief in a political attitude that is ultimately based on empirical and individual experience: 'I think the best and most trustworthy political motive is self-interest'. Ideologically speaking, Amis's mixture of socialistic and individualistic ideas is contradictory, nevertheless, it represents, as we saw in chapter one above, a widespread anxiety over the direction of left-wing politics in the 1950s.

27   Kingsley Amis, *Socialism and the Intellectuals* (London: Fabian Society, 1957), p.1.

The ideological outlook expressed in the Fabian piece is similar to that presented in *Lucky Jim*.[28] In the novel, socialism appears more as a strategic weapon in Dixon's battle against the Welches's upper-class elitism, rather than as any genuine, committed belief. This can be seen in one of the earlier encounters between Dixon and Bertrand. In one passage, after Bertrand has expressed his anti-socialist sentiments, Dixon replies, "'If one man's got ten buns and another's got two, and a bun has got to be given up by one of them, then surely you take it from the man with ten buns'" (51). The simplistic nature of Dixon's version of socialism matches Bertrand's opposition to it, and it becomes clear that this is little more than a gesture on Dixon's part. His attitudes throughout the rest of the text are hardly socialist. In fact his encounters with working-class characters often shows him as condescending and keen to distance himself from that group.[29] However, Dixon does seem to have a more natural alliance with working-class characters, for example, with respect to a pub barmaid he feels 'how much he liked her and had in common with her, and how much she'd have in common with him, if only she knew' (25). He also shows a certain amount of respect for the 'mature' ex-services student, Michie, who clearly has had more worldly experience than Dixon, but also more than Welch, despite the relative seniority of the latter (27–9). The final encounter between Dixon and Michie shows a mutual respect between two 'new men' who have no illusions about the inconsistencies and inequalities of the establishment (231–2).

Despite the (weak) alliance with the working class and socialistic ideas, the celebration of an emergent culture in *Lucky Jim* remains limited and contained. As Brian W. Shaffer argues *Lucky Jim* is 'a

28   It does not necessarily follow, of course, that the leading protagonist in a novel represents the same ideological outlook as the author, but in this case they are certainly close.

29   See, for example, the encounters Dixon has with a taxi driver (133); a bus conductor (243); and a British Rail employee (245–6). These individuals are essentially variations of the same character – the typical working-class Englishman, who in Amis's representation, tends to be unhelpful and naturally antagonistic to one of Dixon's class. Dixon responds by assuming a middle-class superiority in each case.

curious mixture of right wing and left wing proclivities'.[30] It is tempting to say that this is corroborated by Amis's subsequent move to the right as he gets older – his eventual antagonism to socialism, the Welfare state, and feminism.[31] The last of these can certainly be seen in the representation of female characters in the text. The two main women, Margaret and Christine, correspond to two traditional and patronizing representations of women: the manipulator that has to be evaded, and the beauty that is prized. Neither is very convincing as a character. Christine, especially, functions as an emblem of the contest between Dixon and Bertrand rather than the text being particularly interested in her as a fully rounded character. She becomes a feature of the unwritten social conflict between the two men. This can be seen in the first moment that Dixon sees Christine:

> In a few more seconds Dixon had noticed all he needed to notice about this girl: the combination of fair hair, straight and cut short, with brown eyes and no lipstick [...] The sight of her seemed an irresistible attack on his own habits, standards, and ambitions: something designed to put him in his place for good. The notion that women like this were never on view except as the property of men like Bertrand was so familiar to him that it had long since ceased to appear an injustice. (39)

When he persuades her to leave the ball with him he views this as part of his conflict with Bertrand: 'The only thing that he felt at all clear about was that this abduction of her was a blow struck against Bertrand' (134). Christine, then, appears in the novel as an aspect of what Eve Kosofsky Sedgwick describes as a homosocial conflict: the representation of a heterosexual romantic affair that serves primarily not as a relationship between the male and female protagonists, but as a broader contest between two males.[32] Christine functions as little more than the prize that is gained by Dixon through his defeat of Bertrand,

30   Brian W. Shaffer, *Reading the Novel in English 1950–2000* (Oxford: Blackwell, 2006), p.49.
31   For a good account of Kingsley Amis's various positions on cultural, political and literary issues from the 1950s to the 1990s, and how these compare with his son Martin's, see Gavin Keulks, *Father and Son*.
32   Eve Kosofsky-Sedgwick, *Between Men: English Literature and Male Homosocial Desire* (New York: Columbia University Press, 1985).

and as a symbol of his attainment of a higher social position. As Alice Ferrebe notes, 'Within the codes of masculine desire, [...] she [Christine] function[s] as both complimentary to Jim's state of necessarily compromised self-awareness, and utterly discredited by it.'[33] In this respect, *Lucky Jim* is typical of many of the 'Angry' novels of the 1950s.[34]

We can also see in this aspect of the novel that the triangular relationship between Dixon, Bertrand and Christine reveals deeper anxieties produced by Dixon's position as parvenu. Christine, in the quotation above, is perceived by Dixon to be the 'property of men like Bertrand'. Dixon, of course, would also like to *own* someone like Christine and to do so means he has to attain Bertrand's position. This reveals one of the motivations behind Dixon's initial acquiescence of the social impositions placed on him: to become part of the society to which Bertrand belongs means the necessity of becoming like him. Bertrand, in this sense, can be seen as a kind of double for Dixon, an idea that lies at the unconscious root of his antagonism. The scene in which Dixon fights and defeats Bertrand, therefore, is representative of him defeating a potential future self. The moment of the fight is one where Dixon finally rejects the idea of belonging to that order and significantly is another moment in which the inhibitive distance between his private thoughts and his public expression of them is at last removed: 'The bloody old towser-faced boot-faced totem-pole on a crap reservation, Dixon thought. "You bloody old towser-faced boot-faced totem-pole on a crap reservation," he said' (209). This victory over Bertrand is, therefore, another instance of Dixon now being able to express himself freely.[35]

33   Alice Ferrebe, *Masculinity in Male-Authored Fiction 1950–2000* (Houndmills, Basingstoke and New York: Palgrave, 2005), p.37.

34   See Lynne Segal, 'Look Back in Anger: Men in the Fifties', in *Male Order: Unwrapping Masculinity*, ed. by Rowena Chapman and J. Rutherford (London: Lawrence and Wishart, 1988), pp.68–96; Ferrebe, 2005 pp.34–42.

35   Alice Ferrebe produces a convincing reading of the way in which Jim Dixon has two ways of speaking, neither of which are truly authentic, and both of which serve to reassert a masculine form of addressivity; Ferrebe, *Masculinity in Male-Authored Fiction*, pp.34–42.

But not only does Dixon reject the social milieu to which the Welches belong, the text, as a whole, shows their culture to be on the wane. What Dixon comes to realise through the course of the novel is that he is in fact part of an emergent social order. Although he starts by thinking he has to conform to get on, and to mimic the Welches (hence his agreeing to give the 'Merrie England' speech and writing the meaningless article). He comes to realise that, thankfully, their culture is being replaced by his own. This is made clear at the end of the novel where the Welches are perceived as having: 'a look of being Gide and Lytton Strachey, represented in a waxwork form by a prentice hand [...] Dixon allowed Catherine to lead him away up the street' (251). Welch and Bertrand are compared here to Gide and Lytton Strachey to show that they belong to a past culture, one that can be mocked for its anachronistic continuation into the present. Dixon and Christine look back on the Welches as they head off up the street emphasizing their allegiance to the future. Culturally speaking, the text dramatizes the moment of transition in which an emergent culture becomes the new dominant.

Although John Brannigan is right to identify a broadly 'new conservative' outlook for the Movement writers, *Lucky Jim* does contain aspects of a potentially more radical questioning of authority, although this is ultimately diluted by Dixon's readiness to be reintegrated into a class-stratified society through his job with Gore-Urquhart, (Christine's wealthy, businessman uncle) who is another representative of the new social order. Perhaps it is more accurate to see *Lucky Jim*, then, not as a text that represents a 'new conservative' ideology, but as indicative of a new form of liberalism, one that is concerned to shake up the entrenchment of class divisions, whilst falling short of a more radical and wholesale critique of a culturally and economically stratified society. In this sense it corresponds to Alan Sinfield's definition of a subordinate form of culture – one that despite its critique of aspects of contemporary society acts to contain the potentially more radical ideas it might activate in the process.[36]

---

36   Alan Sinfield, *Literature, Politics and Culture in Postwar Britain* (Oxford: Basil Blackwell, 1989), pp.34–5. See the discussion of Sinfield in the introduction to the present book above.

John Wain, *Hurry On Down*

John Wain's first, and most well known novel was published a year before *Lucky Jim*, and he was a fairly established figure in British literary culture by the early 1950s. In 1953 he was appointed editor and presenter of the BCC Third Programme's new literary arts show, *First Reading* and, in fact, was influential in establishing *Lucky Jim* by reading an extract from it on the first broadcast in April 1953, nine months before it was published.[37] As Harry Ritchie has noted, Amis and Wain were inextricably linked in early fifties literary culture as representative of a new breed of irreverential and iconoclastic novelists who were capturing the attitudes of post-war Britain.[38] Yet despite the tendency to link Wain and Amis together, their two debut novels have several important differences in terms of theme, structure and outlook.

Like Amis, Wain was one of the first novelists to be associated with the Movement and was later incorporated as one of the Angry Young Men, although the association of Wain with the Angries is largely misrepresentative of his fiction. There *is* a certain amount of anger in *Hurry On Down*, and it is an unsettling presence, but it is never given any political or ideological direction. In fact, the main protagonist, Charles Lumley, eschews identification with any social group. Alongside the broadly anti-establishment leaning in the text, the main thrust is of an individualistic resistance to all forms of collective activity, including political groupings. In this sense both Amis and Wain represent the inverse side of 1950s culture. Despite the railing against society, the common element is a staunch individualism that in one sense supports an ideology of consumer capitalism

---

37   See Humphrey Carpenter's account of this in his *The Angry Young Men: A Literary Comedy of the 1950s* (London: Penguin 2002), pp.54–5.

38   Ritchie provides an excellent account of the development of the media concepts of the Movement and the Angry Young Men, and Amis and Wain's place within both of these groupings, in his book *Success Stories: Literature and the Media in England, 1950–1959* (London and Boston: Faber & Faber, 1988). See also Carpenter, 2002.

and the free market economy; whilst at the same time being suspicious of the emergent mass culture that that ideology seemed to be producing. However, despite *Hurry On Down* being a novel of containment rather than rebellion, it does reveal aspects of an oppositional culture that resists the prevailing attitudes of 1950s society and culture. As a whole, the novel reveals many of the contradictions and anxieties about the new England that was emerging during the period.

In terms of form, the dominant critical reading of *Hurry On Down* is as a conventionally realist novel.[39] However, it is a realism based on an eighteenth century picaresque model rather than a nineteenth century 'classic' realism. The novel represents a series of adventures for the main character Charles, who, after graduating from University, rejects his middle-class background and becomes involved in various working-class, and sometimes, criminal ventures. These include window cleaner, drug trafficker, hospital porter, chauffeur, and eventually gag-writer for a Radio show. The picaresque form allows Wain to comment critically on several aspects of English society and culture, and the episodic structure of the novel suits the thematic search for freedom of the main character as he continues to resist being reintegrated into the society against which he sets himself. In this way, the novel rejects the typical realist and *bildungsroman* pattern of the adventures of a hero trying to find his place in the social world. It does this by emphasizing that Charles rejects all of the potential social spheres in which he might be contained.

However, It is important to stress that *Hurry On Down* is formally less conventionally realistic than has been assumed and, in fact,

---

39   Although there has been little recent criticism on *Hurry On Down*, most of what there has been places Wain's novel in the broad grouping of anti-experimental fiction of the 1950s. Rubin Rabinovitz, for example, includes Wain in his grouping of fifties novelists who 'show the influence of the nineteenth century novelists by their realistic style', *The Reaction Against Experiment in the English Novel 1950–1960* (New York and London: Columbia University Press, 1967), p.16. Malcolm Bradbury describes the novel as 'realistic picaresque' in *The Modern British Novel 1878–2001*, Revised Edition (Harmondsworth: Penguin, 2001), p.344. Alice Ferrebe notes that the novel deploys 'the omniscient narrator of conventional realism', Ferrebe, *Masculinity in Male-Authored Fiction*, p.28.

uses narrative techniques and strategies that do not eschew an experimental attitude to fiction, despite critical readings to the contrary.[40] One of the main reasons that the novel has been read as conventionally realist is the apparent attack on literary modernism that it contains. A few critics have cited one particular episode as emblematic of this approach.[41] This is the parody of modernist writing presented in the figure of Froulish, the experimental writer with whom Charles lives for a time. At one point Froulish reads from the experimental novel he is working on: 'Clout bell, shout well, pell-mell about a tout, get the hell out. About nowt. Court log wart hogbought a dog' (65). This is clearly a parody of the kind of modernist writing that showed a penchant for over-using poetic techniques within narrative prose, however, the context in which Froulish's novel is presented needs to be reassessed. He has been invited to read his 'Work in Progress' to a provincial literary group, and much of the social satire is directed not at Froulish's modernist style, but at the provincial bourgeois reaction to it. The response of one of the members of this book group, Mr Gunning-Forbes, a local senior English teacher, is tellingly patronizing:

> 'Not a bad touch that' [Gunning-Forbes] commented. 'Illustrate the way the working classes have got above themselves since the war eh?' [...] 'I think its got the makings of a fairly good yarn, providing of course that you cut out this verbal tomfoolery and make it clean-cut [...] A course of Thackeray, that's my prescription – soon weed out these little faults.' (66–8)

In the face of this provincial philistinism, Froulish's experimentalism does not come out as wholly negative.

What might be called a modernist attitude to language is also incorporated into the novel itself. One example of this is the reference

40   Dominic Head, for example, talks of Wain in the context of Movement writing generally, which he describes as an impatience with complexity, symbolism, and opacity *The Cambridge Introduction to Modern British Fiction* (Cambridge: Cambridge University Press, 2002), p.50; whilst Blake Morrison describes the *Hurry On Down* and *Lucky Jim* as 'fiction hostile to "experimentalism"', Morrison, *The Movement*, p.52.

41   See, for example, Andrzej Gasiorek, *Post-War British Fiction: Realism and After* (London: Edward Arnold, 1995), p.4.

to a 'line from a modern poem' that embeds itself into Charles mind: 'And a twister love what I abhor' (29). Charles plays around with this phrase shaping it into different forms ('And twister I, abhorring what I love'; 'Love eye and twist her and what I abhor'). In this motif running through the novel, language loses its referential function and becomes part of a playful concentration of the way in which words are fluid and evade meaning. Unlike the reliance in realism on the referential transparency of language, Wain also makes it apparent that language often adapts itself to the situation in which the main character finds himself. At a particular moment of crisis for Charles towards the end of the novel, the narrative voice slips unannounced into his muddled thoughts, carrying traces of his former experiences:

> Don't worry about me. I can make friends and influence people. And I'm big. I let them influence me in return. Just watch this dial, time the speed in the lower gears. Just clean these windows. A perfectly honest profession. Harry Dogson. Do you know this man? He's harmless. Not like me. Let me be your father. I'm cold, Rosa, Veronica come closer. Sticky newspaper. (228)

In its juxtaposition of phrases taken from different contexts, and the break down of logical thought process, this passage is closer to techniques that would have been recognized as modernist in the 1950s.

This complex attitude to language, and what it represents in ideological terms, is indicative of the contradictions the novel has towards both tradition and the new. Charles's attitude to both is suspicious, although it is certainly the case that his suspicions are, on the whole, directed more towards upholders of tradition such as Gunning-Forbes. Charles's adoption of different identities at different moments in the text, mark him out as representing a new kind of individual, one that is closer to a postmodern model of identity than the 'enlightenment' subject that is conventionally represented in realist fiction.[42] It is also shown that these cultural identities exist *a priori*, in terms of language, to the articulation of them by Charles:

---

42   For a definition of both enlightenment and postmodern models of identity see Stuart Hall, 'The Question of Cultural Identity', in *Modernity and Its Futures* (London: Polity, 1992), pp.274–99.

Charles was reassuring, calling into play that softness and slight hesitancy of speech that the University had made, once upon a time, his normal utterance. He had long since laid it aside in favour of the curter, more aggressive manner of the normal world, but something about Mr Braceweight's helplessness, he found, called it out again despite himself. (169)

Here, Charles is able to 'call into play' ways of speaking that reveal specific social situations. Notice, however, how 'normal' is used for each of the contradictory social spheres, which in effect undermines either as authentic. Both kinds of speech, and all the differing kinds of speech that Charles uses in the course of his experiences, are shown to be constructed and artificial. Also note how these are not fully controlled by the subject: Charles slips into the 'University speech' 'despite himself'. This suggests more of a poststructuralist attitude to language than has generally been thought representative of Wain's style. Despite the attempt by the novel to record authentic experience, there is a self-referential awareness of language (as it relates to social and ideological circumstance) that threatens to undermine the authority of utterance required by a representational medium.

This contradiction is extended to the attitudes the text has towards class. Initially, Charles's attempt to distance himself from the middle class is thrown into disarray by his attraction towards Veronica, the 'niece' of a wealthy businessman he observes in the grandest hotel in Stotwell.[43] After he has begun an affair with her, it emerges that she is in fact the mistress of her so-called 'uncle', who frightens him off. Much like Christine in *Lucky Jim*, Veronica is presented as the property of a wealthy upper-middle-class male, and is initially regarded as something to be attained by Charles despite his antagonism for the middle classes generally.[44]

---

43 Stotwell is described as a typical provincial town/city in the Midlands, and given Wain's background is probably based on Stoke-on-Trent, although, like Amis (and unlike Alan Sillitoe) Wain chooses to not specify the location of his initial setting, suggesting that it could relate to any Northern/Midland English provincial town.

44 This attraction of a lower-class male to an higher-class female also forms the plot of John Braine's *Room at the Top*, another novel that has been misrepresented as an 'Angry' novel. For a more detailed discussion on the representation of masculinity and class in the fifties novel see Lynne Segal, 'Look Back

Perhaps the most open attack on middle-class culture comes in Charles's encounter with Burge (an old college acquaintance) and his friends at a party in a typical suburban house that Charles, somewhat facetiously, dubs 'Stockbroker's Tudor' (170). Burge represents the dominant ruling class in Britain and the argument Charles has with him articulates the central critique the text launches against the prevailing ideology of early fifties society. Burge takes issues with Charles for rejecting his middle-class background by working as a hospital porter (Burge is training to be a doctor):

> 'Yes, you bloody well do understand it,' he [Burge] cried. 'That sort of work ought to be done by people who are born to it. You had some sort of education, some sort of upbringing, though I must say you don't bloody well behave like it. You ought to have taken on some decent job, the sort of thing you were brought up and educated to do, and leave this slop-emptying to people who were brought up and educated for slop-emptying'. (174)

Burge, here, reinforces the dominant belief in a rigid class structure that, at this moment in the text at least, Charles opposes:

> 'No I don't want to know,' Charles retorted. 'And I don't want your silly Edwardian notions of an upper-class Herrenvolk thrown up at me either. By "letting the side down" all you mean is that the nigger-driving sahib oughtn't to do anything that reveals that he shares a common humanity with the niggers he drives. That idea's dead everywhere in practice, and it only survives in theory in the minds of people like you'. (175)

Charles's attack is couched in the language of the end of Empire, and serves to connect two perceived threats to the prevailing order in fifties England: the association of class and 'race', here, marks out the very areas from which the challenge to Burge's privileged lifestyle seems to be generated. Eventually, Charles is ejected from this enclave of traditional privilege, however, the text shows it is firmly on

in Anger: Men in the Fifties'; Ferrebe, *Masculinity in Male-Authored Fiction*; and Susan Brook, 'Engendering Rebellion: The Angry Young Man, Class and Masculinity', in *Posting the Male: Masculinities in Post-War and Contemporary Literature*, ed. by Daniel Lea and Berthold Schone (Amsterdam: Rodopi, 2003), pp.19–34.

the side of his values: 'They frogmarched him to the door and launched him into the air [...] The outsider was outside, and they were inside' (176). Charles is marked, here, as the outsider: a threat to the stability of middle-class values that has to be expunged. However, because of Wain's manipulation of point of view, the reader is persuaded to adopt Charles's outsider position. At this moment in the text, therefore, the belief in a rigid class society is presented as outdated and ideologically suspect.

This attack on the privileged middle class, however, is undermined by Wain's attitude to 1950s working-class society and culture. The second main female character in the novel is Rosa, a working-class woman who works in the hospital where Charles gets a job as a porter. At first, the relationship with Rosa seems to provide him with an escape from the middle-class anxieties of duty, responsibility and ambition, 'Charles felt his search was over. No demands were to be made on him other than merely being there, merely existing' (187). This sentiment, of course, reveals a lack of knowledge of the hardships of working-class life in the early 1950s, and Charles's attitude is based on stereotypical representations of working-class life that are supported by the text as a whole. In fact, there are two forms of working-class culture represented in the novel, both of which reproduce stereotypes: firstly, the older, organic working class represented by Rosa's father; and secondly, the emergent, ambitious, younger working class represented by her brother Stan. In this respect, *Hurry On Down* reinforces prevailing middle-class attitudes to the working class in the 1950s, and reveals some of the anxieties the Movement writers had generally about new class structures alongside nostalgia for the old.[45] Rosa's father, for example, is described in traditional, if patronizing, terms: 'This was Rosa's father's Sunday afternoon, and he had been spending it as he always did, in his armchair by the fire with the *News of the World* on his knee fast asleep' (183); and later, 'Rosa's father had evidently fulfilled his duty towards his children by

45   In this respect, *Hurry On Down* represents a similar dichotomy of working-class culture to that presented in Richard Hoggart's *The Uses of Literacy*, published four years later. See the discussion of Hoggart's book in chapter three above.

begetting them and providing them with food and clothing during their non-productive years, and he seemed vague about other matters' (187). These remarks reveal uninformed, pejorative descriptions of the working class as unambitious, politically apathetic, and irresponsible towards their children. However, despite these derogatory remarks, there is a respect for Rosa's father that contrasts with the scorn placed on his son Stan:

> Charles liked Rosa's father, but he did not like Stan. This was not so much a disappointment as a confirmation of his preferences just now, for Stan was making a fairly determined effort to 'better himself' by rising out of the world of strictly manual work – his father was a foreman at some kind of brickyard or quarry, it was not quite clear which – into the circle immediately above it. This circle seemed, by all accounts, a good deal slimier. At sixty, Stan would have neither the massive good humour nor the genuine dignity of his father, and already he was immersed in learning the technique of cheap smartness. He talked a different language, for one thing; it was demotic English of the mid twentieth century, rapid, slurred, essentially a city dialect and, in origin, essentially American. By contrast it was a pleasure to hear his his father, whose speech had been formed, along with other habits, before 1914. (184–5)

The attitude towards Stan, here, is focalized through Charles, but it also represents the prevailing attitude of the novel as a whole. This can be seen in the use of the word 'preferences' rather than the more appropriate 'prejudices' in describing Charles's evaluation of the two characters. What the passage reveals is anxiety about the new classless society that appeared to be emerging in England after the Second World War. The negative associations attached to the phrases 'better himself' and the acquirement of 'cheap smartness' reveals distaste towards the kind of ambitious and emergent working-class individual Stan represents. The reference to the fear of Americanization articulates an accusation of cultural inauthenticity to this new group in contrast to the heritage of the older working class, formed largely 'before 1914'.[46]

So there would seem to be a contradiction at the heart of Wain's novel in relation to issues of class: the rejection of the old is not

---

46   As we saw in chapter three above, this threat of the Americanization of English working-class culture is also an anxiety underlying Hoggart's book.

balanced by a desire for the new. What is left is a staunch belief in the possibility of an individual's freedom, an escape from the ties that society imposes on the individual. In *Hurry On Down*, this essentially existentialist philosophy is articulated through a desire to evade the rigid class stratification of society, which seems to force individuals into an association with a particular level within society. This individualism is, of course, not ultimately a critique of the prevailing ideological attitudes of 1950s culture, but is in fact the mirror image of middle-class culture. This form of individualism is bound up with the rejection and fear of the consequences of a collective identity emerging from below, and there is no place for collective politics in Wain's rejection of dominant society. Rejection has to be on a personal, rather than a social level. This of course, diffuses any potential for a radical or revolutionary shake-up of society based on collective political action.

So despite the attack on the establishment and conventional ways of life, *Hurry On Down* is unsure about what might replace them. It certainly does not advocate the opening up of society to newly ambitious working-class youth. If it, and Amis's novel, do show anger, it is an anger that is managed or contained by an equal suspicion of the forces that might replace the old order. The description of Amis and Wain, therefore, as Angry Young Men is misleading, especially when compared with novelists in the later 1950s who cover some of the same ground, especially, as we shall see, Alan Sillitoe, Colin MacInnes and Sam Selvon. It is, though, to Muriel Spark that I wish to turn in the next chapter, a writer who reveals a different kind of radical fiction.

Chapter Five
Muriel Spark: Exploring Fictions

Spark in the Fifties and the *Nouveau Roman*

Most discussions of Muriel Spark's early work concentrate on her exploration of essentialist issues such as the role of religion in society (and specifically Catholicism), and the nature of fictional writing. There has been relatively little work done on looking at Muriel Spark from a historicist perspective, and most of what there has been has tended to focus on author biography, rather than linking Spark to broader social and cultural contexts.[1] This chapter attempts to read Spark's 1950s fiction against the historical contexts from which it was produced. In particular, I concentrate on Spark's formal experimentation with the novel, not as part of an ahistorical discussion of narrative fiction, nor how her use of form connects with theological ideas, but as revealing some of the preoccupations of fifties culture and society.

I want to begin this historicist reading of Spark by relating her work to a contemporaneous, although foreign, literary context: the French *nouveau roman*. Several critics have identified a link between Spark's fiction and experimental French writing, however, they tend to cite her mid 1960s and 1970s novels as examples of this influence.[2] In fact, Spark's engagement with some of the techniques, strategies

---

1 For example; Patricia Stubbs, *Muriel Spark* (Harlow: Longman, 1973); Peter Kemp, *Muriel Spark* (London: Paul Elek, 1974); Ruth Whittaker, *The Faith and Fiction of Muriel Spark* London: Macmillan Press, 1982); and Brian Cheyette *Muriel Spark* (Plymouth: Northcote Press, 2000).

2 Kemp, 1974, 128–9 and 146–7; Whittaker, 1982, 8–9; Cheyette, 2000, 71; Martin McQuillan, 'Introduction: "I Don't Know Anything About Freud": Muriel Spark Meets Contemporary Criticism', in Martin McQuillan (ed.) *Theorizing Muriel Spark: Gender, Race, Deconstruction* (London: Palgrave, 2002), pp.1–31; (9–11).

and ideological outlooks of the *nouveau roman* can be identified much earlier – in her fifties novels – especially the three novels covered in this chapter. There is evidence for this influence suggested in an interview Muriel Spark gave to Martin McQuillan in 1998. In responding to a question on the *nouveau roman* Spark says:

> I was thinking the same thoughts that they were thinking, people like Robbe-Grillet. We were influenced by the same, breathing the same informed air. So, I naturally would have a bent towards the *nouveau roman* but in fact I was very influenced by Robbe-Grillet.[3]

Alain Robbe-Grillet was the most recognized proponent of the *nouveau roman* in the 1950s and Spark's acknowledgement of his influence seems to be much earlier than has previously been suggested. In the same interview she mentions *The Ballad of Peckham Rye* as being directly influenced by Robbe-Grillet, which traces the connection back to the late 1950s. As Spark suggests, both writers were affected by a similar social, cultural and intellectual climate and were responding with similar experimental narrative techniques. To employ a theory proposed by Deleuze and Guattari here, a rhizomatic relationship can be identified. For Deleuze and Guattari, 'any point of a rhizome can be connected to any other', but there is a '*plane of consistency* of multiplicities', and it is in this sense that a connection can be made between the narrative style adopted in the *nouveau roman* and Spark's work in the fifties.[4] This connection, of course, resides in the similar social, political and cultural positions of France and Britain during the period; both countries were engaged in a dismantling of their pre-war colonial empires (seen most visibly in their joint political humiliation during the Suez Crisis); both were facing a reduced international political standing in the Cold War stand off between the superpowers of the United States and the Soviet Union; both were suspicious of the cultural influence of Americanization; the intellectual left in both countries was responding to a crisis of faith in

3   '"The Same Informed Air" An Interview with Muriel Spark', in Martin McQuillan, *Theorizing Muriel Spark*, p.216.
4   Gilles Deleuze and Félix Guattari, *A Thousand Plateaus: Capitalism and Schizophrenia* (London and New York: Continuum, 2004), pp.7–9.

158

Marxism after 1956; and both were experiencing new social frameworks due to increases in immigration during the period.[5] There are, of course, differences between the French and British situation but there are enough similarities to make the case that the fiction produced in each country is responding to similar social and cultural conditions.

To explore the way in which Spark's fiction in the 1950s connects rhizomatically with the *nouveau roman* it is necessary to explore some of the positions taken by Alain Robbe-Grillet. The *nouveau roman* represented for many detractors of experimentalism the epitomé of the decline of the novel form during the 1950s. For critics such as C.P. Snow and Kingsley Amis, it represented the culmination of modernist experimentation, and William Cooper described it as 'tedious and arid beyond belief'.[6] Yet the *nouveau roman* represented a narrative form that claimed to retain a radical status whilst rejecting the notions of a committed literature of the type advocated by both socialist realism and a Sartrean *engagement*.

Robbe-Grillet was the main theorist of the *nouveau roman* and the primary target of Cooper's scorn. The French writer developed a critique of the contemporary realist novel in terms of its inability either to represent the contemporary social conditions adequately, or to produce a truly committed literature. In relation to the former, he attacked the situation whereby 'the great novels of the past' are 'set up as the model on which the young writer was supposed to keep his eyes fixed'.[7] He goes on to celebrate 'the writers who are aware of the fact that the systematic repetition of the forms of the past is not only ab-

---

5   For good introductions to French society, politics and culture in the post-war period see Emmanuel Todd, *The Making of Modern France: Ideology, Politics and Culture* (Oxford: Blackwell, 1991); and Henri Mendras with Alistair Cole, *Social Change in Modern France: Towards a Cultural Anthropology of the Fifth Republic* (Cambridge: Cambridge University Press, 1991).

6   William Cooper, 'Reflections on Some Aspects of the Experimental Novel', in *International Literary Review*, No.2, ed. by John Wain (London: John Calder, 1959), pp.29–36, (p.31). See also Rubin Rabinovitz, *The Reaction Against Experiment in the English Novel 1950–1960* (New York and London: Columbia University Press, 1967), pp.2–4.

7   Alain Robbe-Grillet, *Snapshots and Notes Towards a New Novel*, trans. by Barbara Wright (London: Calders and Boyars, 1965), p.43.

surd and sterile, but can even become harmful' (45). He also bemoans the fact that 'The only conception of the novel that is current today is, in fact, that of Balzac' (50).[8] He attempts to challenge this prescriptive ideology of form through foregrounding the textuality of writing, and thus challenge the assumption of the transparency of language accepted in conventional realism. As Stephen Heath comments, the *nouveau roman* represented 'one moment in the development of a radical shift of emphasis in the novel from this monologistic realism to what I shall call *the practice of writing*' (Heath's italics).[9] Heath goes on to stress what he calls a 'hesitation' towards conventional fictional techniques. Following Nathalie Sarraute, Robbe-Grillet suggests that it is the works of proto-realism that in fact should carry the definition 'formalism', because it is those works that uncritically reproduce time honoured formal techniques and structures. In this sense Robbe-Grillet alters the meaning of formalism to 'formulaic'.[10] The concentration on the materiality of text also produces, for Robbe-Grillet, a different *political* agenda that privileges form over content. This reverses the ideological model of literary form being propounded at the time by Georg Lukàcs that stressed that realism was the most appropriate genre for producing politically engaged fiction.[11] For Robbe-Grillet, the conventional nature of realism works ideologically to reproduce, rather than challenge, dominant power structures: the conservatism of literary form mirroring a conservative politics. As Stephen Heath puts it:

> Where once realism, historically, was a question of changing and extending subject-matter and was felt in this way to be radical [...] we now have, in this sense, total realism [...] What is now radical – and this has been the 'scandal'

8   Robbe-Grillet refers to Balzac here because it was this writer who was most often proclaimed by Georg Lukàcs as a primary example of a great realist novelist, exemplifying all the positive elements of classic realism as he [Lukàcs] defined it.

9   Stephen Heath, *The Nouveau Roman: A Study in the Practice of Writing* (London: Elek, 1972), p.22.

10   Robbe-Grillet, *Snapshots*, p.74

11   Goerg Lukàcs, Georg, *The Meaning of Contemporary Realism*, trans. by John and Necke Mander (London: Merlin Press, 1963), first published, in German, in 1956. See the discussion of Lukàcs in chapter two above.

of the nouveau roman – is an activity of reflection on this general writing, on the forms of intelligibility it sustains. To call a novel by Robbe-Grillet 'unreadable' has a precise ideological value that it is the precise aim of the wrtiting of that novel to refuse.[12]

In an essay of 1957 entitled 'On Some Outdated Notions' Robbe-Grillet develops a re-formulated model of committed literature. He accepts the duty of the writer to be politically committed, but he questions how this commitment should manifest itself in the novel. Corresponding to his belief that there is an inter-relation between literature and politics, he accepts the idealism of 'a possible union between an artistic rebirth and a politico-economic revolution' (65), with 'Art and Revolution, advancing hand in hand, fighting for the same cause, going through the same ordeals, facing the same dangers, gradually making the same conquests, and finally attaining the same apotheosis' (66). However, he accepts this alliance of art and revolution only in the abstract – when it comes to 'the practical level, things start to go wrong' (ibid.). He goes on to argue that the contemporary conception of a committed writing is at odds with revolutionary art forms. For Robbe-Grillet, there is a direct antagonism between socialism and experimental art: 'Let us be blunt about it: the socialist Revolution mistrusts revolutionary art' (ibid.). He goes on to suggest that the artist must resist the temptation to impose external political strictures onto his [sic] work: 'Nothing can be more important to the artist than his work [...] the slightest directive from outside paralyses him, to have to pay the slightest attention to didactics [...] is an intolerable constraint' (67).

He goes on to produce a re-formulated model of a committed literature that has three main aspects: firstly, the problematization of the myth of objectivity and the repeated projection of 'man' upon the world in realist texts; secondly, the nature of the new text as self-referential and meta-critical in its awareness of its status as a textual form, and consequently the deconstruction of the myth of the referential and mimetic function of writing; and thirdly, the emphasis on the

---

12   Heath, *The Nouveau Roman*, p.32

multiplicity and indeterminacy of meaning in the literary text. In 'The Use of Theory' he writes:

> it seems that we are [...] moving towards an age of fiction in which the problems of writing will be lucidly envisaged by the novelist, and his concern with critical matters, far from sterilising his creative faculties, will on the contrary supply him with motive power (47).

The self-reflexivity of the *nouveau roman* is identified in Stephen Heath's comments in the preface to his book on the subject: 'To write a book on the *nouveau roman* is already a paradox. How, after all is one to write about a project the whole impetus of which is centred in its aim for foundation as *experience of reading?*'[13] Heath's question should also be asked in terms of the ideological status in which the *nouveau roman* engages with the 'world'. The disruption of conventional assumptions about the practice and function of the written text lead directly, for Robbe-Grillet, to a disruption in the dominant politico-economic frameworks upon which society maintains its power structures. His project is specifically to *alienate* the reader from the text, in an attempt to disrupt the traditional premises upon which reading can take place. This alienation corresponds, therefore, to a foregrounding of a textual 'revolution', but is in direct opposition to a project of dissemination of revolutionary politics in terms of collective action as promoted in socialist and Marxist theories. This is the ideological paradox upon which the *nouveau roman* turns. Its definition of commitment is in direct contrast to a revolutionary literature based on Marxist principles of producing a collectivized, socialist art form, a concern very much to the fore in 1950s writing in England as well as France.

In the context of the fifties, Robbe-Grillet succeeded in producing a theory for the production of 'radical' literature by re-defining the term 'radical' in a literary/ideological context. For him, the concept was understood as a primarily *formal* category, which retained political implications but could not be restricted to a specific political discourse. He developed a theory of the possibility of a radical liter-

---

13   Heath, *The Nouveau Roman*, p.11.

ature outside of a Marxist literary criticism, which freed the 'committed' writer from a privileging of class politics over other forms of radical discourse, and it is here that Robbe-Grillet's work intersects with the formal strategies deployed by Spark. She produced four novels in the late 1950s each of which, in its own way, represents a radical experiment with novelistic form. In the following sections I analyse the nature of the experiment in three of those novels: *The Comforters* published in 1957, *Robinson* which came out a year later, and *The Ballad of Peckham Rye*, published in 1960.[14] With respect to *The Comforters*, I concentrate on Spark's exploration of the ontological relationship between reality and fiction. For *Robinson*, the emphasis shifts to identifying the postcolonial and psychoanalytical aspects of the novel. With *The Ballad of Peckham Rye*, I am interested in her representation of working-class life and the potentially radical disruption caused by the importation of a subversive element, particularly in terms of class, youth and sexuality.

The Comforters

Published in 1957, *The Comforters*, is Muriel Spark's first full-length novel and establishes many of the themes and concerns of her fiction throughout the fifties and beyond. One of these themes is the opening up of a dialogue concerning the conventions of realism; a dialogue grounded in 1950s debates on the philosophical parameters and ideological associations of realist and modernist, or 'experimental', writing. Spark's first novel can be regarded as an experiment in meta-criticism in that it is interested in scrutinizing the limitations and paradoxes in the critical understanding of how imaginative fiction

---

14   *The Comforters* (London: Macmillan, 1957); *Robinson* (London: Macmillan: 1968); *The Ballad of Peckham Rye* (London: Macmillan, 1960). There is a brief discussion of her third novel, *Memento Mori* in chapter one above.

operates.[15] This is achieved in two ways: firstly, through the use of metafictional techniques, and secondly, by presenting parodies of standard devices found in conventional genres, such as characters and plots taken from detective fiction. Spark's critique of realism also engages with other concerns in 1950s culture and society including the rise of youth culture, the role of Britain in a rapidly decolonising world, the place of women in society and, more generally, the questioning of established models of identity.

In *The Comforters*, these concerns are articulated through the central character of Caroline Rose. Caroline is a writer who at the start of the novel has been working on a book project entitled 'Form in the Modern Novel'. The novel has a central metafictional framework: as the novel we are reading proceeds we find her thinking about writing her own work of fiction, a work that essentially becomes the novel we are reading. This represents the first of many paradoxes concerning the processes of writing: given this metafictional framework, what we are reading is not strictly fiction, but Caroline's autobiography. But, of course, Caroline is not a real person, so it is, in fact, fiction. To push this further, Spark alludes, as Brain Cheyette has shown, to events in her own life, and Caroline becoming the fictional stand-in for Spark.[16] This metafictional conundrum allows Spark to explore the nature of writing and of the processes involved in turning experience into fiction. In addition, the questioning of realism as a form adequate in representing experience extends to a questioning of the transparency of writing. As we saw earlier, the *nouveau roman* was concerned with interrogating the mimetic function of writing, which involved the philosophical scrutiny of the materiality of writing, and its function as a communicative tool. In *The Comforters*, Spark addresses these questions by foregrounding different types and processes of writing, most noticeably in two features of the novel: firstly, the figure of the 'ghostly' typist, and secondly, the use of letters.

15 Ruth Whittaker points out that Spark's technique is similar to Jonathan Raban's identification of a style of writing that combines fiction and criticism, that he playfully calls 'criction', *London Magazine* X no.2 (May 1970) pp.89–94.
16 Cheyette, *Muriel Spark*, pp.23–4.

The typing ghost is a figure that Caroline hears at various moments in the novel tapping away at some (at first) undisclosed text. The ontological status of this ghostly ur-author is never established, but Caroline only hears it when she's alone and none of the other characters hear it. What she hears is the tapping of typewriter keys followed by a voice. We see that the voice speaks phrases and sentences that correspond exactly to sections in the third person narration:

> It had struck her in passing that the baron had seemed extraordinarily in interested in Laurence's grandmother [...]
> Through the darkness, from beside the fireplace, Caroline heard a sound. *Tap.* The Typewriter. She sat up as the voices followed:
> *The Baron had seemed extraordinarily interested in Laurence's grandmother.* (52–3)

This is obviously unsettling for Caroline, but it is also unsettling for the reader, whose expectations are disrupted by the typewriter's intrusion into what s/he has been persuaded to think of as a realistic novel.[17] The uncanniness of this device points the reader towards a consideration of the ontological nature of fiction, of writing and of characters as representations of individual identities.

As Cairns Craig suggests, the symbolic use of the typist as Spark's attempt to juxtapose a spiritual narrative alongside the micronarratives of the individual characters, is a manifestation of God, or at least of an alternative deterministic narrative that undercuts the free will of the characters.[18] The typewriter appears just after Caroline's three-week retreat at a Catholic centre in London and perhaps, therefore, represents her self-questioning, and the splitting of the self into two distinct identities. According to this reading, the typewriter is generated not externally but from Caroline's own identity crisis – a form of schizophrenia produced by a moment of revelation. Caroline

17 The novel begins in a conventionally realistic way, describing a visit Caroline's boyfriend Laurence Mander has with his grandmother Louisa Jepp. This opening acts to lull the reader into a false sense of security, making the later deviations from realism all the more surprising.
18 Cairns Craig, *The Modern Scottish Novel: Narrative and the National Imagination* (Edinburgh: Edinburgh University Press, 1999) pp.172–3.

is forced to project this 'other' image of herself externally, so that she can lucidly come to terms with this crisis in identity. As soon as she hears the typewriter she is forced into a questioning of its ontological status:

> Immediately then, shaken as she was, Caroline began to consider the possibilities, whether the sounds she had heard were real or illusory. While the thought terrified her that she was being haunted by people – spirits or things – beings who had read her thoughts, perhaps who could read her very heart, she could not hope for the horrible alternative [...] The question began to appear as one on which she could herself decide; it was like being faced with a choice between sanity and madness. (43–4)

What frightens Caroline is not the thought that these voices are revealing the existence of a transcendental deity, but that they point towards her own madness. The text refuses to offer a final explanation to this central ontological and theological question. However, it does provide clues that suggest that the typewriter is in fact more likely to be a symptom of Caroline's mental state, and therefore, produced internally. For example, earlier in the text we are told how Caroline succeeded in psychologically repressing unpleasant memories:

> In this way, she subjugated St. Philomena's for half an hour. She had devised the technique in the British Museum Reading Room almost a year ago, at a time when her brain was like a Guy Fawkes night, ideas cracking off in all directions, dark idiot-figures jumping round a fiery junk-heap in the centre. (34)

This passage represents Caroline's ability to repress the frightening effects of ideas arriving so rapidly to the brain that no coherence or logical ordering can be achieved. It is significant that this repressed element is articulated metaphorically as a combination between a potential (Catholic) revolutionary, Fawkes, and suppressed devil-like figures. The potential Caroline recognizes, but represses, is the thinking individual's encounter with the irrational and heterogeneous forces of desire lurking behind and below conventional social behaviour. It is also significant that she has developed this technique while researching her book on the form of the 'Realist' novel in the British Museum. The fear she is beginning to recognize is that the realist novel has no form, and, therefore, the thing that it has been trying to represent, that is 'real' life, is also formless. This idea is reversed in the novel to suggest that because life has no form, no order, then the traditional aim of the conventional realist novel to represent life in a logical order is philosophically, aesthetically and rationally mistaken.

A second way in which the novel foregrounds the materiality, or opacity, of writing is in the thematic importance of letters and their relationship to the main text. One example is the letter to Caroline from Laurence (her boyfriend) about his grandmother. The introduction of this letter into the text moves seamlessly from narration and spoken dialogue to epistle form: '"Grandmother has just dozed off again," Laurence wrote, "after looking up to inquire after you"' (22). Here, different types of text follow each other unannounced, with the effect that the textual nature of the whole work is foregrounded. (The letter is, of course, 'textual' in that it is written down by one of the characters, but it appears in the novel as direct speech.) This is an example of what Stephen Heath in referring to the *nouveau roman* calls 'deconstruction of the very "innocence" of realism' through an attention to the 'thickness' of writing.[19] The nature of writing itself is defamiliarized. This denies the attempt by the conventional realist novel to give the lie to the reader that the events and characters being described have a separate corporeal reality distinct from their ontological status as text. This is part of a desire by Spark for us to question our own ontological status – how we ourselves are written texts that communicate with other 'texts' in a cultural and social sense. Spark, here, is foregrounding the ways in which identity is constructed and recognized by others.

Another important letter in the novel that blurs the ontological status of texts and so called real life is the one which ends the novel: 'before he [Laurence] left he sat down at Caroline's desk and wrote her a letter' (232) The letter he writes is then reproduced in the text, which includes his objection of 'being a character in your novel'. But he decides to destroy the letter tearing it into pieces. 'He saw the bits of paper come to rest, some on the scrubby ground, some among the deep weeds, and one piece on a thorn bush; and he did not then fore-

---

19   Heath, *The Nouveau Roman*, pp.22–3

see his later wonder, with a curious rejoicing, how the letter had got into the book.' (238). This passage obviously makes reference to a religious context as, like the words of God, the pieces of the letter fall on stony ground, some of them seemingly crucified on the 'thorn bush', whilst some of them mysteriously take root in the novel itself. The ontological mystery of this letter has been read by Ruth Whittaker as a manifestation of God's transcendental interference in the lives of people, but this reading detracts from a textual one in which the rational impossibility of the letter finding its way into Caroline's novel, in a realist sense, becomes irrelevant in a piece of writing that operates under the very different ontological criteria of a textual world, where anything is possible.

I do not want to dismiss the religious contexts in which Spark's early novels have been read, as they clearly have relevance. But I would argue that it is no coincidence that a novel that is concerned with the ontological status of individuals with respect to spirituality articulates itself at this moment of the 1950s through a questioning or deconstruction of the modes and conventions of the realist novel. Spark's spiritual conversion is tied up with, and not distinct from, the contemporary shaking up of other grand narratives such as patriarchy, the nation, and the generic conventions of literary realism. In this way Spark's writing is radical in a political and ideological sense. Its political engagement manifests itself in a way similar to Robbe-Grillet's arguments for the *nouveau roman*. It achieves this not through the conventions of an openly committed socialist realism, but by destabilizing the reader's understanding of the conventions of society and fixed models of identity, resulting in the questioning of the established social and ideological relationships between people.

The novel that Caroline ultimately produces, a novel also entitled *The Comforters*, is rationally unstable. For Spark, starting out as a novelist in the fifties, a complete rejection of realist forms would inevitably have produced the critical association of her with modernist writing, and thereby serve to re-locate her fiction within recognized generic parameters. Spark's way around the dichotomy of realist/modernist writing, so powerful in the period, is to present realist plots and characters, but to stretch that realism to the extent that it becomes parodic of recognized and generic forms of fiction. In the case of *The*

Comforters, Spark incorporates a conventional detective plot, complete with a criminal gang, blackmail and an amateur detective in the figure of Laurence Manders. But the metafictional framework of the novel alerts us to the self-reflexive use of such conventional plot devices. Spark, therefore, parodies these devices by using unlikely protagonists in each, for example, the head of the diamond smuggling gang is Laurence's grandmother Louisa Jepp. Spark achieves this by defamiliarizing conventional characterizations and plots, for example, in the physical description of Louisa:

> She is short and seen from the side especially, her form resembles a neat double potato just turned up from the soil with its small round head, its body from which hang the roots, her two thin legs below her full brown skirt and corpulence. (7)

This parodic defamiliarization is also registered in conventional representations of the character's history: 'It was a hundred and thirty years after this event that Louisa was sitting down to breakfast with Laurence' (Ibid).

The character of Georgina Hogg also reflects the disrupted ontological nature of characters in Spark's fiction. At one point in the text, other characters observe Georgina physically disappear (211–12). Caroline suggests that this is because she has 'no private life whatsoever'. In the world of fiction, it is suggested, characters do not have an existence other than on the page. Like Samuel Beckett's dramatic characters that only exist when they are on the stage, Georgina only exists when she is being described in writing. This overturns the suspension of disbelief produced in realistic fiction that the characters it presents have a real life existence that continues alongside the plot even if they are not being discussed at that moment in the text. The characters in the novel that are presented as rational are keen to consider the world as a realistic place. As Mervyn says to Louisa Jepp:

> You can't bear to participate in separate worlds. You have the instinct for unity, for coordinating the inconsistent elements of experience; you have the passion for picking up the idle phenomena of life and piecing them together [...] Reality however refuses to accommodate the idealist (18).

Louisa, as a rational character, wants to generate meaning from the chaos of events in order to justify her own existence. It is not surprising then that Laurence, who, like Louisa, is partly a parody of a character in a traditional realistic fiction, dislikes Caroline's metafictional, self-reflexive novel ('"I dislike being a character in your novel"' [233]). This is part of Spark's aim to engage the reader in ontological questions about the way in which we all relate to the world and to others. This questioning is part of a trend in 1950s culture to foreground the nature of existence. If we emphasize the historical contexts informing Spark's writing, it is no surprise that she is producing works that are asking similar questions to Robbe-Grillet in French fiction, Sartre in philosophy, and Beckett in drama. A complex 'rhizome' connects these writers, a rhizome that extends to broader social and cultural movements such as the break-up of empire, the loosening of gender relations and the disruption of traditional social categories such as class, 'race'[20] and age, all of which are central to an understanding of British culture in the fifties. After establishing a radical shift in conventional perceptions of reality through experimenting with realistic form in *The Comforters*, Spark began to explore further these social areas in her subsequent novels.

Robinson

Robinson, Spark's second novel, continues her investigation into the nature of fiction in the contemporary world. It tells the story of a group of air travellers who crash on a small island on their way to the Azores. The narrative is told in the first person by January Marlow, a widowed journalist who happens to be writing an article on threes of things, including, luckily, islands. On the plane with January are 'part-Dutch' Jimmie Waterford, and Tom Wells, an unscrupulous magazine

---

20   Brain Cheyette makes a convincing argument concerning the hybridity of Caroline Rose's ethnic background as a way of showing how the text engages with postcolonial contexts, Cheyette, *Muriel Spark*, pp.25–6.

editor and all round entrepreneur. The island on which they land is named after its main inhabitant, the reclusive Englishman Robinson. Living with Robinson is his adopted son, Miguel, whose biological father was one of the 'Pomegranate Men' who have farmed parts of the island in the past.

As with *The Comforters* this basic realistic framework is put under pressure by Spark's symbolic and parodic approach to fiction. The island location, and the title, obviously point to the classic colonial texts *Robinson Crusoe* and *The Swiss Family Robinson*. However, rather than presenting a novel in which characters of European origin struggle to survive in an alien and dangerous environment, Spark's novel is more concerned with showing the individualistic divisions between people in an enclosed social space. In this sense it is closer to William Golding's *Lord of the Flies* than Defoe and Wyss. As with Golding's novel, *Robinson* traces the psychological relationships between people in extreme circumstances, and goes further than Golding in its use of characters as symbolic representations of psychoanalytic models. *Robinson* is a colonial novel that engages with the historical context of postcolonialism, and implicitly with the contemporary crisis in the 1950s socialist/Marxist ideal of a small community working together towards a common goal. Spark replaces any potential utopian vision of the island society with a dystopian fall into self-interest, mutual suspicion and alienated individuals. With regard to the (post)colonial context, the novel evokes texts that go beyond colonial survival narratives. In particular, Spark implicitly refers to two texts that have attracted postcolonial readings: Shakespeare's *The Tempest* and Joseph Conrad's *Heart of Darkness*.

As we have seen, one of the characteristics of Spark's fiction is her playful reference to other genres and works.[21] The analogies with *The Tempest* are not overt but there are a number of significant similarities between the two works.[22] The island setting is the most obvious of these. Also, Robinson resembles Prospero in that he is the

---

21 In *The Comforters* this is primarily the detective/crime novel; in *The Ballad of Peckham Rye* it is Spark's own take on the fifties working-class novel.

22 Ruth Whittaker also notices a resemblance between the two texts; Whittaker, *The Faith and Fiction of Muriel Spark*, p.53.

initial saviour of the marooned survivors of the air crash, he is the lord of the domain in which he resides, and he eventually sets a test for the other characters by placing them in a situation that serves to bring out their true natures. January reflects on his personality:

> When I think of Robinson now, I think of him as a selfish but well meaning eccentric, but during our last week on the island I felt violently against him […] But really, after all, it was his island, and he probably, at the start, had saved our lives. (171)

Another similarity between the two works is the importance of books for both Prospero and Robinson. Prospero's books, of course, contain his magic, but there is also a magical element to the book belonging to Spark's protagonist (130). Robinson's books are kept behind glass, respected, and sealed off from contact with the world, having a special significance as physical objects, and each of them is stamped with the motto 'Nunquam minus solus quam cum solus' (p.21). In one scene January puts on Robinson's spectacles whilst alone in his room, metaphorically showing her seeing through his eyes. It is at this moment that the books appear to take on magical physical properties:

> The room swung over and round in a swivel movement. The books leaped from the shelves and piled over the carpet. Everything on the tables and the desk whirled on to the floor, and even then did not stay still […] I fixed my eye on the books spread out on the floor. It steadied up, so that I could see the book-plate on the inside cover, and it remained quite still, 'Nunquam minus solus quam cum solus.' I caught sight of Miguel running past the window with a grin on his face. (140)

Although a logical explanation is eventually revealed for the magical effect the glasses produce (it is an earthquake) the uncanny power of the moment represents the shock of seeing from the perspective of the other: an experience that makes the world unstable and forces it to turn 'over and round'. This represents a moment when one character is allowed a brief insight of the alien perspective of another. The Latin phrase that appears to January at this moment translates as 'Never less alone than when alone' and shows the ideological outlook of Robinson – his desire for solitude, which manifests itself as a strident individualism and rejection of society.

The analogy to *The Tempest* can also be seen in Robinson's 'ward' Miguel who, having a more indigenous connection to the island than Robinson, can be seen as a combination of Caliban and Ariel. Robinson has adopted him as the orphan of one of the Pomegranate men who farm the island. Although the Pomegranate men are of Spanish origin, they stand for the now excluded indigenous population of the island: an island that, therefore, comes to represent a colonized space. Miguel's otherness, his keenness to believe in Tom Wells's occultism, for example, is also emphasized to the extent that: 'It was always impossible to know what was exactly going on in his mind' (137). The allusion to the *The Tempest* does work with all the characters, but it is certainly suggested with some of them and in terms of location and plot. At the end of the novel, Robinson is preparing to leave the island as it is gradually sinking into the sea, just as Prospero, Miranda and the rest leave their island at the end of *The Tempest*. The reference to the dream-like quality of the island location is stressed by January on several occasions during the novel, for example she opens her account by referring to it as 'a time and landscape of the mind'. Later, she has an existential and solipsistic crisis when following Miguel, who appears to physically disappear: 'For a moment I thought that perhaps my other companions, too, had disappeared. I though perhaps they had never existed, that Robinson and his household were a dead woman's dream' (34).[23] This seems to echo the dream-like status of the island location and its characters in *The Tempest*.

Another important intertext in *Robinson* is Joseph Conrad's *Heart of Darkness*, which helps to consolidate a reading of Spark's novel as a postcolonial and psychological allegory. January's surname, Marlow, for example, is one of the playful references to Conrad, whose novel, of course, includes a central character with the same

---

23 This reference to the possibility that the narrative we are reading is the imaginings of a woman who has already died evokes another mid-fifties novel, William Golding's *Pincher Martin*, as Brain Cheyette has suggested; Cheyette, *Muriel Spark*, p.33.

name, and the central protagonist in each novel encounters a mysterious other in what might be called a colonial space. Robison, therefore,
can be seen to represent a second allusion alongside Prospero – that of
Kurtz in Conrad's novel, the colonial who has 'gone native', who has
passed over to the position of the other – in both a colonial and
psychological sense. Robinson, for example, is described in terms of a
deep psychological darkness: 'It was the blood which gave me to
think of darkness in Robinson's character' (173). In addition, consider
the way in which Spark emphasizes Robinson's voice from January's
perspective: 'When I sat in Robinson's rooms summoning up his
presence, it was not only the substance of his conversation that
returned to me, but also of his voice, even, rhythmical, almost a chant,
which had a slightly mesmeric effect' (139). This mesmeric effect can
be read as the effect the spoken voice has in a religious ritual: rhythmical and chant-like, but it is also very similar to the way in which
Conrad's Marlow describes Kurtz's voice:

> The man presented himself as a voice […] of all his gifts the one that stood out
> pre-eminently, that carried with it a sense of real presence, was his ability to
> talk, his sense of words – the gift of expression, the bewildering, the
> illuminating, the most exalted and the most contemptible, the pulsating stream
> of light, or the deceitful flow from the heart of an impenetrable darkness.[24]

There is an element of playful allusion here, as Peter Kemp has suggested (as a criticism) of the novel as a whole, and this forms part of
Spark's aim in her 1950s writing to re-address fiction of the past.[25]
Heart of Darkness combines a colonial journey to a distant place of
mystery and darkness with a psychological journey, both of which
emphasize the 'otherness' and dream-like quality of the visited space.
Like William Golding's *Lord of the Flies*, the interest in the colonial
experience is generated as a response to the contemporaneous break-
up of the British Empire, articulated as a dismantling of the myth of

---

24   Joseph Conrad, *Heart of Darkness* (Harmondsworth: Penguin, 1973), first pub-
      lished in 1902, p.83.
25   Kemp, *Muriel Spark*, p.37

English fortitude and fair play.[26] *Heart of Darkness*, therefore, acts as an intertext that foregrounds these issues.

The allusion between the two texts connects Marlow in Conrad's novel to January in *Robinson* as both characters embark on a process of psychological exploration and discovery. Both characters are involved in reassessing their experiences from a point after they have returned to 'civilization'. As with Marlow, January' emphasizes the psychological effect the island-experience has produced, which is again stressed by the dream-like nature of the island, a point she reiterates towards the end of the novel:

> In a sense I had already come to think of the island as a place of the mind [...] It is now, indeed, an apocryphal island. It may be a trick of the mind to sink one's past fear and exasperation in the waters of memory; it may be a truth of the mind. (185)

The only physical reminder she has is the journal that Robinson had urged her to keep when they first crash-landed on the island in which he advised her to 'keep to facts'. The journal, therefore, significantly associated with the rationalist Robinson, represents documentary proof of her experiences. But physical truth is not all that the island-experience has provided for January as her reference to the 'truth of the mind' suggests in the quotation above, and the psychological truth is the more important legacy of her adventure.

This psychological framework operates to a Freudian model, one which emphasizes the use of characters as doubles.[27] These doubles tend to combine one character on the island with one from January's life before the air crash. This suggests that the events on the island allow January to play out anxieties she has in her everyday life by projecting scenarios and characteristics onto the people on the island. In this way the island becomes a kind of dream narrative in which psychological concerns are dramatized and faced up to. An early critic

26   See the discussion of *Lord of the Flies* in chapter one above.
27   See Freud's discussion of the importance of doubles and doubling in his theory of the uncanny: Sigmund Freud, 'The Uncanny', in *The Standard Edition of the Complete Psychological Works of Sigmund Freud*, ed. and trans. by James Strachey, vol. XVII (London: Hogarth, 1953), pp. 219–52.

of the novel, Carol B. Ohmann, identified this psychological frame-work of the novel.[28] Ohmann reads Robinson and Ian Brodie (one of January's brothers-in-law in her pre-island life) as two characters who combine symbolically to represent the super-ego. As Ohmann shows, both characters are sexually repressed and fearful of women, evidenced most openly in their attacks on Mariology, the excessive worship of the Virgin Mary.[29] This anxiety is read as a displacement for a psychological anxiety about the corporality of the mother figure, and by association, the physicality of women generally. In opposition to this, stand the two characters most closely associated with the Id: Tom Wells and Curly Lonsdale (January's second brother-in-law) both of whom are involved in excessive behaviour of some kind – with Lonsdale it is gambling, drinking and womanising, with Wells, it is sham occultism and blackmail. As Peter Kemp points out, though, the doubling is not symmetrical: Ian Brodie and Tom Wells represent more extreme cases than Robinson and Lonsdale.[30]

This doubling of characters can also be extended to January's son Brian, and Robinson's adopted son Miguel. Miguel is influenced at different times by both Robinson and Tom Wells, and this dramatizes January's concerns about her own son's development into mascu-linity. For January, each of the options open to her son appear to be unsatisfactory, whether it is Robinson/Brodie's debilitating repression of desire or Lonsdale/Wells's excessiveness, both of which produce unwanted attitudes towards women. The island space, therefore, repre-sents a projection and playing out of January's anxieties regarding her son's move into adulthood.

This dramatization of psychological models is extended to the symbolic use of the physical space of the island. Early on in the novel January attempts to colonize the island psychologically:

> I must say that through my stay on the island I was more observant of my surroundings than I had ever been before, or have been since. I had often, previously, been accustomed to topographical observations, but that had been

28   Carol B. Ohmann, 'Muriel Spark's *Robinson*', *Critique: Studies in Modern Fiction* VIII, Fall 1965, pp.70–84.
29   See Cheyette, *Muriel Spark*, pp.30–1.
30   Kemp, *Muriel Spark*, pp.31–2.

according to rule, deliberate. Now, without any effort of will, my eye recorded the territory, as if my eyes were an independent and aboriginal body, taking precautions against unknown eventualities. (29–30)

This passage replicates the traditional castaway beginning to survive in a potentially life-threatening environment and is reminiscent of *Robinson Crusoe*. This coming to terms with an alien and hostile landscape is also a form of colonial narrative. Historically, whereas Defoe's novel was produced at the beginning of Britain's colonial period, *Robinson* is written during the break-up of the British Empire. This is reflected in the narrative by the eventual removal of the colonizing force, in this case January, from the island, and indeed the disappearance of the island itself, as it is literally and metaphorically sinking back into the sea at the end of the novel (185). The idea of the island as a postcolonial space is also reflected in Spark's decision to represent the physical geography of the island as a human body. The island has two 'arms' and 'legs' as well as 'the headlands', and is represented diagrammatically at the opening of the novel. Spark avoids a too rigid correlation between parts of the island and parts of the body, but there are playful, yet significant, associations that make certain aspects symbolic. The 'Furnace' at the summit of the island's volcanic mountain, for example, is associated with the heart. It is the place that induces heightened emotions especially when objects are cast into it. The two responses the Furnace makes are a scream and a sigh, representing the two traditional functions of the heart in an imaginative emotional context: fear and love, and as January observes: 'It was impossible to be near the Furnace without being drawn to gaze into it' (119). When January and the others enter into the caves towards the end of the novel, they are symbolically entering the 'body' of the island. The passage where they enter the first of the caves is loaded with a combined symbolism of corporeality and traditional notions of the underworld as a devilish space. This connects the psychological and physical allegory of entering into the deeper recesses of the mind and the body, suggesting that the psychological truth of one's identity is placed inside the self. Psychological truth is symbolically located at a geographical extremity based on a Euro-centric model of the world: not only on an alien island location, but within the body of that island. It is significant that Miguel is at home in this subterranean environment and he takes on devilish characteristics, which re-emphasizes his otherness: 'By this light Miguel's dark skin and lean figure showed up fiendishly' (116); and later, 'Miguel splashed over to the far wall and seemed to melt into it' (117). In fact, all of the characters take on an other-worldly appearance in the caves, heightening the air of suspicion between them: 'Jimmie's head was in darkness, and I could only see the dim red glow of the man's long body. Very much later, thinking over the scene, it occurred to me that I too must have looked ghoulish in the caves' (116). The caves, then, represent the extreme point of January's physical and psychological journey. It is here that she hides her journal (164–5) and that she comes closest to death in her last encounter with the blackmailer Tom Wells (166). It is also, of course, the place where she stands up to Wells who, as we have seen, represents a physical manifestation of the Id: the threat of unrepressed desire.

It is historically significant, then, that Spark chooses to locate her psychological drama in a colonial space just at the moment when Britain is going through a rapid process of decolonization. The extremity of location reveals a space outside of everyday behaviour and is articulated in a metaphorical framework that represents a geographical and psychological otherness that corresponds with Edward Said's identification of an orientalizing tendency in western writing.[31] The location of psychological crisis in a (de)colonized space, therefore, implicitly dramatizes the crisis of national identity in Britain in the 1950s and represents a coming to terms with a crisis of identity: psychological, social and national.

31 See Edward Said, *Orientalism: Western Conceptions of the Orient* (Harmonds-worth: Penguin, 1991).

The Ballad of Peckham Rye

Spark's fourth novel, *The Ballad of Peckham Rye*, was published in 1960 but is still very much located in the world of 1950s England. It could be described as Spark's contribution to the trend in the late fifties for working-class fiction in that it is located in an industrial area of south London and deals primarily with working-class people and culture. Novelists like Alan Sillitoe, Keith Waterhouse, Alexander Trocchi, Colin MacInnes and Sam Selvon had already published novels that had depicted working-class life in the fifties, and alongside these fictional representations, there was, as we saw in chapter three, the increasing interest amongst New Left writers to investigate and record contemporary working-class culture.

Spark's novel, however, offers her own distinctive approach to the working-class novel, an approach that reflects her suspicions about the role of such 'human researchers', and her continued suspicion of the veracity and transparency of the realist novel. Spark was influenced more by the *nouveau roman* than she was by the Angry Young Men and the British New Left, and as noted earlier, she has explicitly referred to *The Ballad of Peckham Rye* as being influenced by this French connection: 'What I loved about Robbe-Grillet – I tried it of course in *The Ballad of Peckham Rye* and I think it came off – he would write a book without once saying "he or she thought" or "he or she felt".'[32] Cairns Craig, for one, has identified the strict economy of language in the novel: 'The novel is immersed in an almost self-destructive restriction of language to the mere repetition of reality, reduced to a "standard" set of terms that is like the grey "ash" left over from a living world.'[33] Although Craig does not refer to the *nouveau roman* specifically, the style he is identifying in Spark is similar to the paring down of language advocated by Robbe-Grillet.

Spark's novel, therefore, represents what many commentators on fiction in the 1950s would deem as antithetical: the representation of the urban English working class, but in a radical experimental style.

32   McQuillan, *Theorizing Muriel Spark*, p.216.
33   Craig, *The Modern Scottish Novel*, p.177.

This opposition connects formal with thematic and ideological issues. Most of the working-class fiction of the period, based as it was on models developed in the 1930s, had tended to use realistic forms of narrative to evoke the gritty realism of working-class life.[34] However, Spark continued to be suspicious of realistic conventions. She employs techniques in *The Ballad of Peckham Rye* that Georg Lukàcs, for example, would recognize as modernist, rather than realist. Despite, and in many ways because of this, Spark provides her own form of radical disruption of the conventional moral, ethical and ideological codes of the period. One of the key characteristics of Spark's writing is that it purposely evades didacticism, despite many critics linking her to a tradition of Catholic morality writers.[35] Her characterization, in particular, emphasizes a non-realistic approach.

One of the formal characteristics of the novel is suggested by the title – the 'ballad' tradition, an oral narrative form appropriate to the working-class setting. However, for Spark, this reference to the ballad contains a parodic self-reflexiveness. She goes to great pains to emphasize the way in which the events of the novel are ultimately subsumed within a quasi-mythical narrative, one that tells the story of the man who 'had answered "No" at his wedding' (202). The status this story achieves in Peckham culture exceeds the 'facts' of the narrative. Stylistically, Spark also disrupts the conventional narrative parameters of the realist novel by the use of frequent flashbacks and prolepsis. This approach is encapsulated in the first chapter, which essentially relates the full story to the reader in the space of a few pages: 'The affair was a legend referred to from time to time in the pubs when the conversation took a matrimonial turn' (12).

The novel revolves around the enigmatic and mischievous Dougal Douglas. Dougal, on one level, represents a parody of the kind of middle-class anthropologist that has immersed himself into a close-

34   We shall see in the next chapters that Alan Sillitoe, Colin MacInnes and Sam Selvon prove problematic in this context.
35   See Whittaker, *The Faith and Fiction of Muriel Spark*; Malcolm Bradbury, 'Muriel Spark's Fingernails', *Critical Quarterly*, 14 (1972), pp.242–3; Frank Kermode, 'Muriel Spark' in *Modern Essays* (London: Fontana, 1990), pp.267–83. See also Martin McQuillan's critique of the reductive effect of reading Spark as a Catholic writer; McQuillan, *Theorizing Muriel Spark*.

knit working-class community. He moves to Peckham to take up a position at a textile-manufacturing firm, Meadows, Meade & Grindley as an assistant to the Personnel manager. The job has been newly created and represents a response to fifties concerns with maintaining good industrial relations between workers and employers, and to open up industry to the Arts. '"Industry and the Arts must walk hand in hand"' (13) says Mr Druce, Dougal's direct employer. Dougal is allowed to define his role: '"It will be my job to take the pulse of the people and plumb the industrial depths of Peckham"' (16). The phrasing of this is interesting in that it suggests a psychological as well as a social and cultural aim. The distinction between his job at Meadows, Meades & Grindley and his overall function in the novel is important. He eventually reports his findings to Mr Druce in the shape of a systematic analysis of Peckham culture: '"There are four types of morality observable in Peckham," he said. "One, emotional. Two, functional. Three, puritanical. Four, Christian"' (114–5). However, the effects he has on people in carrying out his 'research' exceed the remit he has been given by the company. The official findings represent an implicit critique of the systematic generalizations produced by the cultural studies/social anthropological approach as exemplified during the period by Richard Hoggart, Raymond Williams and others associated with the New Left. But the unofficial effects he has show a deeper moral, ethical and psychological approach.

In this sense it significant that Dougal is an outsider to the culture in which he is placed. As an Edinburgh University Arts graduate he is representative of the middle-class culture of the academy, as well as of a different 'nationality' to the enclosed world of working-class Peckham (a point that is often referred to by the Peckham people). His national difference is also expressed in racial terms – his red hair and his Celtic origins being foregrounded. In addition to his ethnic otherness, his physical deformity, his 'crooked' shoulder, is also represented by the text as a mark of his difference. In fact, Dougal's *difference* is repeatedly referred to: '"He's just different. Says funny things. You have to laugh," Dixie said [...] Humphrey knew that Douglas was different' (28); '"One thing about you I'll admit," she [Elaine] said, "you're different"' (84); '"But you can't help but like him. He's different"' (97); '"You're unnatural," said Mr Weedin'

(101). Brain Cheyette suggests that what is different about Dougal is his 'radical singularity', his refusal to adhere to the codes of conventional behaviour.[36] This 'difference' is extended beyond a realistic framework to suggest that Dougal has other-worldly characteristics. He refers to the 'bumps on his head' as devil's horns that he has had surgically removed, inviting several characters to feel them. It is never established whether Dougal is in fact a devil, or that this is part of his playing with the beliefs of the Peckham people, but his radical otherness is established irrespective of his actual ontological status within the text. This otherness is established as crucial to his role of unsettling and disrupting the conventional lives of the Peckhamites he encounters.

As in *The Comforters*, Spark's main protagonist represents the figure of the novelist as a fabricator of stories. With Dougal, this fabrication includes his own character, which is constantly changing as it adapts to its environment and the guise best suited to draw out his interlocutors. 'Dougal changed his shape and *became* a professor [...] Dougal leaned forward and *became* a television interviewer' (14–15, my italics). One of his several 'jobs' in the novel is to act as a 'ghost' writer for Miss Maria Cheeseman, whose so-called autobiography he sprinkles with events garnered from the real-life stories of others he hears during his 'human research' in Peckham. Spark, here, is once more playing with the notion of reality and fiction in that real life stories are transferred to another person, which, therefore, take on a fictional status, but are presented to the world as 'real' autobiography. As in her first novel, the *mis-en-abeyme* of this real-fictional paradox serves to undermine the realism/modernism debates that, as we saw in chapter two, were dominating fifties literary criticism.

This playfulness with the real/fictional opposition extends to Dougal as a character. His ontological status remains questionable throughout. Spark refuses to pin him down as either a fantasist within an essentially realistic setting, or as an actual angel-devil disrupting the realist framework of the text. Dougal often refers to himself as the devil, but this could be another fictionalization of himself as a ploy to cause more mischief. We are provided with another example of this

36 Cheyette, *Muriel Spark*, p.46.

when he entices the gossip-mongering culture of Peckham society by spreading the rumour (which he has started) that he is a police informer "'I'm in with the cops, tell them'" (160). Maybe the devil story is of a similar kind, maybe not; what is certain is that the novel retains an ambiguity over Dougal's ontological status:

> 'I have the powers of exorcism,' Dougal said, 'that's all.'
> 'What's that?'
> 'The ability to drive devils out of people'
> 'I thought you said you were a devil yourself'
> 'The two states are not incompatable'. (142)

The radical nature of the text, then, is focused primarily in the figure of Dougal. He represents a subversive force that at times appears to be Carnivalesque and at other times demonic. He induces lethargy, sexual release, laughter, violence and eventually murder, and he succeeds in thoroughly shaking up the closed cultural and behavioural practices of the working-class urban community. As Dixie, the jilted bride, states towards the end of the novel,

> 'I'm glad he's cleared off [...] You never know what he might have done. He might have gone mad among the guests showing off the bumps on his head. He might hade made a speech. He might have jumped and done something rude' (199).

The fear he causes is generated by his uncontrollable nature and his unpredictability, and ultimately, his indeterminacy. In Bakhtinian terms, Dougal acts as a conduit for the release of desire in a repressed society, bowed down as they are by the restrictions of industrialized work. Absenteeism, for example, increases significantly at Meadows, Meade & Grindley after Dougal's arrival (86). He also succeeds in drawing out the sexual desires of several characters, even the very prim and proper Miss Frierne, who is persuaded by Dougal to tell of a previous encounter on the Rye with a Highland soldier. When walking with Merle Coverdale, he points out the presence of a pram on a balcony that she had never seen before, although as Dougal makes clear, it has been there all the time. Kemp suggests that this passage refers to the fact that Dougal makes people see things that were not there before.[37] This is true, but the fact that it is a pram surely relates to Merle's anxieties as a thirty-eight year old woman in the 1950s who feels she has missed out on family life by giving herself as a mistress to the exploitative Mr. Druce. (Dixie later refers to Merle as a 'disappointed spinster' [42]). The text also makes clear that Dougal generates sexual feeling in Merle that exceeds the very mechanical sexual relations that she has with Druce: 'Then she laughed her laugh from her chest, and Dougal pulled that blonde front lock of her otherwise brown hair, while she gave him a hefty push as she had not done to a man for twenty years' (41).

The laughter that Dougal produces in Merle is an effect he has on many other characters. So much so that it becomes a significant and symbolic response to the subversive force Dougal offers. He draws Humphrey into laughter by replicating the sound his surreptitious love-making with Dixie has made on the cupboard connecting his and Humphrey's room: 'Dougal bent his knees apart as before and leapt into the air. "Creak-oop, creak-oop," he said [...] Humphrey laughed deeply with his head thrown back' (64). In such scenes Dougal's banter takes on a demonic form, which in part encourages the transgressive nature of the laughter he produces. The laughter itself often becomes demonic, for example, in the scene where after Miss Frierne, Dougal's prim landlady, discovers the death of her long lost brother (whom she has denied association with) Dougal puts on a darkly comic tableau of death:

> 'Ever seen a corpse?' He lolled his head back, closed his eyes and opened his mouth so that the bottom jaw was sunken rigid.
> 'You're callous, that's what you are,' Miss Frierne said. Then she screamed with hysterical mirth. (173)

Often, the laughter is followed quickly by tears, suggesting a close connection between the two emotional responses: both caused by being shocked out of everyday existence, and of learning something about the self that had previously been repressed: 'Merle began to laugh from her chest. Suddenly she began to cry. "God!" she said.

37   Kemp, *Muriel Spark*, p.53.

"Dougal, I've had a rotten life".' (586). This kind of response is closer to an opening up to previously repressed psychological feelings, than it is to a Bakhtinian release of socio-economic restrictions on human behaviour (although, the two are closely linked in Spark's work). Laughter is produced by the sudden revelation of socially taboo subjects: by death, by guilt and by sexual suggestiveness.

This kind of response is reminiscent of Georges Bataille's analysis of the release of heterogeneous forces within the socially policed homogeneity of dominant culture and society.[38] As with Bataille, the effect Dougal has on those he encounters is ambivalent. As many critics have identified, Dougal's actions remain difficult to assess within a moral or religious framework, and that also holds true in terms of ideology. After all he provides the means whereby several characters are able to confront their real selves, their true natures that have up until then remained hidden or repressed by social pressure. As Humphrey realises through his contact with Dougal, '"There's a dirty swine in every man"' (1). This realisation stands in opposition to the restrictions placed on Peckham society, and by extension, to the dominant codes of behaviour in Britain in the 1950s. This restrictiveness is maintained by a society's self-constructed methods of surveillance. The idea of the internal surveillance of a society by its constituent members is a theme repeated throughout the novel, and one of the fears and excitements that Dougal produces in people is his lack of regard for what other people think of him. As Merle Coverdale sums it up: '"Watch out, people are looking"' (140). The characters most susceptible to this self-surveillance are the very ones who are most immersed within the dominant economic and cultural codes of Peckham society, for example, Dixie. The model of self-surveillance represented in the text is reminiscent of Michel Foucault's symbol of the panopticon, an incarcatory system of social control whereby people

---

38   Georges Bataille, 'The Psychological Structure of Fascism', in *Visions of Excess; Selected Writing, 1927–1939*, ed. by Allan Stoekl, trans. by Allan Stoekl, with Carl R. Lovitt and Donald M. Leslie, Jr. (Minneapolis: University of Minnesota Press, 1985) pp.137–60. For a reading of Spark with reference to Bataille, see Jeremy Idle, 'Muriel Spark's Uselessness', in McQuillan, *Theorizing Muriel Spark*, pp.141–54.

agree to socially defined codes of acceptable behaviour because of the possibility of being observed acting deviantly by others: 'Mr Weedin rose to hit him [Dougal], but since the walls of his office were made mostly of glass, he was prevented in the act by an overwhelming sense of being looked at from all sides' (102). Here, the perception of social observation represses Weedin's real desire to inflict violence upon Dougal. Foucault's prison metaphor is, here, significantly transferred to a business environment, suggesting the incarcatory nature of prevailing lifestyles in the 1950s.[39]

It is also tempting to see Dougal in psychoanalytic terms: as a figure of the Id counterbalancing the repressive forces of the superego. In this sense Dougal can be seen as a similar character to Tom Wells and Curly Lonsdale in *Robinson*. As in that novel, the Id has both a negative and positive influence on the lives of the characters it affects and the same can be said of Dougal in the later novel. His effects on Humphrey, for example, seem to be positive, allowing him to evade a marriage in which his sexual desires and his masculinity would be threatened by Dixie's over-anxious thriftiness:

> 'I know what's the matter with you' he [Humphrey] said. 'You're losing all your sex. It's all this saving up to get married and looking to the lolly all the time, it takes the sex out of a girl. It stands to reason, it's only psychological'. (74)

It is not coincidental, I think, that this relationship encapsulates many of the gender concerns of socially contained masculinity explored by many of the Angry writers. As Lynne Segal has pointed out, many of the Angry texts of the 1950s were responses to male writers' anxieties over the reduced role of masculinity in the post war period.[40] For

39   Michel Foucault, 'Discipline Three: Panopticism' in *Discipline and Punish: The Birth of the Prison*, trans by Alan Sheridan (London and New York: Vintage, 1995), pp.195–228.

40   Lynne Segal, 'Look Back in Anger: Men in the 1950s', in *Male Order: Unwrapping Masculinity*, ed. by Rowena Chapman and Jonathan Rutherford (London: Lawrence and Wishart, 1988), pp.68–96. See also Susan Brook, 'Engendering Rebellion: The Angry Young Man, Class and Masculinity' in *Posting the Male: Masculinities in Post-War and Contemporary Literatture*, ed. by Daniel Lea and Berthold Schone (Amsterdam: Rodopi, 2003), pp.19–34.

Humphrey, therefore, Dougal represents a release from the anxieties of being contained, sexually, emotionally and financially within the family structure. Humphrey, of course, returns to Dixie, after the subversive influence of Dougal has been removed.

However, it is not as simple as to see Dougal's effects as a positive force shaking up a morally and ideologically inauthentic culture. It has to be observed that most of the victims of Dougal's machinations are women. Dixie is left standing at the altar; Molly Mahone, because of her association with Dougal, is physically assaulted by the three representatives of delinquent youth culture in the novel: Trevor Lomas, Collie and Leslie Morse; Miss Frierne suffers a stroke, induced by the realization that she has denied her brother's existence; and, the most extreme case is the murder of Merle Coverdale by Mr Druce, a direct effect of Dougal's influence on their relationship. So in one sense *The Ballad of Peckham Rye* is about the dangerous effects of subversion and the irresponsibility of releasing the heterogeneous within a community. That this affects women more than men is a comment on the limitations of the radicalizing scope of the Angry Young Men; that this kind of radicalism is needed to shake up moral, political and ideological laxity in fifties culture, but that, as Bataille recognized, once released, these radical forces can be dangerous.[41]

In fact the novel openly addresses issues of masculinity as they are reflected in 1950s culture and especially in youth culture. Dougal threatens to overturn conventional codes of masculinity. He is referred to as a 'pansy' on a number of occasions, mainly due to his crying about the loss of his former girlfriend in front of the women workers at Meadows, Meade & Grindley (51–2). It is difficulty to know whether Dougal is genuinely upset at this moment or whether he is staging this response to undercut the conventional behaviour for young men in fifties working-class society. This disruption of the conventional codes of masculinity is replicated in the scene where he induces a similar response from Mr Druce. It becomes apparent, in fact, that Druce is attracted to Dougal, revealing a latent homosexuality 'Mr Druce could not keep his eyes off Dougal' (14); and

41   Bataille, 'The Psychological Structure of Fascism'.

later, "'You fancy yourself" / "No, Mr Druce does that"' (139). Dougal also identifies the contemporary cultural codes of masculinity as historically contingent: "'Does you good," Dougal said, "a wee greet. A hundred years ago all chaps used to cry regardless"' (91).

But the main target for the critique of conventional masculinity is Trevor Lomas. Trevor represents the typical Americanized fifties Teddy Boy (125). This is shown by his language and behaviour, "'Come and wriggle, snake"' (76), which is later mocked by Dougal ('Come and leap, leopard'; 'Got a pain, panda'; 'Feeling frail, night-ingale?' [81–3]). Trevor is drawn in by Dougal's behaviour and responds in a typical way by mocking Dougal's apparent lack of masculinity. After the crying episode in the factory, Trevor mocks Dougal, who responds by challenging him to a fight on the Rye, the place demarcated by the community for transgressive behaviour (al-though this belies a deeper conventionality, in that it is a location sanctioned by dominant society for the release of tensions). The fact that Dougal responds in the way that is deemed to be standard mascu-line behaviour shows him to be mocking Trevor by mimicking him: "'He does Trevor to a T"' (154). Trevor, of course, is too dim to rec-ognize this mirroring of his own behaviour and is drawn in by Dougal.

It is interesting that Spark chooses Trevor as the final repre-sentative of conventional working-class culture, as in one sense his 'type', the aggressive working-class youth was, during the 1950s, being represented in the popular media, and by critics such as Hoggart, as a threat to traditional society. There seems to be a cor-respondence here between Spark's construction of Trevor and Hog-gart's anxieties over youth culture as an insidious form of replicating and extending a new commodity-fetishized working-class society. Compare, for example, the similarlity between Hoggart's description of young males with Spark: 'Most of the men looked as if they had not properly woken from deep sleep, but glided as if drugged, and with half closed lids, towards their chosen partner' (76). It is not difficult to equate the dream-like state in which these examples of youth culture are described and the ideological false consciousness with which

Hoggart imbues the 'juke-box boys'.[42] Far from being radical, youth culture is presented by Spark as part of the overall nexus of conventional, and therefore, stultifying behaviour.

However, Spark's representation of youth culture is more complex. One remarkable passage that reveals this complexity is the fight scene on the Rye. Here, Dougal and Trevor, and a group of other young people have gathered to engage in a staged fight. However, the fight unexpectedly turns into a mock dance or 'jive' instigated by Elaine because she observes policemen coming towards them. The shift from fight to jive, though, is presented with an element of uncanniness, foregrounding the strangeness of both forms of behaviour:

> The confusion stopped. Elaine started to sing in the same tone as her screaming, joylessly, and as if in continuation of it. The other girls, seeming to take a signal from her, sidled their wails into a song [...] In a few seconds everyone except Dougal was singing, performing the twisting jive, merging the motions of the fight into those of the frantic dance. (60)

This uncanny transference of fight to jive is initiated by the surveillance of the police, and represents a symbolic containment of the transgressive forces of violence into the pseudo-jouissance of the 'frantic dance'. However, the dance is presented as joyless, artificial and ultimately macabre ('Dougal saw Humphrey's face as his neck swooped upwards. It was frightened' [60]). So the dance is presented, not as part of a youth culture of resistance, but as a simulation of excess; an excess that is paradoxically re-contained by the surveillance of official power. Seen in this light, the initial fight also becomes part of a stock reaction to a repeatable set of social circumstances. Dougal agrees to fight Trevor because that is how he is expected to behave. Youth culture is represented in the novel as responding in stereotypically ways. However, this is not that Spark is simply reproducing these stereotypes, but showing that people's reactions to social situations follow already established codes of protocol, often ritualistically. In this sense, Trevor Lomas is the main representative of a youth culture that has the veneer of subversion and transgression, but

42   Richard Hoggart, *The Uses of Literacy* (Harmondsworth: Penguin, 1958), first published 1957, pp.246–50.

is in fact seen to operate as an additional force in the continuation of prevailing ideological power relationships. Trevor is Dougal's nemesis: the force that needs to be defeated in order for the heterogenous to defeat the homogenous power of conventional society.

It is significant that Trevor is the one that ultimately expels Dougal from Peckham. Their unlikely last encounter (unlikely, at least, in a conventional realist novel) is loaded with symbolic value. They meet in the tunnel that is part of the archaeological excavations of an old nunnery under the police station. They fight with bones belonging to long-dead nuns that they find in the tunnel. The result is that Dougal is wounded in the eye and Trevor is knocked out. That this location is underground, like the use of space in *Robinson*, suggests a psychological analogy. The tunnel is exposed to the Peckham public for only a few days and then closed 'owing to three scandals ensuing from its being frequented by the Secondary Modern Mixed School' (197). Trevor, in fighting with Dougal, is symbolically defeating the Id that threatens to disrupt the collective ego (or superego) of Peckham society. The weapons he uses are relics from a past religious morality, wielded unknowingly by this unlikely champion of conventional morality. And all this takes place underneath the police station, the most visible force for containment of transgressive behaviour. Dougal is ultimately stabbed in the eye with a nun's bone, generating mythopoeic references from Samson to Oedipus (198).[43]

Spark's characterization, then, plays with the stereotypes that 1950s culture re-presents to itself in its cultural and media productions: stereotypes that are self-consciously presented as acting in expected and generic ways. The result is that 'real' people, if presented with those cultural stereotypes often enough, begin to act in stereotypical, pre-constructed ways. Her fiction cleverly problematizes the relationship between free will and the unquestioned following of accepted codes of respectable social behaviour. In Spark's world,

---

43   It is worth mentioning that Spark ends each of the three novels discussed here with a final battle between the main protagonist and a character who is identified as their enemy. In *The Comforters*, Georgina Hogg drowns when Caroline struggles to free herself from her (224–5), whilst, as we have seen, January fights Tom Wells in the caves in *Robinson*.

realism is inverted: rather than presenting a world in which fictional characters behave as real people, we are made to think of the ways in which real people act in everyday life as if they are taking part in fictions. As Cairns Craig observes: 'Spark's fiction plays with type precisely to defy the limitation of the world to a series of one-dimensional types for whom it is possible to say there was another world than this.'[44] It is not difficult to see how this reading is close to an Althusserian model of ideology in which individual behaviour is socially conditioned. As many critics have observed the image of another, non-ideological, truly conscious world is only glimpsed at the end of the novel: 'The Rye for an instant looking like a cloud of green and gold, the people seeming to ride upon it, as you might say there was another world than this' (202). Richard Kane interprets this as an image of a religious afterlife, but I see it more as an indication of a potential material world that can be attained once the conventional codes of behaviour have been removed.[45] Humphrey has glimpsed this alternative, radically subversive world, but has chosen to reject it in favour of his marriage to Dixie. The other characters that have embraced this alternative reality are either dead, have turned into murderers or have been driven insane. In Spark's world, however, these are not necessarily negative qualities.

In this chapter, I have stressed that Spark's writing in the 1950s was responding to specific social and cultural forces. Decolonization, the nature of national identity in the post war world, issues over the relationship between men and women and between the classes are all addressed by Spark in ways that are distinctly different from the norm in 1950s fiction. These 'social' concerns are mirrored in the exploration of the nature of fiction and, in particular, in the critique of the value and adequacy of the realist form for reflecting the 'truth' of the world.

---

44   Craig, *The Modern Scottish Novel*, p.179.
45   Richard C. Kane *Iris Murdoch, Muriel Spark and John Fowles: Didactic Demons in Modern Fiction* (London and Toronto: Associated University Presses, 1988), p.76. On the transcendent moment at the ending of *The Ballad of Peckham Rye* see Kemp, *Muriel Spark*, pp.58–9; Whittaker, 1982, 59; Craig, *The Modern Scottish Novel*, p.179.

Chapter Six
Alan Sillitoe: Realism and the (Ir)responsibility of Writing

Alan Sillitoe's two 1950s texts *Saturday Night and Sunday Morning* and *The Loneliness of the Long Distance Runner* in many ways have come to epitomize the representation of the British working class in the 1950s. The narratives of disaffected working-class youth move through an imaginative landscape of factories, pubs, back-to-back houses and borstal. In many ways, Sillitoe's fifties texts have suffered from their own success: critics have tended to locate them firmly within their historical period and their sociological environment. They have been associated in turn with the Angry Young Man novel;[1] as continuing in a tradition of the working-class realism;[2] as texts that represent the emergence of a new youth culture influenced by the economic boom in the 1950s;[3] and as existential novels that present marginalized individuals who resist dominant society by attempting to

---

1   Robert Hewison, *In Anger: Culture in the Cold War* (London: Weidenfeld and Nicolson, 1981); David Lodge, *Modes of Modern Writing: Metaphor, Metonymy and the Typology of Modern Literature* (London: Edward Arnold, 1979); Michael Barber, 'Love on a Slag Heap', Radio Four broadcast, May 22, Part 2 of *The Angry Decade*, 1987.

2   David Craig, 'The Roots of Sillitoe's Fiction', in *The British Working-class Novel*, ed. by Jeremy Hawthorn (London: Edward Arnold, 1984), pp.95–110; Stanley S. Atherton, *Alan Sillitoe: A Critical Assessment* (London: W.H. Allen, 1979); Nigel Gray, 'Life is What You Make It', in *The Silent Majority: A Study of the Working-class in Post-War British Fiction* (London, Vision, 1973), pp.101–32; Ronald Paul, *'Fire in Our Hearts': A Study of the Portrayal of Youth in a Selection of Post-War British Working-Class Fiction* (Gothenburg: Acta Universitatis Gothoburgensis, 1982); Stuart Laing, *Representations of Working-class Life 1957–1964* (London: Macmillan, 1986).

3   Paul, *Fire in Our Hearts*; Laing, *Representations of Working-class Life*.

construct their own identities.[4] However, each of these readings is reductive and serves to contain the texts within generic boundaries: appropriating them as (contained, subordinate) novels of social critique. Each of these readings, in fact, serves to obscure the more radical aspects of the fiction, recognized in particular through the formal experiments Sillitoe uses, as well as the characters and events he describes. In this chapter, I want to 'reopen' Sillitoe's fiction through a close reading of his narrative techniques. I will argue that *Saturday Night and Sunday Morning* and *The Loneliness of the Long Distance Runner* combine a radical, marginalized discourse of a subcultural identity, in a form that pushes the boundaries of realist modes of fiction.

Self-Reflexivity and The Subcultural 'Other' in *The Loneliness of the Long Distance Runner*

At one point in *The Loneliness of the Long Distance Runner*, the teenage narrator of the text, Smith, writes (in parentheses):

> (Its a good job I can only think of these things as fast as I can write with this stub of pencil that's clutched in my paw, otherwise I'd have dropped the whole thing weeks ago).[5]

This moment of reflexivity in the text, the text foregrounding its own nature as text, reveals a central tension within Sillitoe's writing. It is placed in parenthesis because it reveals something, not about the 'events' of the text, but about the text itself, about the nature of writing in relation to the specific context of 'authorship'. Its paren-

---

4   William Hutchings, 'Proletarian Byronism: Alan Sillitoe and the Romantic Tradition' in *English Romanticism and Modern Fiction*, ed. by Allan Chavkin (New York: AMS Press, 1993), pp.83–112.

5   Alan Sillitoe, *The Loneliness of the Long Distance Runner* (London: Panther, 1985), first published 1959, p.18.

thetical status represents a moment of mediation between the text and the outside 'world', a world that includes the projected reader. The 'stub of pencil' with which Smith writes represents the contextual constraints upon the incarcerated narrator. This becomes emblematic of society's neglect of this individual, and the position of the 'writer' outside the pale of dominant literary practice. This also foregrounds a central problematic in the ontological status of Sillitoe's texts as examples of working-class literature, raising specific questions in terms of justifying the text to the reader. For example, why is this teenage 'delinquent' writing this text: for whom; for what purpose? Why does the narrator of the text need to justify its writing? How could an individual who clearly has had inadequate educational opportunities produce such a piece of writing? Why would this individual choose a 'literary' form in which to express his grievances with the system? The tension of the work lies in its own improbability, its implausible existence as a text. The ideological significance of *The Loneliness of the Long Distance Runner*, therefore, is produced in the tension between the unlikeliness of the text (theoretically) as a literary discourse and its actual existence on the page.

The self-reflexive moments appear more than once in *The Loneliness of the Long Distance Runner*, which suggests it is an issue of some importance. Sillitoe is aware of the improbability of Smith's discourse, in terms of the mode of narration he has chosen. The attempt to voice the internal monologue of this particular type of individual foregrounds the medium in which the voice would, in ideological terms, express itself. This corresponds to Jacques Derrida's discussion of the critical function of self-reflexivity in literary texts. Derrida suggests that 'They [self-reflexive texts] operate a turning back, they *are* themselves a sort of turning back on the literary institution.'[6] Sillitoe's self-reflexive strategy within *The Loneliness of the Long Distance Runner* functions as a questioning of the range and scope of the body of writing designated as 'literature' produced in

6   Jacques Derrida, '"This Strange Institution Called Literature": An Interview with Jacques Derrida', in *Acts of Literature*, ed. by Derek Attridge, trans. by Geoffrey Bennington and Rachel Bowlby (London and New York: Routledge, 1992), pp.33–75, (p.41).

Britain in the 1950s in terms of an 'interpretative community'. As Peter Hitchcock suggests, Sillitoe's writing represents 'a literature that challenges and to some extent undermines predominant notions of the literary'.[7] Sillitoe's deployment of this self-reflexive technique thus serves to question the dominant construction of the literary institution in place in Britain during the 1950s through the representation of a narrative voice that lies 'outside' the experience of the institution.[8] Through choosing a literary form 'belonging' to that institution, the short story, he succeeds in foregrounding the basis upon which the literary is constructed. In this sense, Sillitoe's fiction corresponds with Derrida's description of texts that 'are very sensitive to this crisis of the literary institution (which is more than, and other than, a crisis), to what is called "the end of literature"'.[9] The 'end of literature' in Sillitoe is gestured towards in terms of the class construction of the literary institution: rather an 'end' to a particular ideological framework for the production and reception of 'literary texts'.

The short story ends on another self-reflexive point:

> In the meantime (as they say in one or two books I've read since, useless though because all of them ended on a winning post and didn't teach me a thing) I'm going to give this story to a pal of mine and tell him that if I do get captured again by the coppers he can try and get it put into a book or something, because I'd like to see the governor's face when he reads it, if he does, which I don't suppose he will; even if he did read it though I don't think he'd know what it was all about. And if I don't get caught the bloke I give this story to will never give me away; he's lived in our terrace for as long as I can remember, and he's my pal. That I do know. (54)

This is a remarkable passage that reveals several of the textual and ideological problems suggested above. It begins by foregrounding the institution of literature in the West as an essentially bourgeois art form (again in parentheses) that fails to represent the moral, ethical and behavioural preoccupations of (white, male) English working-

---

7   Peter Hitchcock, *Working-Class Fiction in Theory and Practice: A Reading of Alan Sillitoe* (Ann Arbor/London: UMI Research Press, 1989), p.1.

8   I discuss the 'institution' of literature in terms of literary form and ideology in chapter two above.

9   Derrida, 'This Strange Institution Called Literature', p.42.

class youth. It goes on to envisage a specific reader, the 'governor', and therefore places the function of the text as a repetition of the act of rebellion represented by the events of the story: the written text reinforces the radical stand taken by the teenage narrator. However, the text also undercuts its function through the denial of the message reaching the specific reader at which it is aimed: namely, the governor. It could be described as an open letter that will never reach its recipient, but through its public expression (re)writes its oppositional discourse. The text, therefore, represents a performative act of rebellion.

The passage also suggests the construction of an intermediary, an individual who will act as a messenger, or postman, delivering the message from this subcultural, and 'sub-textual', world to the dominant culture. The desire here is to identify this named 'pal' of the teenager as a representation of Sillitoe, the radical author whose duty it is to represent this minority culture. However, the passage also foregrounds the dominant ideological framework in which the production of texts is dependent on the systems of class and representation within that hegemonic system. This represents a problematic in the theories concerning the ideological nature of literary texts. Etienne Balibar and Pierre Macherey, for example, argue that 'the literary text is the agent for the reproduction of ideology in its ensemble [...] it induces by the literary effect the production of "new" discourses which always reproduce [...] the same ideology'.[10] This suggests that the dominant education system would preclude the possibility of this text, or at least reduce its radical content to a (new) form of reproduction of the dominant ideology. Therefore, the radical voice it represents should, according to Balibar and Macherey's model, have been subsumed into the dominant linguistic frameworks available to the narrator through his experience of educational and penal institutions. This is, of course, precisely what happens when the cultural establishment positions the

10   Etienne Balibar and Pierre Macherey, 'On Literature as an Ideological Form',
      in *Untying the Text: A Post-Structuralist* Reader, ed. by Robert Young (London
      and New York: Routledge and Kegan Paul, 1981) p.96.

text as 'working-class' fiction or an Angry Young Man novel.[11] These classifications serve to contain the radicalism of the text, to place it in a position of (contained) subordination. And yet the narrative maintains its radical discourse through the act of writing itself. For the teenage delinquent, writing is an operation that contradicts the stereotypical construction or perception of this 'class' of individual. To write, in these circumstances, is a gesture of resistance against the imposition of a particular identity upon this individual as a representative of his particular subculture.[12] This is why it is necessary for the text to announce itself emphatically as a text.

One function of Sillitoe's fifties texts is to represent the previously unrepresented in subcultural terms. To retrieve the '(hi)story' of the delinquent teenager of *The Loneliness of the Long Distance Runner* is a political function that attempts to resist the possibility that this experience may 'disappear irretrievably'.[13] The text's existence is justified through its attempt to record the unrecorded, to bear witness and to rescue the teenager's narrative from the oblivion of non-representation. But this begs the question of who is being represented to whom? Is the function of the text to indicate a textual solidarity between the narrator of the text and like-minded individuals who would represent a particular subcultural identity in opposition to dominant codes of behaviour and ideology? Or is the text aimed towards a 'reader' whose experience lies outside the experience of the narrator, who would be part of what the text itself would implicitly designate as a liberal, middle-class readership? In the latter case, the text becomes an anthropological investigation into the belief system

11 I refer to the positioning of Sillitoe as a 'working-class' writer by critics such as Gray, 'Life is What You Make It'; Paul, *Fire in Our Hearts*; Craig, 'The Roots of Sillitoe's Fiction'; and Laing, *Representations of Working-class Life*.

12 As we saw in chapter three above the approach adopted by New Left analyses of youth tended to homogenize subcultural identity within specific categories. See also Gary Clarke's critique of this tendency in the New Left, 'Defending Ski-Jumpers: A Critique of Theories of Youth Subcultures', in *The Subcultures Reader*, ed. by Ken Gelder and Sarah Thornton (London and New York: Routledge, 1997), pp.175–80.

13 Walter Benjamin, *Illuminations*, ed. by Hannah Arendt, trans. by Harry Zohn (London: Fontana, 1977), p.247.

198

of a particular 'other': that of the white, working-class, teenage 'delinquent'. In fact, it provides both these functions. In terms of 'reading', the text envisages two distinct addressees, and thereby two distinct aims: to record *and* analyze a particular subcultural identity. In this sense the texts negotiate the imposed category of 'working-class' fiction.

Writing the Working Class in the 1950s

J.P. Keating argues that working-class writing flourishes at moments of social and political crisis. (He cites the 1840s/50s Chartist novel, the 1880s/90s and the 1920s/30s as examples of this).[14] This is one reason for the apparent rise in working-class literature in the late 1950s. Sillitoe's texts engage with specific social, cultural and political concerns during the period as seen in the attention paid to the subject by the emerging New Left and in a range of literary texts. John Braine, Stan Barstow, Arnold Wesker, Colin Wilson, Keith Waterhouse, Shelagh Delaney and Doris Lessing all produced texts that attempted to represent working-class life. This explosion of writing is concerned to represent the working classes as a distinct social and cultural group in opposition to what the texts themselves posit as 'middle-class' culture. Many of these texts (Braine, Delaney, Waterhouse, Barstow)[15] claim a distinct working-class culture and ethics, which, with a Benjaminian imperative of recording for posterity, necessitates *textual* representation to give it an equal validity to

14 J.P.Keating, *The Working-class in Victorian Fiction* (London: Allen and Unwin, 1971), p.124.
15 John Braine, *Room at the Top* (Harmondsworth: Penguin, 1957); Shelagh Delaney, *A Taste of Honey* (London: Methuen, 1959); Keith Waterhouse, *Billy Liar* (Michael Joseph, 1959); Stan Barstow, *A Kind of Loving* (London: Michael Joseph, 1960).

the dominant 'middle-class' novel and thereby challenge dominant cultural formations.[16]

However, there are palpable differences between the kind of anger expressed in Sillitoe's texts than in the Movement novels of Amis and Wain and the writers cited above. As we have seen, the heroes in most Movement and Angry fiction tend to be ambitious social climbers who are railing against the inconsistencies of the British class system, rather than threatening to overturn it. Sillitoe's texts are different in that his characters are firmly ensconced within a working-class culture and thoroughly reject, whether through choice or necessity, the moral, ethical and cultural codes imposed upon them by dominant society. As William Hutchings argues, Sillitoe's characters, through celebrating aspects of working-class culture and completely rejecting the attempt to escape into the middle classes, represent an: 'increasingly ardent [...] interest in an ideology of revolution.'[17]

Despite this 'revolutionary' potential, however, it is also clear that Sillitoe's texts reject the primary political opposition to Britain's hegemonic structure in the 1950s, namely communism. In *Saturday Night and Sunday Morning*, there are various references to the merits and demerits of communism from the perspective of Arthur Seaton, the text's central character. For example, the following passage reveals Seaton's equivocal approach:

> 'You was only telling me you believed in communism the other week,' Jack said reproachfully, 'And now you talk about luck and superstition. The comrades wouldn't like that,' he ended with a dry laugh.
> 'Well,' Arthur said, his mouth full of second sandwich and tea, 'if they don't like it, they can lump it [...] I ain't a communist, I tell you. I like 'em though, because they're different from these big fat Tory bastards in parliament. And them Labour bleeders too'.[18]

---

16   It is also significant that the classic working-class novel, *The Ragged Trousered Philanthropists* by Robert Tressell, was first published in its unabridged version in 1955, although an abridged version had been published in 1914.
17   Hutchings, 'Proletarian Byronism', pp.90–1.
18   Alan Sillitoe, *Saturday Night and Sunday Morning* (London: Flamingo, 1994), first published 1958, p.28.

This passage articulates the political ambivalence of the contemporary, rebellious working-class youth. According to Sillitoe's representation, they reject mainstream politics outright, but also reject the main form of organized radical discourse against the dominant power group. This can be seen as indicative of the contemporary 'crisis' in Marxist and communist politics in Britain in the 1950s. The radicalism that replaces communism for Seaton is a rebellious individualism, which refuses to collectivize itself into active political action. Despite a certain sympathy towards communism in *Saturday Night and Sunday Morning*, Arthur ultimately rejects collective action in favour of an anarchic individualism. As Arthur suggests:

> In the Army it was: 'F___ you, Jack, I'm all right.' Out of the army it was: Every man for himself. It amounted to the same thing. Opinions didn't matter. Intelligent co-operation meant falling for a slip-knot, getting yourself caught in a half nelson. (132)

Here, rebellion is articulated as a personal attitude and release against the harshness and constraints of society. In this sense, the text represents a 'post-Marxist' discourse that is concerned to reject the notion of the working class as a mass homogenized group with identical beliefs and aspirations, and to celebrate the anarchic and unstructured spirit of resistance against dominant society.

However, by rejecting official communism and Marxism as sites for resistance, the plight of Arthur's class seems inescapable in the context of the localized society represented in the text. All the means of escape from, or happiness within, the system in which the hero finds himself are rejected: whether it be through social advancement as exemplified by the character Robboe, Arthur's foreman; crime, as represented by the deceased Doddoe and his sons; or conformity, as represented by his work colleague Jack. The text opens up the oppositional model of working-class culture as suggested in much New Left writing of the period, but Sillitoe's construction of the working class is heterogeneous and identifies a range of ideological positions *within* the working class. The representation of Arthur's culture as emergent as opposed to the residual culture and ideology of his father's generation, further pluralizes the construction of the working class in

Sillitoe's writing. This rejection of a model of homogenized working-class culture means that, for Arthur, the only 'political' option is an irresponsible rebelliousness encapsulated in his motto: 'Don't let the bastards grind you down' (40).

This individualized rejection of the dominant system *and* the primary form of oppositional politics has lead many critics to identify the links between Sillitoe and the French existentialist writings of Sartre and Camus.[19] Arthur, like the central characters of *Nausea* and *The Outsider*, is representative of the individual's struggle against the hegemonic constraints of dominant society.[20] This is represented dramatically in *Saturday Night and Sunday Morning* in the scene that describes Arthur's fight with the two 'squaddies':

> His back was again to the wall. They rushed him together [...] He drove his fists back hard against one or the other of them [...] But four fists against two began to tell [...] the world had shrunk for him to a struggle being decided in the space of a few square yards [... he] slipped down in a dead faint, feeling the world pressing its enormous booted foot on to his head (174–6).

This fight, coming at the end of the first of the two sections of the novel, represents the institutionalized power of the system defeating the existential hero, and it is after this event that Arthur resigns himself to marriage with Doreen, and finishes his affairs with Brenda and Winnie. This episode can be read in Althusserian terms as the ultimate victory of the dominant ideological state apparatuses over the rebellious and wayward individual. However, Arthur, and the teenage narrator in *The Loneliness of the Long Distance Runner*, maintain

19   William Hutchings identifies the 'existential commitment' of *The Loneliness of the Long Distance Runner*, Hutchings, 'Proletarian Byronism', p.93; Atherton also stresses the connection, Atherton, *Alan Sillitoe*, pp.48–57. Also, in a radio interview, Sillitoe refers to his reading of the French avant-garde at the time he was writing *Saturday Night and Sunday Morning*, Barber, 'Love on a Slag Heap'. See also: Anna Ryan Nardella, 'The Existential Dilemmas of Alan Sillitoe's Working-class Heroes', in *Studies in the Novel* 5, Winter 1973, pp.469–82.

20   Jean-Paul Sartre, *Nausea*, trans. by L. Alexander (London: Hamilton, 1962); Albert Camus, *The Outsider*, trans. by Joseph Laredo (Harmondsworth: Penguin, 1982), first published 1942; English translation, 1946.

their dignity despite their defeat by the system: the freedom they eventually achieve is an individualized freedom within a fixed confinement, similar to Camus's image of the freedom of the condemned man, or the slave.

It is apparent, then, that Sillitoe's texts engage with the diversity of representations of the working class in the 1950s. This cannot be detached from the formal aspects of the text and the following section is concerned to reveal the way in which Sillitoe uses narrative techniques and strategies to emphasize his ideological aims.

Narrative Strategies of Empowerment in *Saturday Night and Sunday Morning*

As suggested at the beginning of this chapter, Sillitoe's texts of the 1950s have been categorized formally as working in the realist mode. Most readings have emphasized the influence of a heritage of twentieth-century working-class fiction going back to Robert Tressell's *The Ragged Trousered Philanthropists* and Walter Greenwood's *Love on the Dole*.[21] David Lodge, for example, includes Sillitoe in a group of fifties realist writers who he argues were: 'content to use, only with slight modifications, the conventions of 1930s and Edwardian realism' (213). David Craig writes, 'the mode of the book is still apparently realism,'[22] while Stanley Atherton devotes a whole chapter of his study of Sillitoe to 'Touch stones of Reality' in the early fiction.[23] Christopher Taylor has written on, 'Realism and the Language of Realism in the works of Alan Sillitoe', and makes the point that his

---

21   Robert Tressell, *The Ragged Trousered Philanthropists* (London; Lawrence and Wishart, 1955), the abridged version of the text was first published in 1914, while the first full-length version was not published until 1955. The paperback edition of 1965 included a preface by Sillitoe. Walter Greenwood, *Love on the Dole* (Harmondsworth: Penguin, 1969), first published 1933.
22   Craig, 'The Roots of Sillitoe's Fiction', p.99.
23   Atherton, *Alan Sillitoe*, pp.90–109.

realism is different to nineteenth-century patterns, but he maintains that the dominant form of the fiction is still realism.[24] By looking closely at the narrative techniques used in *Saturday Night and Sunday Morning* I want to question this consensus on Sillitoe's formal approach to his fiction and suggest that he departs significantly from models of realism as suggested by Lodge, Georg Lukàcs and others.[25]

Sillitoe, in his introduction to the 1973 edition of the novel, stresses that he attempted 'the sweat of writing clearly and truthfully, the work of trying to portray ordinary people as I knew them, and in such a way as they would recognize themselves'.[26] In this respect, Arthur Seaton, the novel's central character, has been seen as a faithful portrait of working-class youth in the late 1950s, and the Nottingham presented in the text a realistic description of an existing place. This is partly related to the traditional form of the working-class novel, which develops from the nineteenth-century realist novel.[27] The 'working-class' novel has been viewed traditionally as a sub-genre of the 'condition of England' novel, which again has been equated with conventional realist modes. Added to this function of the novel as social and political commentary are Sillitoe's own views on

24   Christopher Taylor, 'Realism and the Language of Realism in the Works of Alan Sillitoe', in *Four Fits of Anger: Essays on the Angry Young Men*, ed. by Brady and others (Zeta Universita: Campanotto Editore, 1986) pp.100–49 (pp.100–5).

25   Lodge, *Modes of Modern Writing*; Georg Lukàcs, *The Meaning of Contemporary Realism*, trans. by John and Necke Mander (London: Merlin Books, 1963), first published in German, 1957; Rubin Rabinovitz, Ruben, *The Reaction Against Experiment in the English Novel: 1950–1960* (New York and London: Columbia UP, 1967); Ronald Dee Vaverka, 'Realism and the Fictional World of Sillitoe', in *Commitment as Art: A Marxist Critique of a Selection of Alan Sillitoe's Political Fiction* (Uppsala: Almqvist & Wiksell International, 1978), pp.23–30. See also the discussion of Lukàcs's theories on literary form and ideology in chapter two above.

26   Alan Sillitoe, 'Introduction' to *Saturday Night and Sunday Morning* (London and New York: W.H.Allen, 1973), p.8.

27   Accounts of Sillitoe's influences have stressed his reading of conventional realist writers, for example Atherton identifies Arnold Bennett and Tolstoy as influences; Atherton, *Alan Sillitoe*, p.29.

the commitment of the novel to press for social reform. As Atherton observes:

> The serious writer today has a two-fold duty, according to Sillitoe. First he should concern himself with themes which reflect contemporary social injustice, and second he should continually remind his readers of the need for reform.[28]

According to this account, the realist mode is most suited to Sillitoe's aims. Sillitoe stresses that the writer should be a 'rebel' and should 'communicate in realities', but he also argues that the writer should be a 'threat to the monolithic order'.[29] This would suggest that the writer should strive not only for justice in society but also for a writing that is critical of dominant power structures. Sillitoe identifies this in a discussion on the relationship between literary form and socio-political frameworks:

> Something new has got to come. I'm not sure what it's going to be, but it's got to be something powerful and immediate to everyone [...] I keep asking myself what; but I haven't come up with a satisfactory answer yet.[30]

This suggests that Sillitoe was engaged in searching for a new form to represent adequately the new social and cultural realities he was observing during the period and this new form would move beyond the conventions of the realist mode as they were recognized at the time.

Of course, the debates around the ideology and commitment of specific literary forms in the 1950s are partly to blame for this placing of Sillitoe within a realist tradition. The perceived socialist agenda of Sillitoe's fiction has meant that most have emphasized the realism (conventional, socialist or critical) of the fiction, but this has distracted attention from the experimental techniques he uses. However, there are various narrative techniques used in Sillitoe's novel that that

28   Ibid., p.48.
29   Alan Sillitoe, 'Johnny Livens Up Grim Schooldays', in *Reynold's News*, No.31 January 1960, p.11.
30   Ibid.

205

constitute an experimental approach to realism. In particular, the fluid relationship between the third-person narrative voice and the central character; the use of free indirect speech and internal monologue; and the rejection of linear plot construction in the texts are techniques that Lodge, for example, has identified as representative of modernist rather than realist fiction.[31]

One of the main ways in which *Saturday Night and Sunday Morning* uses modernist narrative techniques is in the use of dramatic monologue. Consider the following passage:

> I'm just too lucky for this world, Arthur told himself as he set the lathe going, too lucky by half, so I'd better enjoy it while I can. I don't suppose Jack's told Brenda yet about going on nights, but I'll bet she'll die laughing at the good news when he does. I might not see her at weekends, but I'll get there every night, which is even better. Turn to chamfer, then to drill, the blade-chamfer. Done. Take out and fix in a new piece, checking now and again for size because I'd hate to do a thousand and get them slung back at me by the viewers. Forty-five bob don't grow on trees. Turn to chamfer and drill, then blade-chamfer, swing the turret until my arms are heavy and dead. Quick as lightening. Take out and fix in, shout for the trolley to take it away and bring more on, jotting down another hundred, not noticing the sud smells any more or the belts over my head that gave me the screaming ab-dabs when I first came to the factory at fifteen, slapping and twisting and thumping and changing direction like Robboe the foreman's mind. It's a hard life if you don't weaken, if you grab like owt to earn a few quid, to take Brenda boozing and back to bed, or to the footpaths and woods up Strelley, passing the big council estate where Margaret my sister has a house and three kids from her useless husband, taking Brenda by all that to a broken-down shepherd's cottage that I've known since I was a kid and laying her on the straw and both of us so loving to each other that we can hardly wait. Only less of this or there'll be another handle on the lathe that I won't know what to do with and another gallon of suds that will jam the works. Time flies and no mistake. (37–8)

In this passage, Sillitoe's aim is to record the mental processes involved by an individual engaged in a semi-skilled manual job. The narration moves smoothly from the extradiegetic narrative voice of the text to expression in the idiom of the central character ('too lucky

31   Lodge, *Modes of Modern Writing*.

by half', 'Forty-five bob don't grow on trees').[32] Arthur's internal monologue, or rather a representation of his continuous train of thought as he works at the capstan lathe, is detached from a specific temporal framework. There is juxtaposition of concerns from the immediate focus on the technical aspects of the job in hand: 'Turn to chamfer and drill, the blade-chamfer. Done'; and projection to future events: 'I'll bet she'll die laughing at the news'; to past memory snatches: 'gave me the screaming ad-dabs when I first came to the factory at fifteen'. This represents the range of mental activity of the factory worker that resists the monotony of the physical task in which he is engaged. Although the passage is not quite self-consistent in terms of voice (for example, would Arthur really need to tell himself that Margaret is his sister?), it nevertheless attempts to record the actuality of Arthur's job through his thought processes. This use of free indirect speech and internal monologue functions ideologically to represent the internal thoughts of a class that had previously been under-represented in literary texts, and to counteract the externalized representation of the manual factory worker. As David Craig argues, this is the first passage 'in our literature [...] that evokes a factory-worker's experiences from the inside'.[33] This aspect of the text would appear to corresponds to Lukàcs's definition of socialist realism, as it: 'describes the forces working towards socialism *from the inside*' (Lukàcs's italics).[34] However, the political and ideological function of the text to represent a previously unrepresented class experience is achieved precisely through the deployment of narrative techniques that Lukàcs (and David Lodge) would associate with modernist rather

---

32 I am using the terms 'extradiegetic' and 'homodiegetic' to categorize the style of narration deployed here in reference to Rimmon-Kenan's definition of the terms (following Gerard Genette's typology of narrators). An extradiegetic narrator, according to Rimmon-Kenan, is one which is 'above' the narration; a homodiegetic (in this case at the points where Seaton takes over the narration) is one which is involved in the events of the story, Shlomith Rimmon-Kenan, *Narrative Fiction: Contemporary Poetics* (London and New York: Routledge, 1983), pp.94–6.

33 Craig, 'The Roots of Sillitoe's Fiction', p.103.

34 Lukàcs, *The Meaning of Contemporary Realism*, p.93.

than realist techniques, thus disrupting the traditional classification of the text as realist.

Other narrative techniques used in the text disrupt the distance between the extradiegetic narrator and Arthur's homodiegetic narration. For example, chapter two begins with the external narrator's voice: 'He lifted a pair of clean overalls from the bedrail and pulled them over his big white feet' (24), but then shifts, unannounced, into Arthur's voice: 'Black Monday. Then there would be more sense in it, when you felt your head big from boozing, throat sore from singing' (24). This use of free indirect speech serves to unhinge the distinction between third-person narration and narrated object/character.[35] This technique is used to upset the grounding of the moral and ethical centre of the text, and prevents the reader from distancing him/herself from the marginalized subject being represented.

The technique of reducing the distance between narrator and character is also identified *within* the third person narrative in terms of the specific use of metaphor. Although supplied by the external narrator, metaphor is often constructed in the register and style of the focalized character:

> His footsteps led between trade-marked houses, two up and two down, with digital chimneys like pigs' tits on the rooftops [...] Stars hid like snipers, taking aim now and again when clouds gave them a loophole [...] each dark street patted his shoulder and became a friend. (166)

In this passage, the external, non-participating narrator describes the scene, but this is articulated through metaphors taken directly from Arthur's experience. This again reduces the distance between narrator

---

35   The technique of free indirect speech corresponds here to Rimmon-Kenan's (following Banfield and MacHale) fourth function of FID: 'Because of its capacity to reproduce the idiolect of a character's speech or thought – some would add: pre-verbal perceptions, whether visual, auditory or tactile – within the narrator's reporting language, FID is a convenient vehicle for representing stream of consciousness, mainly for the variety called "indirect interior monologue"', Rimmon-Kenan, *Narrative Fiction*, p.114.

and character as they share a similar mode of expression: a distance that tends to be maintained in accounts of conventional realism.[36]

Saturday Night and Sunday Morning has been criticized for this lack of distance between the extradiegetic narrative voice and the main character. Atherton, for example, has written of 'Sillitoe's lack of detachment from his hero, for it is particularly evident in his continued failure to condemn any of Seaton's actions'.[37] Nigel Gray has identified a 'radical instability' in the narrative point of view in the text, suggesting that this inconsistency is a failing.[38] Similarly, Dominic Head suggests that the 'technical difficulty' and 'inscrutability' of the novel resides in the inconsistencies of the narrative voice and its relationship towards the main protagonist. He argues that: 'The technical "tinkering" with realism, to convey [...] a quasi-existentialist helplessness for Arthur Seaton, demonstrates the apparent impossibility of regenerating a constructive working-class realism.'[39] However, these criticisms betray a basic misunderstanding of the nature and function of the narrative voice of the text. By refusing to either advocate or criticize the behaviour of the central character, the novel operates at a level of detachment from conventional moral and ethical points of view. The basis of this criticism lies in the fact that, on the whole, both Gray and Head are judging the text against the conventions of a realist mode of narrative in which a hierarchy of discourses is established and acts as a framework for the moral judgment of characters and events by the reader. However, the 'tinkering' with realism in *Saturday Night and Sunday Morning* is far more pronounced than Head assumes. Rather than advocating Arthur's rebelliousness the novel presents a more radically unstable ambivalence to his actions. Sillitoe, in fact, reduces the distance between narrator and subject in an attempt to engage the reader in the

---

36   This hierarchical distinction between narrator and characters in realist modes is identified by several critics including Lukàcs and Belsey, especially in the latter's model of a 'hierarchy of discourses' in 'classic' realism. Catherine Belsey, *Critical Practice* (London and New York: Routledge, 1980), pp.67–84.

37   Atherton, *Alan Sillitoe*, p.116.

38   Gray, 'Life is What You Make It', p.131.

39   Dominic Head, *The Cambridge Introduction to Modern British Fiction, 1950– 2000* (Cambridge: Cambridge University Press, 2002), pp.67–8.

moral and ethical dilemmas that are raised by his central character's actions and beliefs.

This can be approached by looking at the way the novel produces a 'collective' narrative voice that belongs neither solely to the homodiegetic narrator nor to Arthur, but, by the use of the collective second-person pronoun, seems to indicate a collective identity: 'The minute you stepped out of the factory gates you thought no more about work. But the funniest thing was neither did you think about work when you were standing at your machine' (38). This *suggests* the experience of the main character, but does not describe it in Arthur's idiosyncratic voice. The narrative address presents a plural 'you', which incorporates Arthur, the extradiegetic narrator, the representation of a collectivized subcultural voice, and, presumably, the projected reader(s) of the text into a shared position of observation on the society in which all reside. Peter Hitchcock argues that:

> Sillitoe shifts language styles, consciously or not, according to the perspective in which Arthur can best be communicated – for Arthur is the central character of the story and in altering the relative position of the reader in relation to the represented consciousness of Arthur, this character becomes the central challenge of the book.[40]

Hitchcock goes on to suggest that Sillitoe distances Arthur from the narrative by switching from the collective second-person to the first-person producing an ironic response in the reader to the character's politics. However, the ambivalence of the homodiegetic narrative voice disrupts any fixed position of addressivity by which a model of parodic distance might be constructed. Arthur's political inconsistencies are treated as indicative of a radical 'irresponsibility', which, as we shall see in the next section, produces a different form of oppositional ideology, but which is hardly reduced by a distancing function of the narrative as Hitchcock suggests.

This deployment of a 'collective' narrative voice corresponds to Deleuze and Guattari's definition of one of the functions of a 'minor

---

40   Hitchcock, *Working-Class Fiction in Theory and Practice*, p.64.

literature', in which the political content of the text strives towards the representation of a minority culture.[41] As they argue:

> The third characteristic of a minor literature is that everything takes on a collective value [...] what each other says individually already constitutes a common action, and what he or she says or does is necessarily political [...] literature finds itself positively charged with the role and function of collective, and even revolutionary, enunciation. It is literature that produces an active solidarity in spite of skepticism; and if the writer is in the margins or completely outside of his fragile community, this situation allows the writer all the more the possibility to express another possible community and to forge the means for another consciousness and another sensibility. (17)

The narrative techniques deployed by Sillitoe represent an attempt by the author to empower a marginalized subcultural voice, that of white English working-class youth, through the collectivizing effects of its mode of addressivity.[42] A solidarity of ethical outlook is produced through the incorporation of the external narrative voice, the central character and the direct addressee(s) of the discourse, here (re)constructed as the radical and emergent working-class reader. This addressee is constructed by the text through a combination of recording a specific range of experiential activity that places the text in a specific socio-economic and cultural space, and the incorporation, through the deployment of inclusive narrative techniques, of the reader into that collective identity.

Ultimately, however, the fluidity of narrative voice represents an undecidability in terms of the possibility of producing a fixed ideological and ethical interpretation of the text. The narrative articulates an inconsistency between the commitment to collective political action, as advocated by contemporary communist and Marxist discourses, and the individualistic rejection of the system that tends towards an existential empowerment of the central character. The

41   Gilles Deleuze and Felix Guattari, *Kafka: Toward a Minor Literature*, trans. by Dana Polan (Minneapolis, University of Minnesota Press, 1986), pp.16–27.

42   I am using the concept of addressivity as defined by Steven Connor in *The Novel in History 1950–1995* (London and New York: Routledge, 1996), pp.8–13.

political and cultural concerns of the text are thus reproduced in its narrative form.

In terms of the plot, it is also problematic to describe Sillitoe's technique as conventionally realist. There are elements of a realist approach in terms of subject matter, as the novel deals with what Sillitoe identifies as the attempt to: 'write clearly and truthfully [… and] portray ordinary people as I knew them'.[43] This can be identified in the chain of events that describe Arthur's various sexual encounters with Brenda, Winnie and Doreen (the three main female characters in the novel): the pregnancy and abortion of Brenda and Arthur's child; dodging detection in his adulterous affairs, which ultimately results in the encounter with the squaddies; and his gradual acceptance of the merits of marriage to Doreen.[44] However, *Saturday Night and Sunday Morning* rejects conventional realist enplotment. The novel, in fact, was criticized, soon after publication, for its lack of linear plot by John Wain, who observed that while 'there is plenty of action', there is 'no real "plot"'. In addition, Irving Howe described it as 'a series of vignettes, like a succession of movie stills without much continuity'.[45] These criticisms, however, are based on evaluating the novel against an assumed model of classic realism.

The rejection of the heavily enplotted narrative characteristic of the conventional realist novel, as defined, for example, by David Lodge, is in fact part of an attempt to produce an oppositional aesthetic by Sillitoe based on a distinction within the texts between

43   Alan Sillitoe, 'Introduction', p.8.
44   These 'events' correspond more to a reading of the novel as picaresque rather than 'classically' realist, a point that William Hutchings makes; Hutchings, 'Proletarian Byronism', 92.
45   John Wain, 'Possible Worlds', in *The Observer*, 12 October 1958, p.20; Irving Howe, 'The Worker as a Young Tough', in *New Republic*, 24 August 1958, pp.27–8. Howe is one of the first critics to identify a connection between the 'angry young men' in Britain and the Beat writers in San Francisco (although he does not mention Sillitoe specifically), foregrounding the oppositional function of these literary groups to the dominant cultural establishment in their respective countries; Irving Howe, 'Mass Society and Postmodernist Fiction', in *Decline of the New* (London: Victor Gollancz, 1971), pp.204–5.

212

working and middle-class forms of expression.[46] This aesthetic is based upon the recounting of specific anecdotal stories, often exaggerated and celebratory of the (mock) heroic deeds of the central character, and can be traced in a tradition of working-class novels back to Robert Tressell's *The Ragged Trousered Philanthropists*.[47] This suggests a correspondence to an older oral tradition within working-class culture, which operates under different criteria to the 'bourgeois' novel form. As Walter Benjamin argues, the expression of a proletarian identity is more easily produced not through the bourgeois form of the novel, but through access to older forms of oral narrative.[48] In Sillitoe's novel, the aim to represent 'ordinary people' is articulated through the presentation of disparate anecdotal stories, with focalization through Arthur as the linking device. The novel is constructed as a series of episodes describing the exploits of the central character, or people with whom he is closely connected: for example, the story of Arthur's uncle Doddoe's romanticized death in a motor-cycling accident (74–5), or the incident that recounts Arthur shooting Mrs Bull, the local gossip, with an air-rifle (118–27). This representation of individual stories about the same group of characters works ideologically to construct a specific cultural identity. The exaggerated myth-making and celebration of Arthur's activities functions as a form of empowerment for a member of a subjected class, and again problematizes the categorization of Sillitoe's writing as realist.

In conjunction with the linear drive of the narrative, there is a stronger cyclical narrative, enhanced by the fragmentary episodes that form the whole. The rhythm of the novel revolves around the artificial rhythm of the working week, hence the thematic importance of

46   David Lodge, *Working With Structuralism* (London: Routledge and Kegan Paul, 1981). See also Seymour Chatman, *Story and Discourse: Narrative Structure in Fiction and Film* (New York: Ithaca, 1978), p.48.

47   Tressell, *The Ragged Trousered Philanthropists*. Sillitoe makes reference to the influence of this text in his early writing in his introduction to the 1965 edition.

48   Walter Benjamin, 'The Storyteller: Reflections on the Work of Nikolai Leskov', in *Illuminations*, pp.84–7. See also Peter Hitchcock's discussion of the relationships between 'oral narrative', working-class fiction, and *Saturday Night and Sunday Morning*, Hitchcock, *Working-Class Fiction in Theory and Practice*, pp.91–4.

Saturdays and Sundays: 'For it was Saturday night, the best and bingiest glad-time of the week, one of the fifty-two holidays in the slow-turning Big Wheel of the year, a violent preamble to a prostrate Sabbath' (9). This rhythm of the week forms the structural framework of the plot and represents the inescapable world of manual labour for the central characters. In doing so, the novel formally as well as thematically emphasizes the arbitrary structure of existence which is enforced by capitalist working practices: 'Living in a town and working in a factory, only a calendar gave any real indication of passing time, for it was difficult to follow the changing seasons' (129). The cyclical structure of the novel corresponds to the experience of time passing in this distinct cultural group. Sillitoe rejects the enplotted form of the middle-class novel and replaces it with the enclosed space of the cyclical narrative, representing the self-contained world of the working-class community. This narrative structure thereby corresponds to other thematic elements in the novel; for example, Arthur's rejection of middle-class aspirations and his ultimate re-integration into the closed world of the working-class community. Therefore, the rejection of a plot-driven narrative structure represents a rejection of the accumulative aspirations of middle-class culture. The representation of Arthur's subcultural identity removes the desire to escape – a desire characteristic of other, less radical, Angry novels of the period.[49]

As we have seen *Saturday Night and Sunday Morning* exceeds realist modes of writing, and yet it still contains a political agenda that engages with fifties socialism. Therefore, rather than an example of socialist realism it might be more accurate to use Rob Pope's category of 'socialist modernism' with regard to Silliotoe's fiction.[50] Pope cites Brecht's 'epic theatre' as the paradigm for socialist (post) modernism,

49   For example, John Braine's *Room at the Top*, and as we saw in chapter four above, Wain's *Hurry On Down* and Amis's *Lucky Jim*. One text that focuses on this desire for escape from working-class provincial culture is Keith Waterhouse's *Billy Liar*. Although the eponymous hero eventually rejects the move out of his working-class culture, the dramatic drive of the text revolves around the repeated repression of his desire to leave.

50   Rob Pope, *The English Studies Book: An Introduction to Language, Literature and Culture*, 2nd Edition (London: Routledge, 2002), p.107

but I would argue that Sillitoe's texts produce a similar effect in relation to narrative fiction. Sillitoe's writing is certainly closer to a Brechtian model of realism, which identifies a certain amount of experimentation with the form, than a Lukàcsian model of 'critical' or 'socialist' realism.[51]

Irresponsibility and Transgression in *Saturday Night and Sunday Morning*

In 'This Strange Institution Called Literature', Derrida suggests that literature in the West has the special privilege of being allowed to say anything.[52] This licence in 'literary' texts, he argues, can produce radical oppositional discourses that challenge dominant ideological frameworks. This 'freedom' is allowed through the institutional status of the literary in Western society, and although, as he suggests, this can and often does re-instate hegemonic power relationships, it can also produce a radical 'irresponsibility' that works ideologically to challenge those frameworks: 'This duty of irresponsibility, of refusing to reply for one's thought or writing to constituted powers, is perhaps the highest form of responsibility.'[53] Derrida argues that this irresponsibility is produced through both the play of language and the representation of irresponsible actions in a literary text.

Now I believe this concept of irresponsibility is a useful way of addressing what is at stake in *Saturday Night and Sunday Morning*, and it can be traced in three ways. First, in the 'irresponsibility' of the linguistic and narrative forms articulated in the text; second, in terms of the 'irresponsible' relationship established between the ambivalent authorial narrative and the central character; and third, in the exces-

---

51 Brecht, Bertolt, 'Against Georg Lukacs', trans. by Stuart Hood, in *Aesthetics and Politics*, ed. by Ronald Taylor and others (London: New Left Books, 1977), pp.68–85. See the discussion of Lukàcs in chapter two above.
52 Derrida, 'This Strange Institution Called Literature'.
53 Ibid., p.38.

sive and transgressive actions in which Arthur Seaton engages. Derrida's discourse of irresponsibility intersects with two other models in critical theory: Jean Baudrillard's discussion of the revolutionary potential of the artist/poet in Western culture, and Georges Bataille's discussion of the radical role of transgressive behaviour as a challenge to dominant society and ideology. All of these theoretical discourses connect with Sillitoe's writing.

In *Saturday Night and Sunday Morning* Arthur's rebellion is registered in his arbitrary acts of violence against the emblems of the ruling class and through his non-conforming attitudes to sexuality through his adultery and promiscuity. The first of these can be identified in the following passage:

> When I'm on my fifteen days' training and I lay on my guts behind a sand-bag shooting at a target board whose faces I've got in my sights every time the new rifle cracks off. Yes. The bastards that put the gun in my hands [...] Crack-crack-crack-crack-crack-crack. Other faces as well: the snot-gobbling gett that teks my income tax, the swivel-eyed swine that collects our rent, the big-headed bastard that gets my goat when he asks me to go to union meetings or sign a paper against what's happening in Kenya. (132)

As can be seen form this passage, Arthur's rebellion is directed towards figures that impact on him directly. His resistance to authority, therefore, is what we might call post-ideological in a 1950s context in that he is equally antagonistic to the union official as to the rent collector. His rebellion is never contained within an organized collective movement of resistance, but is articulated as an individual and irresponsible rebellion against all authority figures.

This irresponsibility manifests itself in two acts of violence in the novel, firstly, the smashing of a jewellery shop window by an unnamed character that Arthur encounters: 'it synthesized all the anarchism within him [Arthur]' (108); and secondly, the scene in which Arthur and his cousin Fred overturn a parked car: 'Though locked in a revengeful act they felt a sublime team-spirit of effort filling their hearts with a radiant light of unique power and value, of achievement and hope for greater and better things' (116). These acts of violence, focused on emblems of the consumer society, reproduce for the protagonists an inverse image of 'power', 'value' and

216

'achievement' normally associated with the act of work. As these individuals are alienated, in Marxist terms, from the produce of their labour in the factory, the pleasure of achievement is projected upon this act of vandalism. It is also significant that Arthur and Fred act with 'team-spirit', producing a communal solidarity in their 'illicit' actions.

This aspect of the novel corresponds with Jean Baudrillard's model of the 'true revolutionary', one who goes beyond Marx's pre-occupation with production. As he writes: 'this subversion directed against the axiomatic of productive rationality itself (including its internal contradictions) is no longer accounted for by a Marxist analysis of class and mode of production' (152). For Baudrillard:

> Revolt emerged against the integration of labor power as a factor of production. The new social groups, de facto dropouts, on the contrary, proved the incapacity of the system to 'socialize the society' [...] And it is on the basis of their *total irresponsibility* that these marginal generations carry on the revolt.[54]

Although the acts of destruction represent a rejection of the objects of consumer society, they also represent a rejection of the main organized resistance to capitalist ideology in the 1950s. Sillitoe's portrayal of an anarchic revolutionary force is post-Marxist and, as such, is as much a representation of a crisis in fifties Marxism, as it is a challenge to the dominant ideology.

The novel, then, reveals the ideological function of the irresponsible and transgressive in relation to two aspects: firstly, the celebration by the central character of various violent and rebellious actions; and second, the ambivalent representation of Arthur's contradictory political positions. It also foregrounds the transgressive and irresponsible in terms of Arthur's sexuality, and this element of the text needs to be interpreted in the context of a wider discourse of masculinity present in the 1950s. Many of the Movement and Angry novels of the 1950s emphasize the masculinity of their central characters as a form of resistance to what was perceived to be an

---

54   Jean Baudrillard, *The Mirror of Production*, trans. by Mark Poster (St. Louis: telos Press, 1975, p.133.

effeminate element within middle-class culture. Osborne's *Look Back in Anger*, Braine's *Room at the Top* and Storey's *This Sporting Life* all present characters whose masculinity is emphasized as a strategy of resistance to dominant society and culture.[55] The 'masculinity' of Angry fiction of the period is in part influenced by contemporary American literature and film. In particular, American Beat writing, alongside its discourse of homosexuality, also expresses a celebration of masculine power, a characteristic that Doris Lessing identifies as 'mensch'.[56] One of the ways in which this discourse of masculinity was articulated in the fiction was through the representation of casual and promiscuous sexual relationships, often with the emphasis on a cold efficiency in male sexual performance. This was represented as a resistance to the perceived restrictions of the nuclear family structure, which was regarded as one of the ways in which dominant society contained the potentially revolutionary aspects of an unrestricted sexuality.

The representation of strong masculine physicality and acts of violence by the central characters in Sillitoe's texts engage with this trope in 1950s culture. In *Saturday Night and Sunday Morning*, it is represented through Arthur Seaton's sexual encounters with the three main female characters of the novel: Brenda, her sister Winnie (both of whom are married), and Arthur's eventual fiancée Doreen. The relationships Arthur has with these women are used to display various aspects of sexual behaviour that would appear transgressive to dominant moral and ethical codes in the late 1950s. Arthur's adulterous affairs with Brenda and her sister Winnie are two instances of a challenge to the dominant family unit that underlies both conventional middle and working-class culture of the period. At one point, Arthur is having affairs with all three of the female characters, foregrounding another taboo and anxiety for dominant society in the 1950s: that of the promiscuity of contemporary youth, and the effects this might

---

55   John Osborne, *Look Back in Anger* (London: Faber & Faber, 1956); Braine, *Room at the Top*; John Storey, *This Sporting Life* (Harmondsworth: Penguin, 1962), first published 1960.

56   Doris Lessing, *Walking in the Shade: Part Two of My Autobiography 1949–1962* (London: Harper Collins, 1997), pp.151–62.

have on future society. In addition to this, the text raises the social taboo of abortion through the narrative of events between Brenda and Arthur, and this is presented in the text as a further challenge to the bourgeois family structure. Peter Hitchcock has noted that this taboo is so strong in fifties culture that the text refuses to name it out-right, relying on a series of euphemisms.[57]

It is significant, however, that the text often presents Arthur's engagement in heterosexual relationships in terms of violence and struggle. For the theorist Georges Bataille, trangressive sexual behaviour represnts an ideological as well as a cultural challenge to dominant society. In 'The Psychological Structure of Fascism', he distinguishes between 'homogenous' and 'heterogeneous' social existence: the former corresponding to dominant hegemonic society and culture, the latter to 'the numerous elements or social forms that *homogeneous* society is powerless to assimilate'.[58] He goes on to suggest:

> *Violence, excess, delirium, madness* characterize heterogeneous elements to varying degrees: active as persons or mobs, they result from breaking the laws of social *homogeneity* [...] *Heterogeneous* reality is that of a force or shock ... [and] takes on the form of a challenge to reason.[59]

Here, Bataille argues that the heterogeneous forces of society react against homogenizing forces through transgressive acts of violence and excess, and that this manifests itself in acts that go beyond the 'reasonable' in conventional terms. For Bataille, 'acts having a suggestive erotic value' and 'different types of violent individuals or at least those who refuse the rule (madmen, leaders, poets etc.)' are both included in his category of the heterogeneous.[60] For Arthur Seaton, as for Bataille, sex, violence and resistance to dominant ideology

---

57   Hitchcock, *Working-Class Fiction in Theory and Practice*, pp.71–2.
58   Georges Bataille, 'The Psychological Structure of Fascism', in *Visions of Excess; Selected Writing, 1927–1939*, ed. by Allan Stoekl, trans. by Allan Stoekl, with Carl R. Lovitt and Donald M. Leslie, Jr. (Minneapolis: University of Minnesota Press, 1985), p.142.
59   Ibid., pp.142–4.
60   Ibid., p.142.

are connected, and the radical nature of Bataille's heterogeneous corresponds to the provocative representation of sexuality in Sillitoe's text.[61] However, Bataille traces two distinct forms of the heterogeneous: the 'impure', which is a celebration of the 'untouchable' and 'excretions' of society formulated in terms of a potentially liberating and revolutionary force; and the 'imperative', which equates to the 'noble', 'superior' and 'individual', and which ultimately tends, he suggests, towards fascism.[62] In Sillitoe's texts, the implication of the celebration of an overt sexuality can lead in both directions. In terms of an act of resistance to dominant culture and the attempt to produce an empowerment of white working-class male youth subculture, the nature of the heterogeneous is towards Bataille's notion of the celebration of the impure. However, in terms of the social and cultural position of other marginalized identities, and in particular working-class women, it leads towards the re-imposition of repressive and restrictive structures. I will return to this point later.

The celebration of the heterogeneous foregrounds what can be designated as the *ethical* or ideological framework of the text. Arthur's transgressive violence, immorality, misogyny, and 'irresponsibility' are never challenged by the extradiegetic narrative voice. The external narrator remains ambivalent in the representation of these events (and Arthur's internalized interpretation of his actions), refusing moralistic or ethical commentary. This ambivalence in the narration produces the articulation of an emergent form of working-class ethics that is distinct from competing representations of working-class life in the 1950s, such as that found in Hoggart and other New Left texts. The representation of the individualistic young white working-class male in Sillitoe's fiction represents an emergent form of working-class oppositional culture that no longer believes in

61   The same conjunction of features can also be identified in other British texts of the period including John Braine's *Room at the Top*; and more emphatically in Alexander Trocchi's *Young Adam* whose pornographic passages are interwoven with violence and an existential radical critique of society's institutional apparatuses (Edinburgh: Rebel Inc., 1996), first published 1954.
62   Bataille, 'The Psychological Structure of Fascism', pp.143–4.

the ability of collectivized oppositional political action to alleviate the conditions in which the individual is placed.

The perspective of representation is crucial here. Anthony West recognized that *Saturday Night and Sunday Morning* offered a new voice in English literature: that of the English working class from the inside.[63] Most writers, argued West, who had previously written on working-class life had done so as external observers, and this corresponds to the kind of working-class analysis being offered in the contemporary sociological analyses. Sillitoe's novel, according to West, offered a view from *within* the culture so that the reader (or addressee) and the narrator are placed inside the world of the text and can only judge actions and characters from within that enclosed perspective. However, West identifies Arthur as a representation of the *whole* of the working class, when in fact the character is more representative of a specific emergent subculture within that class. This fracturing and fragmentation within the oppositional framework of the working class in the 1950s disrupts the model of a homogenous or holistic 'way of life' suggested by Raymond Williams's contemporaneous model of working-class culture.[64] As we have seen this disruption corresponds to Sillitoe's experiment with realist forms. Sillitoe's use of internal monologue, focalization, free indirect discourse, floating narrative perspective, and minimal and ambivalent authorial commentary function to 'defamiliarize' the 'realistic' representation of working-class life. In this sense, Sillitoe's formal techniques correspond more to a Brechtian understanding of realism, than to a Lukàcsian model. The positioning of Arthur as a doubly marginalized figure distanced from both dominant society, and conventional (or adult) working-class culture, identifies the multiple discourses that the text articulates and provides a basis for the formal experiments Sillitoe produces.

63   Anthony West, 'On the Inside Looking In', in *New Yorker*, 5 September 1959, pp.99–100.
64   As propounded in *Culture and Society* (London: Hogarth, 1987), first published by Chatto and Windus in 1957; and *The Long Revolution* (London: Chatto and Windus, 1961). See the discussion of Williams's model and its influence on New Left writing in chapter three above.

This complicates the interpretation of the text in terms of the projected readership or addressee the text encodes. Arthur's acts of irresponsibility and transgression produce a central tension in the text between the main characters, the authorial voice and the projected addressees. The ambiguity of distance between narrator and narrated subject offers a moral and ethical dilemma to the 'dominant' addressee. Should the reader celebrate or denigrate the exploits of the central characters? How are we meant to judge the robbery, adultery, vandalism, violence, and seemingly mindless rebelliousness perpetrated by the two anti-heroes? These questions can be addressed in terms of a model of multiple addressees. On one level, Arthur's irresponsibility in *Saturday Night and Sunday Morning* can be identified as a mindless, anarchistic and self-defeating rejection of dominant culture *and* residual working-class society that leaves the central character isolated. However, the actions of the central character simultaneously represent an attempt to empower, through written articulation, the anger and anxieties of a specific emergent and marginalized group within the contemporary working class that could potentially represent a political radicalism that would threaten dominant power relationships. This can be approached in terms of the range of groups represented in the text: middle-class culture, residual working-class culture, and the emergent white working-class youth subcultures. These addressees correspond to Alan Sinfield's model of dominant, subordinate and radical cultures and can be projected onto similar distinct categories in terms of the addressivity of the text.[65] The ambivalent narrative address that Sillitoe produces results in a range of ideological interpretations dependent on the kind of addressee we posit for the text. A pluralized model of identity, therefore, generates multiple ideological significance in Sillitoe's writing. This distances the text from the differing forms of either 'socialist' or 'critical' realism as identified by Lukàcs as the production of ideological meaning is far more complex.

65   Alan Sinfield, *Literature, Politics and Culture in Postwar Britain* (Oxford: Basil Blackwell, 1989). I discuss Sinfield's model in greater detail in the introduction to this book.

In conjunction with the elements of the text that suggest the articulation of an empowering discourse for an emergent subculture, Sillitoe's text also negotiates other marginalized identities. However, the attempt to create an individualized form of resistance against dominant society produces a discourse that often rejects a 'chain of equivalence' with other marginalized groups.[66] In particular, Sillitoe's texts fail to acknowledge similarities between a working-class subcultural position and that of black subcultures, and the subordinated position of (working-class) women within the dominant ideology. *Saturday Night and Sunday Morning* engages with both these marginalized discourses, but refuses to identify corresponding levels of marginalization.

In terms of the representation of black identity, the text engages with Britain's contemporary position as a post-imperial state. Published a year after the Suez Crisis, two characters from the declining empire are included in the text. The first is Sam, a Ghanaian friend of Arthur's brother in the army. A range of responses to this black character is produced: Arthur's cousin Bert represents a racist element within the culture through a series of jokes that foreground Sam's physical characteristics (191), however, Bert is regarded as anomalous to the overall acceptance of Sam within the white working-class home. In this sense, Sillitoe suggests an easy alliance between two oppressed groups, a feature of much English working-class writing.[67] The second 'foreign' figure in the novel is the 'Indian' who is living with Doreen's mother. This character remains significantly nameless and silenced in the text (he does not speak English), and there is less of a connection made between the narrative voice and this character. However, Arthur does reflect on the loneliness of this exiled figure

---

66   Here I am re-deploying Laclau and Mouffe's theory of the strategic development of a 'chain of equivalence' between the radical discourses of Marxism (with its privileging of the category of class) and other minority and radical discourses focused on gender, ethnicity, sexuality and age. Ernesto Laclau and Chantal Mouffe, *Hegemony and Socialist Strategy* (London: Verso, 1985).

67   Tony Harrison attempts a similar link in 'On Not Being Milton', in Tony Harrison, *Selected Poems*, 2nd edn. (Harmondsworth: Penguin, 1987), p.112. James Kelman has also identified the correspondence between working-class and black radical politics.

(211–12). These postcolonial encounters articulate a contemporary concern with decolonization that introduces alternative representations of identity from other marginalized positions, and identifies a range of responses to black identities from within the white working class in the 1950s. It suggests complex issues related to ethnicity that rejects the stereotypical image of the English working class as racist.[68]

The strategic 'irresponsibility' of Sillitoe's texts results in the subjugation of another 'minority', or unrepresented cultural group in Britain, that of working-class women. All the women represented in the text are working class, but their portrayal defines them collectively as a group that is to be feared by the central character, rather than their doubly subordinated position to be regarded as a basis for an equivalent association of marginality and resistance. Towards the end of the text, Arthur reflects:

> And trouble for me it'll be, fighting every day until I die. Why do they make soldiers out of us when we're fighting up to the hilt as it is? Fighting with mothers and wives, landlords and gaffers, coppers, army, government (219).

Here, Arthur places working-class women alongside the ideological state apparatuses arraigned against him. His position is particularly articulated in terms of the family: it is wives and mothers that repre-

---

68 This generalized interpretation of the English working class is reproduced in contemporary New Left studies during the period. For example, the series of articles on the Notting Hill riots in *ULR 5* (Autumn, 1958) presents English working-class youth as profoundly racist. These are discussed further in chapter three above. Phil Cohen's 'Subcultural Conflict and Working-class Community', and in Tony Jefferson's 'Cultural Responses of the Teds', the portrayal of Ted cultures reproducing the racism of their parent culture also supports this misreading (Cohen's article is in Gelder, *The Subcultures Reader*, pp.90–9; Jefferson's in John Clarke et al., *Resistance Through Rituals* (London: Routledge, 1993), pp.81–6. I am not suggesting that there are not elements of racism within English working-class culture, but rather that this is one of a range of attitudes to other 'races' in working-class culture that includes tolerance, acceptance and even celebration of the multicultural diversity of the British working class. Hebdige records this negotiation between white subcultures and other racial identities in *Subculture: The Meaning of Style* (London and New York: Routledge, 1979).

sent the main restrictive forces on the hero. When he discusses women in the text, there is no recognition of the class status of women, as there is with the male characters, rather women from all classes appear as a collective group that Arthur feels is attempting to restrict his liberty and his transgressive activities.

The social and cultural context of the late 1950s needs to be explored to understand this aspect of Sillitoe's text. In her essay 'Look Back in Anger: Men in the Fifties', Lynne Segal identifies the tendency in 'Angry' fiction to position women as representatives of the system of control rather than as an equivalent subjugated group: 'What was really happening in so many of these novels was that class hostility was suppressed and twisted into new forms of sexual hostility.'[69] Although it is not the case that class hostility is suppressed in Sillitoe, it is certainly true that his texts reveal a certain amount of sexual hostility. His view of women falls into the traditional working-class dual stereotype of either 'warm wonderful creatures that needed and deserved to be looked after', or 'with battleship faces and hearts as tough as nails who rattle a big fist at you and roar: "Do this, do that, do the other, or else"' (44).[70] As Nigel Gray has written, 'Arthur is against all authority – except the authority of men over women.'[71] A potential chain of equivalence between the subaltern positions of working-class women and men is not made.

69   Lynne Segal, 'Look Back in Anger: Men in the Fifties', in *Male Order: Unwrapping Masculinity*, ed. by Rowena Chapman and J. Rutherford (London: Lawrence and Wishart, 1988), pp.68–96, (p.82).

70   Gilbert and Gubar's identification of the 'angel' and 'monster' opposition in nineteenth century constructions of female identity is reproduced here in a fifties working-class context. See Sandra Gilbert and Susan Gubar, *The Madwoman in the Attic: The Woman Writer and the Nineteenth-Century Literary Imagination* (New Haven and New York: Yale University Press, 1979), pp.16–36.

71   Gray, 'Life is What You Make It', p.129.

Gone Fishing: The Future of Arthur Seaton

It is apparent, then, that Sillitoe's fiction negotiates the ideological framework for the production of 'literary' texts in Britain in the 1950s. This raises a few important questions. How are the texts to be positioned within the ideological nexus produced through their reception and incorporation into the 'institution' of literature? Do Sillitoe's texts of this period represent a Deleuzean and Guattarian empowerment of a minority discourse; a Bataillean radicalization of the transgressive; or a Derridean or Baudrillardian celebration of the irresponsible? Or do they reveal the limits of a radical discourse as suggested by Macherey and Balibar's theory on the ideological saturation of language and literary production? These questions, as Peter Hitchcock has suggested, relate to the whole categorization of working-class fiction and Sillitoe's texts as representative of that category.[72] To approach these closing questions, I will focus upon the ending of *Saturday Night and Sunday Morning*.

The ending is far more ambiguous than most commentators have suggested. In the last scene, Arthur is fishing in the local canal and we learn that he is to be married to Doreen in three weeks. Despite this, he re-states his rebellious outlook on life: 'Well it's a good life [...] if you don't weaken, and if you know the big wide world hasn't heard from you yet, no, not by a long way' (219). Critics have offered two readings of this ending: firstly, that Arthur ceases his rebellion against society and finally chooses to conform; secondly, that despite his re-integration into society by way of his marriage to Doreen, he will maintain his openly rebellious attitude towards society.[73] The former suggests the archetypal realist pattern for the ending of the novel, with a marriage and the main protagonist being re-integrated into society. The latter tends to a more modernist ending, anticipating continued

---

72   Peter Hitchcock, 'The Theory and Practice of Working-Class Fiction', in Hitchcock, *Working-Class Fiction in Theory and Practice*, pp.89–103.

73   Atherton discusses the former of these readings, citing Anthony West and John Braine, whilst offering the latter reading himself, in Atherton, *Alan Sillitoe*, pp.114–15.

struggle, and a continuation of the alienation of the central character from society.[74] The ending is in fact subtler than both these readings. Arthur, alone, fishing, suggests something of the existential nature of the character and is in stark contrast to the opening scene of the novel.[75] The emblem of fishing can also be interpreted in relation to the ideological meanings the text produces. This is achieved through an identification between Arthur and the fish he catches, which suggests a complex power relationship in which the victim is the perpetrator of his own victimization: 'Whenever you caught a fish, the fish caught you, in a way of speaking, and it was the same with anything else you caught, like the measles or a woman' (216). In this sense, Arthur self-reflexively causes his own defeat, maybe through an unconscious need for re-integration, precipitated by the warm family celebrations at his aunt's house recounted in the penultimate chapter. However, the ending also defines the inevitable power of society and the powerlessness of the individual. The ending reminds us of Orwell's *Nineteen-Eighty-Four* in which the hero is finally and incontrovertibly defeated by the system against which he has been struggling throughout. In Althusser's terms this interpretation represents an 'imaginary reconciliation of real contradictions'.[76] However, in a Brechtian sense, it also attempts to engage the political sensibilities of the addressees to which it is aimed by resisting the closure of the conventional realist text and by opening up an ideological debate in the 'real' world. This self-reflexive, ideologically informed ending invites the reader to reflect upon the nature of power, powerlessness and the individual in terms of the containment of the radical within dominant society.

---

74   Here, I am referring to David Lodge's crude dichotomy of 'realist' and 'modernist' endings, which he equates to closed and open endings respectively, Lodge, *Modes of Modern Writing*, p.226.

75   The novel begins with Arthur in a crowded club scene in which he falls down a flight of stairs due to the: 'eleven pints of beer and seven small gins playing hide and seek inside his stomach' (5).

76   Hitchcock, *Working-Class Fiction in Theory and Practice*, p.13; see also Louis Althusser, 'Ideology and Ideological State Apparatuses', in *Lenin and Philosophy: and Other Essays*, 2nd. edn., trans. by Ben Brewster (London: New Left Books, 1977), pp.152–65.

In conclusion, it is clear that Sillitoe's fifties fiction attempts to record the characteristics and codes of a specific subcultural identity within working-class culture, and to present this as a competing representation to other contemporary studies of the working class. In doing so, it attempts to produce a discourse of resistance and empowerment in opposition to the dominant socio-cultural group against which it positions itself. It also negotiates different levels of oppositional culture by identifying an emergent working-class culture that is distinct from an older or residual form. As distinct from Hoggart, Sillitoe is concerned to produce a narrative that articulates and accepts this emergent culture, and attempts to find a potentially political force within it. Sillitoe achieves this through the deployment of narrative techniques that create what Deleuze and Guattari designate as a 'minor' literature, through the creation of a collective oppositional voice. However, the radicalism of the texts has to be placed against the effects of the institution of literature upon them. As Peter Hitchcock argues, the status of working-class fiction is always problematic in terms of the articulation of radical positions and the counter-force of containment that the dominant ideology, through the institutional framework of the literary, re-imposes on individual texts.

As noted earlier, J.P. Keating argues that working-class fiction flourishes at times of political crisis. This can be developed in relation to Gramsci's concept of hegemony. According to Gramsci, dominant systems maintain their power base through a combination of force and consent by the members of society. But at moments of political crisis the desire and imperative to articulate radical positions increases, and the novel represents a significant site in this process because of its privileged position within Western society. The articulation of radicalism is thus *allowed* in fiction; however, it is always already an act of self-containment. In the process of articulating the radical in a form that is privileged in Western culture, a complex process of re-consent is established. Nevertheless, the text repeatedly engages the reader in a continuous struggle between the radical potential to disrupt prevailing ideologies and the attempt by dominant discourses to restrict that radicalism. The dominant cultural institutions thereby deploy techniques of framing, appropriating and subordinating the text to contain

228

its radical potential. Sillitoe's texts have been framed within the acceptable generic boundaries of 'working-class' fiction, or youth cult fiction, or the 'Angry' novel, and these sub-genres serve to make the radical palatable for a readership that fundamentally accepts the dominant power structures of contemporary society. The existence of such sub-genres persuades the liberal reader that there is a place for the expression of discontent within the dominant system, but the process functions to reduce the impact of the radical messages of the text in terms of actually altering power structures.[77] Nevertheless there remains a radical questioning of the dominant modes of Western literary production in Sillitoe's fiction. As Peter Hitchcock argues: 'The war over words traced through the work of Alan Sillitoe under-lines that the dialogism of the oppressed is not merely a quirk of history, but an active component of contemporary struggle.'[78] This suggests, and I would agree, that Sillitoe's texts, through their articulation of a radical oppositional politics focused on working-class youth subculture, maintain their relevance and radicalism in a contemporary context.[79]

77 I am alluding to the subversion/containment debate that is prevalent in much cultural materialist criticism: Jonathan Dollimore, 'Introduction: Shakespeare, Cultural Materialism and the New Criticism', in *Political Shakespeare: Essays in Cultural Materialism*, ed. by Jonathan Dollimore and Alan Sinfield, Second Edition (Manchester: Manchester University Press, 1994), pp.2–17, (pp.10–15). See also the discussion of this in chapter four above.

78 Hitchcock, *Working-Class Fiction in Theory and Practice*, p.100.

79 Sillitoe has since published *Birthday* (London: Flamingo, 2001) which is a sequel both to *Saturday Night and Sunday Morning* and *Key to the Door* (London: W.H. Allen, 1961). The latter novel follows the exploits in the army and in Nottingham of Arthur's brother Brian. The recent novel is not as power-ful as the earlier works, but it shows Sillitoe still experimenting with the use of voice, especially in the use of the second person pronoun in the chapters that are focalized through Arthur.

Chapter Seven
Colin MacInnes: Subcultural Fictions

Colin MacInnes is a fifties writer who has until recently been largely overlooked in critical analyses of the period.[1] His writing represents a radical experiment with narrative forms and genres that corresponds to his investigation of the submerged worlds of 1950s subcultures, a writing that sits uneasily with the dominant critical readings of the period. This chapter discusses two of MacInnes's novels in relation to four specific issues and is divided into four corresponding sections. Firstly, it will analyze the use of narrative techniques in two of MacInnes's 'London' novels: *City of Spades* and *Absolute Beginners*.[2] The second section concentrates on *Absolute Beginners* and discusses MacInnes's narrative strategies against the wider context of a 'crisis' in the construction of Englishness in the 1950s. Section three also concentrates on *Absolute Beginners* and identifies MacInnes's aim to produce a contesting representation of youth to those offered in mainstream cultural writing and by the early New Left. The fourth

1   Critical work on MacInnes has been restricted to Tony Gould's biographical/ critical appraisal *Inside Outsider: The Life and Times of Colin MacInnes* (London: Allison and Busby, 1983); Harriet Blodgett, 'City of Other Worlds: The London Novels of Colin MacInnes', in *Critique: Studies in Modern Fiction*, 18:1, 1976, pp.105–18; Alan Sinfield, *Literature, Politics and Culture in Postwar Britain* (Oxford: Blackwell, 1989), pp.127–8, and 169–71; and Steven Connor, *The English Novel in History, 1950–1995* (London and New York: Routledge, 1996), pp.89–95. However, interest has been gathering recently in MacInnes's fiftes novels, *City of Spades* and *Absolute Beginners*; see, for example, John Brannigan's discussion of the former and Alice Ferrebe on the latter: John Brannigan, *Literature, Culture and Society in Postwar England, 1945–1965* (New York: Edwin Mellen Press, 2002) pp.180–3; Alice Ferrebe, *Masculinity in Male-Authored Fiction 1950–2000* (Houndmills, Basingstoke and New York: Palgrave, 2005), pp.143–50.

2   Colin MacInnes, *City of Spades* (London and New York: Allison and Busby, 1980), first published 1957; *Absolute Beginners* (Harmondsworth: Penguin, 1964), first published 1959.

section focuses on the construction of black immigrant identity in *City of Spades*.

Free Form: Narrative Strategies in *Absolute Beginners* and *City of Spades*

Colin MacInnes produces a body of writing in the late 1950s and early 1960s that attempts to combine the documentary with the fictional. Alongside the novels, he produced articles for many of the most important literary and cultural journals and magazines of the period such as *Encounter*, *The Twentieth Century* and *The New Left Review*.[3] There is a journalistic and sociological impulse charging MacInnes's fifties fiction. He was responding to what he considered to be a misrepresentation of youth and black subcultures in both the mainstream media and in New Left analyses. In a 1959 review of Shelagh Delaney's *A Taste of Honey*, he wrote:

> As one skips through contemporary novels, or scans the acreage of fish-and-chip dailies and the very square footage of the very predictable weeklies, as one blinks unbelievingly at 'British' films and stares boss-eyed at the frantic race against time that constitutes telly, it is amazing – it really is – how very little one can learn about life in England here and now.[4]

He goes on to stress how little 'we' have learned, through the cultural sites he cites above, of 'working-class child mothers, ageing semi-professional whores, the authentic agonies of homosexual love, and the new race of English born coloured boys [...] the millions of teen-agers [...] the Teds [...] the multitudinous Commonwealth minorities in our midst' (206). Responding, therefore, to this lack of representation, one of MacInnes's aims in his novels is to fill the gap he

3   Most of these are gathered in *England, Half English* (London: Chatto and Windus, 1986).
4   Colin MacInnes, 'A Taste of Reality', in ibid., p.206. The article was first published in *Encounter*, April 1959.

identifies in contemporary literature and journalism concerning these alternative lifestyles. *Absolute Beginners* details the experiences and outlook of a nineteen-year-old photographer as he moves through the submerged worlds of 1950s London. It is narrated in the first person in a style that attempts to authentically represent the voice of a 1950s teenager. *City of Spades* uses similar first person narration although in this novel the narrative is divided between two characters: Montgomery Pew, a white, middle-class civil servant who is working as an 'Assistant Welfare Officer' for the 'Colonial Department'; and Johnny Fortune, a black student who has just arrived in London from Nigeria. MacInnes attempts to reproduce an authentic black voice for Fortune to represent his marginalized status.

In *Absolute Beginners*, the impulse behind the use of first person narration is to avoid the distancing of observer and observed that, as we saw in chapter two above, much New Left and sociological writing on youth produced. MacInnes thereby constructs an idiosyncratic narrative voice that attempts to represent the teenage subculture's style of speaking directly:

> He didn't wig this, so giving me a kindly smile, he stepped away to make himself respectable again. I put a disc on to his hi-fi, my choice being Billie H., who sends me even more than Ella does, but only when, as now, I'm tired, and also, what with seeing Suze again, and working hard with my Rolleiflex and then this moronic conversation, graveyard gloomy. But Lady Day has suffered so much in her life she carries it all for you, and soon I was quite a cheerful cat again. (27–8)

Here, the incorporation of unofficial and unlicensed language ('wig', 'sends', 'cat') and references to the insider's knowledge of a specific subcultural interpretive community ('Billie H', 'Ella', 'Lady Day'), creates a disruption of Standard English that acts as a linguistic statement of opposition to dominant culture. Although this does not represent the authentic voice of actual teenagers in an ethnographic sense, it produces, through its performative presentation of stylized subcultural language, the ideological function of style in youth subcultures. This use of language corresponds to Dick Hebdige's analysis of the function of subcultural style: 'The communication of a significant *difference*, then (and the parallel communication of a group

identity), is the "point" behind the style of all spectacular subcultures.'[5] The construction of the teenager's voice in MacInnes's novel,
through its foregrounding of an alternative stylistic discourse, is a
textual representation of subcultures to distance themselves from the
mainstream, and operates as a process of identity-forming empowerment.

The decision to make the teenager hero a photographer has
thematic importance as it foregrounds the 'documentary' nature of the
text: the photographer's job being to record and document events and
practices, but from a certain distance, from a point of detached observation.[6] The teenager's narrative represents this detached function
for most of the text, as the 'photo-journalist' remains distanced from
the cultural practices he describes. Therefore, he is not responsible for
the things he records, but exists on the margins of this subculture, not
(he initially believes) exploited by the culture, but maintaining a
hustling independent existence on the edges of it. The text includes
several passages which represent this 'sociological' or 'documentary'
function of the text, for example, the description of teenage fashion
and the specific and multiple identities within youth culture in the
long description of the differences in dress between the skiffle and
trad jazz uniform of the Misery Kid and his cultural opposite 'number'
the 'sharp mod jazz' Dean Swift (70). The narrative perspective at the
opening of the novel represents the social observer who is familiar
with the culture he is observing. This duality of narrative perspective
represents a negotiation of distance and proximity to the world of the
teenage subculture. The significance of this methodological approach
is foregrounded towards the end of the novel, when the teenager is
forced to confront directly the racial violence evidenced in the description of the Notting Hill riots. At this point in the text he ceases to
be an external observer and becomes part of the action, refusing to
exploit the culture he is part of in favour of direct action within it,

5   Dick Hebdige, *Subcultures: The Meaning of Style* (London and New York:
     Routledge, 1979), p.102.
6   Several critics have identified the 'journalistic impulse' in MacInnes's novels:
     Sinfield, *Literature, Politics and Culture in Postwar Britain*, p.169; Gould,
     Inside Outsider, p.176.

represented through the rejection of his camera: 'I took up my Rolleiflex, but put it down again, because it didn't seem useful any longer.' (218).

Similar to Sillitoe's *Saturday Night and Sunday Morning*, *Absolute Beginners* rejects the plot-driven narrative associated with the conventional realist novel in favour of an episodic form that allows the teenage narrator to reveal different aspects of the subcultural world he inhabits. Steven Connor has identified the episodic form as indicative of the fragmentary nature of subcultural existence and representation, and this corresponds to its function in MacInnes's novel.[7] As with Sillitoe, this structural device works ideologically to reject the form of the realist linear narrative in favour of a structure that reflects an oral culture. MacInnes's deployment of this narrative technique attempts to produce a public communication of the experience of youth subcultures corresponding to Walter Benjamin's definition of the art of the story-teller, which Benjamin claims has been lost due to the rise of the middle-class novel.[8] MacInnes's narrator also functions in Benjamin's dual 'interpenetration' role of the storyteller as 'peasant' and 'seaman', as the narrator is steeped in the oral culture of his location within the subcultural space of fifties youth, but also communicates the 'distant' experience of this environment to the uninitiated addressee.[9] This 'oral' narrative is achieved through the representation of disconnected (in terms of plot) descriptions and short exaggerated 'stories' of various aspects of teenage practice and culture. The linking function of plot is thereby replaced by the text's subject matter: the representation of the subculture itself. The narrative foregrounds this as an empowering discourse through the teenager's exoticization of the subcultural world he describes. This empowering discourse is manipulated and controlled by the teenager's voice as it leads the uninitiated reader through the fragmented subcultural world. Therefore, the reader is introduced to characters and

7   Connor, *The English Novel in History*, p.90.
8   Walter Benjamin, 'The Storyteller' in *Illuminations*, ed. by Hannah Arendt, trans. by Harry Zohn (London: Fontana, 1973) pp.83–107.
9   Ibid., pp.84–5.

situations that are unfamiliar without the traditional aid of the linear plot by which that reader might gain orientation within this 'world'.

However, the text not only speaks to the uninitiated reader, it also attempts to speak directly to the subculture itself. The inside/outside dual narrative perspective is achieved by MacInnes's deployment of a specific type of narrative voice. Because the teenager's homodiegetic[10] narrative maintains control, the reader is never quite sure whether the events being described are faithful recordings or the over-imaginative consciousness of its hero. The reliability of the narrative voice for the reader may be questionable in terms of strict veracity, but this undecidability establishes a site of empowerment for the teenager. The teenager retains a power over the narrative, which only an insider of the subcultural world being described could verify. This unreliability is not due to 'limited knowledge' (as Rimmon-Kenan describes one function of an unreliable narrative voice[11]) but represents a control over the information communicated by the narrator to the reader. The narrative, therefore, represents the 'subaltern' voice of youth, and the inscription of this voice problematizes the 'hierarchy of discourses' produced in 'classic realism'.[12] The uninitiated reader is persuaded to accept the teenager's idiom as a faithful (though stylized) narrative, and that they are allowed access to the inner experience of this subcultural world.

However, there are tensions here concerning the multiple functions of the text in terms of authenticity and style. The text actually produces a paradoxical verification of the authenticity and authority of the narrative perspective through the construction of a stylized narra-

---

10 As defined by Genette's typology of narrators; Gerard Genette, *Narrative Discourse*, trans. by Jane E. Lewin (Oxford: Blackwell, 1980), pp.255–6; see also Shlomith Rimmon-Kenan, *Narrative Fiction: Contemporary Poetics* (London and New York: Routledge, 1989), pp.94–105.

11 Rimmon-Kenan, *Narrative Fiction*, p.100.

12 See Catherine Belsey's definition of 'classic realism' and its deployment of a 'hierarchy of discourses' in *Critical Practice* (London and New York: Routledge, 1980), pp.70–2. This disruption in realist form complements the ideological significance of the text as a written challenge to discourses of authority. The 'author' of this narrative is presumed to be the teenager, thus wresting control from the omniscient narrator of conventional realism.

tive. The text does not transparently 'reflect' the language style used by fifties teenage subcultures, rather it re-constructs, in a textual form, the *function* of style, and the deployment of unofficial language in the positioning of subcultural identity *vis-à-vis* dominant culture. As Steven Connor suggests, this form creates an exclusionary and inclusionary relationship with the reader, whereby the addressee is excluded from the subcultural world that is being described, but at the same time is being invited to enter into that world through association with its construction within the text.[13]

As suggested earlier, though, the text constructs a dual narrative address. It is the mainstream reader who is the true absolute beginner in this environment, whilst the narrative voice represents itself as confident of its place within its own subcultural world, and projects directly to perceived 'members' of that marginalized group. The deployment of a first-person narration from within the culture becomes a strategic technique that allows the text to engage in a discussion of the teenage 'world' without resorting to a form that externalizes the narrative voice of the text. Therefore, the text internally constructs a dual set of 'implied' readers. Firstly, a 'reader' who is part of the teenage subculture who will recognize the situations, characters and world of the text, and will feel included by the narrative address. Potentially, this produces a narrative of empowerment as the textual recording (for the first time) of this subcultural world and identity is structured as a collective address. And secondly, a 'reader' who is excluded, who is part of the dominant culture to which the text is simultaneously addressed as a revelatory discourse of the culture of a specific subcultural 'other'.[14]

Absolute Beginners, then, has two specific narrative functions that recognize two distinct 'interpretive communities', which, in turn reveals the intersection of subcultural and national identity. The text, on one level, represents a radical social critique that aims to educate the white adult English population about youth and black subcultures of which the majority of English people had been given a false under-

13   Connor, *The English Novel in History*, p.90.
14   The narrative structure thereby produces a dual narrative of inclusion and exclusion in relation to Connor's model of 'addressivity', ibid., pp.8–13.

standing by the media. It also attempts to warn white English society of its implicit prejudices against youth and black subcultures. These prejudices were beginning to surface in mainstream culture in the fifties, and gain public expression in the so-called 'race riots' in Nottingham and Notting Hill in September 1958. The intersection of youth and black subcultural identities is foregrounded in MacInnes's fiction through a discourse of the nation, and reveals contemporary cultural anxieties about youth, 'race' and Englishness.[15]

These concerns are also evident in *City of Spades* and again are articulated through the deployment of a dual narrative address. In this text, this is more overtly identified by the split first-person homodiegetic narration of the two central characters, Montgomery Pew and Johnny Fortune. The dual narrative structure of this novel allows MacInnes to represent the voice of a particular minority subculture, that of the black immigrant living in London in the 1950s, but also to represent dominant white middle-class culture (albeit a 'liberal' representative). Again, this technique reflects the dual function of the text in terms of its addressivity. It attempts to represent black subcultures through the paradoxical construction of an 'authentic' subcultural voice that functions to articulate the case of the marginalized group, whilst at the same time alerting dominant white society to the actualities of racism in fifties England.

City of Spades also includes a third-person extradiegetic narrative voice in the two 'interludes' of the text, which act as textual 'hinges' between the two homodiegetic narratives. The first of these sections entitled 'Idyll of miscegenation on the river' describes a trip on a Thames pleasure steamer taken by Johnny Fortune and his white lover, Muriel MacPherson. The trip describes an idyllic escape from urban London to the pleasant surroundings of Greenwich Palace, and is represented formally as a 'textual' escape from the limited perspective of the two first-person narratives. It also represents the possibility of an escape from the social constraints upon the 'mixed-race' couple in which they dream of a future married life together. This section, therefore, also engages with anxieties in fifties mainstream

---

15   This connection between youth and black subcultural identity is identified in particular by Hebdige, *Subcultures*.

culture about the presence of black individuals within English society and the threat of miscegenation.[16]

The second extradiegetic interlude, '"Let justice be done (and seen to be)!"', records the institutionalized racism of the English legal system, both in terms of the police and the judiciary. In the court scene towards the end of the novel, Johnny Fortune's use of non-Standard English confirms his 'alien' identity to the judiciary:

> 'Listen to me, sir. I live some few week when I have no money with this woman.' [Johnny Fortune]
> 'So you *did* live with her? You admit that?'
> The judge croaked again. 'There's just a point here, Mr Gillespie [the prosecuting counsel], I think. It's possible the language difficulty, you know.' (219)

Here, the institutionalized racism of the judicial system is identified in terms of both Fortune's colour and his 'unofficial' mode of expression, and although he is eventually acquitted of the charge of 'living off the immoral earnings of a woman', it is made apparent that this is only because of the intervention of Theodora Pace, the upper-middle-class white BBC journalist, who speaks on his behalf. As she says: 'I heard Mr. Fortune giving evidence this morning. English is not his mother tongue, and an African has greater difficulty in expressing himself clearly than many of us realize' (225). The 'us' of this passage positions Fortune as the ethnic 'other' who can only 'speak' legitimately in the court surroundings when represented by a 'white' spokesperson. The subaltern status of black racial and cultural identity makes it necessary that Fortune's 'authentic' voice is replaced by the 'official' voice of dominant white culture. Theodora Pace, therefore, speaks *for* Fortune. The novel also makes it clear that Fortune's acquittal is unusual in this situation, and that in the vast majority of such cases the court would convict the black defendant precisely on grounds of 'race'. The section ends, significantly, with the eventual imprisonment of Fortune despite his initial acquittal, representing the power of the police over an individual whom they have decided beforehand should be convicted: 'A week later, Johnny

16   I discuss this issue in greater detail in the section on *City of Spades* below.

Fortune was re-arrested on the charge of being in possession of Indian hemp [...] and Johnny went to prison for a month' (229).

These two extradiegetic narrative interludes represent racism in practice, both popular and institutionalized. They are placed in juxtaposition with the two homodiegetic narratives to foreground the initially naive attitudes of the two sides of the racial encounter. Both Montgomery Pew and Johnny Fortune begin the novel in the belief that there is very little racial antagonism in England, but the narrative movement of the novel gradually reveals the falsity of this belief, and this point is emphasized by MacInnes's manipulation of narrative voice.

The representative function of the teenager's voice in *Absolute Beginners* and Johnny Fortune's narrative in *City of Spades*, therefore, exceeds the portrayal of individual characters. Their narratives are a representation of collective subcultural identities that attempt to articulate a discourse of empowerment for particular marginalized groups in fifties society. As with Sillitoe's texts, this collective narrative technique corresponds to the ideological function identified by Deleuze and Guattari, in what they call 'minor literature', as the political representation of marginalized discourses in a fictional form.[17]

Cool Britannia: Reconstructing Englishness

As identified in chapter one and above, the 1950s represents a period in which traditional ideas of Englishness were undergoing reappraisal and re-negotiation.[18] Anxieties concerning what it meant to be English

---

17   Gilles Deleuze and Felix Guattari, *Kafka: Toward a Minor Literature*, trans. by Dana Polan (Minneapolis: University of Minnesota Press, 1986), pp.16–18. See also the discussion of Deleuze and Guattari in relation to Sillitoe in chapter six above.

18   MacInnes's position as a 'postcolonial' writer appears to contribute to his fascination with English national identity. MacInnes, son of author Angela Thirkell, was born in London in 1914, but was brought up in Australia from

in the contemporary world were affected by the perceived threat of foreign influences, most notably by the perceived threat of Americanization in popular and youth culture, and by the effects of an increasing immigrant population. These factors are represented in MacInnes's novels by contradictory attitudes towards Englishness.

Following Tom Nairn's description of the nation as 'the modern Janus',[19] Homi Bhabha has identified the 'janus-faced ambivalence' of the discourse and language of national culture. He writes:

> The 'locality' of national culture is neither unified nor unitary in relation to itself, nor must it be seen simply as 'other' in relation to what is outside or beyond it. The boundary is Janus-faced and the problem of outside/inside must always be a process of hybridity, incorporating new 'people' in relation to the body politic, generating other sites of meaning and, inevitably, in the political process, producing unmanned sites of political antagonism and unpredictable forces for political representation.[20]

In this passage, Bhabha identifies the fluid construction of the nation and suggests that national identity is never fixed but is in a constant process of reconstruction and re-negotiation. A similar model of the nation is also assumed in *Absolute Beginners*. MacInnes's novel attempts to construct the 'other sites' identified by Bhabha both in terms of meaning and through the construction of identities that engage in the ideological construction of an emergent Englishness. However, the text is also concerned to retain certain aspects of a residual Englishness. The position of the narrative voice as simultaneously inside and outside in relation to youth subcultures corresponds to this negotiated construction of the nation. The narrative occupies a liminal position from which it attempts to reconstruct a new national identity by re-positioning the narrative, and the reader, in relation to a moral judgment on the construction of Englishness in relation to the other 'geographies' of youth and 'race'.

1919 onwards, returning to London in 1936. Tony Gould's biography provides a good account of MacInnes's life and works.

19   Tom Nairn, *The Break-up of Britain* (London: Verso, 1981), p.348.

20   Homi K. Bhabha, 'Introduction', in *Nation and Narration*, ed. by Homi K. Bhabha (London and New York: Routledge, 1990) p.4.

The text's contradictory attitude towards the nature of English identity is registered through the central consciousness of the teenager, who is unclear about which aspects of the nation he can support, and which he would prefer to reject. This 'undecidability' of national identity is articulated in the conversation the teenager has with a South American diplomat who is in the process of writing a report on 'British-folk ways': "'So you've not much to tell me of Britain and her position." ["O]nly," I said, "that her position is that she hasn't found her position"' (25–7). This description of the nation as fluid and unstable is informed by the contemporary 'crisis' of Britain's loss of colonial and international power, and foregrounds a moment of transition in English national identity by observing and commenting on both residual and emergent forms of Englishness.[21] However, it is not the case that MacInnes's teenager simply rejects the residual and celebrates the emergent aspects of the contemporary national culture; a more complex attitude is presented by way of a reconstruction of the nation through a re-negotiation of traditional and new cultural forms and practices. As the teenager comments: "'You bet I'm a patriot!" I exclaimed. "It's because I'm a patriot, that I can't bear our country"' (59).

There *is* plenty of invective about residual forms of Englishness in the novel, especially in relation to out-of-date colonial attitudes that retain the pretence that Britain is still a major world power. For example, the teenager tells the South American diplomat, referring to the English:

> If they'd stick to their housekeeping, which is the only back-yard they can move freely in to any purpose, and stopped playing Winston Churchill and the Great Armada when there's no tin soldiers left to play with any more, then no one would despise them, because no one would even notice them. (26)

---

21 The shift between British and English here is, of course, problematic, but is not addressed in MacInnes's novel. In many ways MacInnes regards the 'Empire' as English rather than British, which may have something to do with his Scottish and Australian background.

This passage reveals the text's critique of the residual forms of colonial power, which are also identified by the teenager in Britain's recent failures in international power broking:

> 'The war,' said Vern [the teenager's elder half-brother], 'was Britain's finest hour.'
> 'What war? You mean Cyprus, boy? Or Suez? Or Korea?'
> 'No, stupid. I mean the *real* war, you don't remember.'
> 'Well Vernon,' I said, 'please believe me I'm glad I don't. All of you oldies certainly seem to try to keep it well in mind, because every time I open a newspaper, or pick up a paperback, or go to the Odeon, I hear nothing but war, war, war. You pensioners certainly seem to love that old struggle'. (35)

The teenager bases his critique on the fact that residual forms of Englishness fail to accept the nation's declined status in the postcolonial world.

In addition, the text argues that England has failed to take responsibility for its colonial heritage, and to recognize that it is implicated in its colonial history precisely because the exploitation of subject peoples has taken place *elsewhere*, away from the colonial centre:

> For centuries [...] the English have been rich, and the price of riches is that you export reality to where it is you get your money from. And now that the marketplaces overseas are closing one by one, reality comes home again to roost, but no one notices it, although it's settled in to stay beside them. (98)

The process of decolonization in the 1950s as represented by MacInnes corresponds to Sartre's comments on this process in which the guilt of the colonial power is revisited upon the centre. Sartre writes: 'today violence, blocked everywhere, comes back to us through our soldiers, comes inside and takes possession of us. Involution starts; the native recreates himself, and we, settlers and white Europeans, ultras and liberals, we break up'.[22] According to MacInnes, the construction of an emergent, 'postcolonial' Englishness must accept

---

22   See Sartre's introduction to Frantz Fanon, *The Wretched of the Earth*, trans. by Constance Farrington (Harmondsworth: Penguin, 1967), first published in French in 1961, first published in English 1965, p.23.

the inevitable consequences of decolonization and the effect this process has on the old colonial 'centre'.

The failure to respond to the changing contemporary situation is shown in the text's fictional description of the Notting Hill riots of 1958. In the novel, this eruption of violence is represented as a spontaneous and collective psychological reaction to contemporary anxieties about national identity amongst the dominant white population. This leads the teenager to reject residual and entrenched forms of Englishness:

> Because in this moment, I must tell you, I'd fallen right out of love with England. And even with London, which I'd loved like my mother, in a way. As far as I was concerned, the whole dam [sic.] group of islands could sink under the sea, and all I wanted was to shake my feet off of them, and take off somewhere and get naturalized, and settle (228).

However, parallel to this critique of residual forms of the nation, the text simultaneously offers a celebration of other traditional forms of national identity, which appear to be under threat from the new social and cultural forces. For example, in contrast to the text's focus on the emergent musical form of jazz, the operettas of Gilbert and Sullivan are celebrated as a cultural expression of a residual, yet still important element of Englishness (132–3). Gilbert and Sullivan function in the text as a cultural signifier of traditional, 'liberal' England, representing an honest, ordered and tolerant society. In one section, the teenager goes on a boat trip with his father (who represents a gentle, quietly spoken, but solid English character) and he celebrates older narratives of Englishness by appropriating royalist and pastoral images:

> Up there behind us, was the enormous castle, just as you see it on screen when they play 'the Queen' [...] and there out in front of us were fields and trees and cows and things and sunlight, and a huge big sky filled with acres of fresh air, and I thought my heavens! if this is the country, why haven't I shaken hands with it before – it's glorious! (172)

This nostalgic celebration of an English pastoral scene seems at odds with the teenager's encounters with the new forms of teenage and black subcultures that pervade most of the text. However, this aspect represents an attempt to reconstruct a positive, emergent national identity that is acceptable not only to the new subcultural identities the novel records, but also to the mainstream culture. This ambivalence in terms of national identity serves to envisage a reconstruction of Englishness that will incorporate mainstream *and* the new identities of youth and black subcultures. The novel, therefore, attempts to appropriate these new cultures by representing them to an audience that has come to perceive them as wholly threatening to traditional national values. If MacInnes's teenager can respond to the implicit worth of certain aspects of an older English identity, then it is more palatable for dominant English culture to include these new subcultural forces into an emergent reconstruction of Englishness. It thus anticipates later discourses of a 'Cool Britannia' that appropriates youth and black subcultures in a vibrant and forward-looking construction of the nation. It is for this reason that the text ends with the poignant image of a new group of immigrants landing in England, full of hope and a reliance on the very English myths that the teenager has reproduced:

> They all looked so dam [sic.] pleased to be in England, at the end of their long journey, that I was heartbroken at all the disappointments that were in store for them [...] 'Welcome to London! Greetings from England! Meet your first teenager! We're all going up to Napoli to have a ball!' (234–5)

This contradictory attitude to the construction of Englishness reveals the novel's engagement with contemporaneous debates on the social and political experience of Britain in the post-war period. The text enters a contemporary cultural debate concerned to identify a national identity that has been loosened from its traditional certainties, one which is no longer the property of the dominant cultural institutions, but is in the process of being reconstructed from below. There is a radical instability and undecidability in the text concerning the form this new national identity might take, which again corresponds to contemporary anxieties about Britain's present and future international status and role. Following Timothy Brennan's argument that the 'national longing for form' is represented in the narrativization of a country's national identity, the instability of the construction of

Englishness (and the experimentation with realist form in terms of a dual narrative address) in *Absolute Beginners* represents these contemporary anxieties.[23] The novel celebrates certain aspects of the new cultural forces, but it also acknowledges an uncertainty over the consequences and nature of the emergent cultural forms. The danger of the new manifests itself in *Absolute Beginners* as an outpouring of racial violence, precipitated precisely through the crisis in national identity engendered in segments of white English youth.

The Young Ones: Ambivalent Youth Cultures in *Absolute Beginners*

As argued in chapter three above, the range of analytical models adopted by the New Left and sociological studies of youth in the fifties tended to be informed by Marxist and/or class-based approaches. This kind of analysis tended to distance the object of study and, consequently, to interpret youth subcultures as indicative of the effects of new consumption-based economic models and as indicative of a 'false consciousness' on the part of the participants. One of MacInnes's aims in *Absolute Beginners* was to offer an alternative reading of 1950s youth culture that, firstly, foregrounded the radical potential of youth to challenge dominant culture, and secondly, would allow youth to speak in (a textual representation of) its own voice.

Despite rejecting its analytical approaches, *Absolute Beginners* is concerned to cover much of the same ground as the New Left and later British cultural studies, and MacInnes reproduces similar readings of youth subcultures in which they are represented as reconstituted forms of dominant cultural ideologies. For example, Phil Cohen's writing on white working-class youth subculture in fifties London argues that youth represents, in different forms, the same anxieties as the parent culture, which is thus revealed through a strong

23   Timothy Brennan, 'The National Longing for Form', in Bhabha, *Nation and Narration*, pp.44–70.

sense of territorialization and racist practices. Youth, in Cohen's analysis, is read as a 'sub-section' of dominant culture.[24] Similarly, Hoggart identifies 'youth', through a discourse of Americanization, as a contemporary indication of the preponderance of a new form of consumer capitalism.[25] Both these positions are, to a certain extent, represented and negotiated in MacInnes's novel.

One of the problems of these approaches, however, is that they construct 'youth' subculture as an homogenous group that consequently is read in relation to the dominant or the 'parent' culture. MacInnes's text offers a contrasting representation of youth by identifying multiple subcultures within the homogenizing term 'youth'. The representations of Teds, Mods (although this description had not yet been coined when *Absolute Beginners* was published), 'trad' and 'mod' jazz followers, as well as the younger 'teen' cultures, problematize the singular definition of youth subculture and achieve a complexity that is lacking in Cohen's and Hoggart's writing. *Absolute Beginners* offers a more contradictory, unstable and ambivalent reading of youth that combines an anxiety and attraction towards the new teenage phenomenon.

MacInnes's teenager is convinced that the teenage phenomenon carries the *possibility* of a radical disruption of dominant power relationships:

> youth has power, a kind of divine power straight from mother nature [...] As for the boys and girls, the dear young absolute beginners, I sometimes feel that if they only *knew* this fact, this very simple fact, namely how powerful they really are, then they could rise up overnight and enslave the old tax-payers, the whole dam lot of them. (13)

However, this power is significantly circumscribed by the fact that the teenagers are unaware of their revolutionary potential. This passage significantly, in terms of the political climate of the 1950s, deploys a

24   Cohen, Phil, 'Subcultural Conflict and Working-class Community', in *The Subcultures Reader*, ed by Ken Gelder and Sarah Thornton (London and New York: Routledge, 1997), pp.90–9.
25   Hoggart, Richard, *The Uses of Literacy* (Harmondsworth: Penguin, 1958), first published 1957, pp.246–72.

traditional Marxist vocabulary that represents youth as a subjugated group rising up to overthrow the dominant system, but this language of revolution is moved from a category of class distinction to one of age. This image is repeated in the following passage:

> even here in this Soho, the headquarters of the adult mafia, you could every-where see the signs of un-silent teenage revolution. The disc shops with those lovely sleeves set in their windows, the most original thing to come out in our lifetime, and the kids inside them purchasing guitars, or spending fortunes on the songs of the Top Twenty. The shirt-stores and bra-stores with cine-star photos in the window selling all the exclusive teenage drag I've been describ-ing. The hair-style saloons where they inflict the blow-wave torture on the kids for hours on end. The cosmetic shops – to make girls of seventeen, fifteen, even thirteen, look like pale rinsed-out sophisticates. Scooters and bubble-cars driven madly down the roads by kids who, a few years ago, were pushing toy ones on the pavement. And everywhere you go the narrow coffee bars and darkened cellars with the kids packed tight, just whispering, like bees inside the hive waiting for a glorious queen bee to appear. (74)

The focus on style here, as signifying the radical aesthetics of youth subcultures, is close to Dick Hebdige's reading of the radical potential of youth. Hebdige writes: 'We should [...] not underestimate the signi-fying power of the spectacular subculture not only as a metaphor for potential anarchy "out there" but as an actual mechanism of semiotic disorder.'[26] What is significant in MacInnes, however, is that the weapons of this new teenage revolution are precisely the consumer products that will ensure that it fails to threaten the dominant *eco-nomic* ideology, and therefore, in class terms, can never successfully achieve any fundamental challenge to dominant power structures. Again, as Hebdige writes: 'It is difficult [...] to maintain any absolute distinction between commercial exploitation on the one hand and creativity/originality on the other.'[27] MacInnes also identifies the way in which any original authentic teenage culture is gradually appro-priated through commodification: '"They buy us younger every year"' (10). Therefore, the radical potential of the teenage 'revolution' is ultimately diluted through its incorporation into hegemonic capitalist

26   Hebdige, *Subcultures*, p.90.
27   Ibid., p.95.

power structures. As Alice Ferrebe notes: 'one of the radical characteristics of the narator's male teenage-hood is his easy, guilt free adoption and exploitation of the principles of the consumer market'.[28] This is identified, in particular, by the very young, yet experienced character, the Wizard, who epitomizes the darker undercurrent of teenage subculture. As he observes:

> It's been a two-way twist, this teenage party. Exploitation of the kiddoes by the conscripts, and exploitation of themselves by the crafty little absolute beginners. The net result? 'Teenager''s become a dirty word or, at any rate, a square one. (10)

Nevertheless, the text simultaneously envisages the possibility of a more radical, 'utopian' subcultural discourse that rejects the codes of the dominant culture. This discourse is necessarily underground, existing as it does on the margins of dominant society, and finds its evocation in the musical and cultural expression of jazz. The importance of musical styles as signifying ideological positions is crucial in *Absolute Beginners*, and again corresponds to Hebdige's reading of the aesthetics of youth culture.[29] Jazz, in MacInnes's text, represents the potential revolutionary spirit that idealistically removes all prejudices of class, age, ethnicity, gender and sexuality. The text suggests that this utopian vision was contained in the original impulse for the teenage culture, that it was once 'pure', uncontaminated by commercialism:

> This teenage ball had a real splendour in the days when the kids discovered that, for the first time since centuries of kingdom-come, they'd money, which hitherto had always been denied to us at the best time in life to use it, namely, when you're young and strong, and also before the newspapers and telly got hold of this teenage fable and prostituted it as conscripts seem to do to everything they touch. Yes, I tell you, it had had a real savage splendour [...] our world was to be our world. (10–11)

---

28 Ferrebe, *Masculinity in Male-Authored Fiction*, 146
29 Hebdige reads the 'moment' of fifties jazz as an 'unprecedented convergence of black and white', Hebdige, *Subcultures*, p.47.

Here, teenage youth culture is defined as a real, though lost, vehicle for radical social change. At the moment the novel takes place, the mantle of this potentially radical power has been taken over by jazz:

> But the great thing about the jazz world, and all the kids that enter into it, is that no one, not a soul, cares what your class is, or what your race is, or what your income, or if you're boy, or girl, or bent, or versatile, or what you are – so long as you behave yourself, and have left all that crap behind you, too, when you come in the jazz club door. (68–9)

MacInnes here projects a radical construction of community that incorporates differences in class, 'race', gender and sexual orientation, and offers an alternative form of 'community' to Raymond Williams's model, which, as we have seen, was influential in early New Left discourse.[30]

The jazz world, however, also represents a radical 'irresponsibility' in terms of its rejection and exclusion of the specific societal problems of 1950s culture. As with Sillitoe, MacInnes inscribes within his text the political and ideological function of an irresponsibility that corresponds to both Derrida's and Baudrillard's use of the term.[31] This irresponsibility is written in *Absolute Beginners* as a specifically political and textual gesture against dominant culture. The utopian environment of the jazz club corresponds to Baudrillard's reading of 'utopia' as the 'very speech of communism', written by the 'cursed poet' and 'non-official art[ist]'.[32] Baudrillard argues that: 'Poetry and the utopian revolt have this radical presentness in common [...] this actualization of desire no longer relegated to future liberation, but demanded here, immediately' (165). The radical space of the jazz world articulates the radicalism inherent in the rejection of dominant culture, and of any responsibility for the practices and beliefs of that

30   Raymond Williams, *The Long Revolution* (London: Chatto and Windus, 1961), pp.41–53.
31   Jacques Derrida, '"This Strange Institution Called Literature": An Interview with Jacques Derrida', in *Acts of Literature*, ed. by Derek Attridge (London and New York: Routledge, 1992), pp.33–75, (p.38); Jean Baudrillard, *The Mirror of Production*, trans. by Mark Poster (St. Louis: Telos Press, 1975). See the discussion of irresponsibility in chapter six above.
32   Baudrillard, *The Mirror of Production*, p.164.

culture. It also places that moment of radical opposition in the present by placing the moment of revolution in the transgressive immediacy of the jazz club experience.

It is apparent, though, that MacInnes's novel exceeds a reading of the radicalism of youth subcultures as a primarily 'utopian' move. MacInnes offers a more (politically) ambivalent reading of youth that stresses 1950s anxieties about the instability and undecidability of the release of these radical forces. It is useful here to return to Bataille's theory on the relationship between the 'heterogeneous' and 'homogeneous' forces of society.[33] In Bataillean terms, youth culture can be read as representing a heterogeneous force that destabilizes the homogeneity of dominant society. For Bataille, '*Violence, excess, delirium, madness* characterize heterogeneous elements to varying degrees: active as persons or mobs, they result from breaking the laws of social *homogeneity*' (142). The transgressive nature, the violence and the excess of the subcultural world described by MacInnes's teenager represents a textual unleashing of the underground, rejected and re-pressed forces of society, and the jazz world represents the model of excess and non-productive consumption that Bataille identifies as the 'heterogeneous': forces of human psychology that represent the excluded components, the detritus of homogeneous bourgeois society. For Bataille, as Fred Botting and Scott Wilson have pointed out, the heterogeneous forces of non-productive consumption are revealed when 'the unproductive expenditure of energy [...] is released from within homogeneous society by sacrifices and festival'.[34] In *Absolute Beginners*, the heterogeneous excess is 'spent' through the dual sub-cultural modes of empowerment represented by the consumption of subcultural artifacts: fashion, music, appearance; and consumption of the jazz club experience.

33   In particular see the essays, 'The Use Value of D.A.F. de Sade' and 'The Psychological Structure of Fascism', in Georges Bataille, *Visions of Excess: Selected Writings, 1927–1939*, trans. by Allan Stoekl (Minneapolis: University of Minnesota Press, 1985), pp.91–102 and pp.137–60.
34   Fred Botting and Scott Wilson, *The Bataille Reader* (Oxford: Blackwell, 1997), p.22.

However, the Bataillean concept of the heterogeneous also reveals a negative function that problematizes the ideological construction of the radical nature of heterogeneous excess. In 'The Psychological Structure of Fascism', Bataille presents an alternative product of the release of the heterogeneous in terms of the creation of a general unification of prohibited forces onto the figure of a 'fascist' leader as the 'transcendent object of collective affinity'.[35] This process 'amounts to a negation of the fundamental revolutionary effervescence' of the heterogeneous, combining it with residual elements of the homogeneous such as 'duty, discipline and obedience' (139). In *Absolute Beginners*, this 'negative' aspect of the heterogeneous is represented by the existence of the neo-Nazi group that the teenager visits and of which his former friend Wizard is a member:

> Then I looked at Wizard. And on my friend's face, as he stared up at this orator [from the White Protection League], I saw an expression that made me shiver [...] his wiry little body was all clenched, and something was staring through his eyes that came from God knows where, and he raised on his toes, and shot up his arms all rigid, and he cried out, shrill like a final cry, 'Keep England White'. (220)

Wizard represents the liberatory potential of youth culture perverted from a discourse of equality towards a discourse of racial prejudice that re-subjugates black culture in the process of empowering white English working-class youth. This character, therefore, articulates contemporary anxieties in the collective psychology of the nation in relation to the presence of black subcultures in the colonial 'centre', and points towards the worrying rise of racism in Britain in the 1950s.[36]

In Bataillean terms, it is significant that the moment of exalted and sublime pleasure experienced by the teenage narrator at the jazz concert is precisely the same moment in which he learns of the obverse effects of this released subversive energy, namely the 'race riots' in Nottingham (189). The teenager's excess is thereby revisited as a sense of guilt, specifically as guilt for his nation's (including

35   Bataille, 'The Psychological Structure of Fascism', p.139.
36   See Cohen, 'Subcultural Conflict and Working-class Community'.

white English youth's) violence towards black immigrants, reinforcing his position as implicated ideologically in his nation's socio-political framework. The riots remind him that he cannot ignore the ideologies of the society in which he is placed, no matter how much he despises some of the attitudes and actions of that society, and no matter how far he desires to distance himself from them.

This aspect of the text has echoes of Phil Cohen's reading of the racist practices of fifties white London youth as a displacement of the 'parent' culture's anxieties about social change articulated as a xenophobic attitude to immigrant black communities. However, it also represents a moment in which the repressed forces of the heterogeneous surface as a fascistic form of mob violence. The text is unequivocal about the negativity of this aspect of youth culture and justifies MacInnes's division of youth into the (sub-)subcultures of the Teds and jazz followers, the former representing the upsurge of racist attitudes. At this moment of crucial decision, the text rejects a complete irresponsibility in its attempt to justify the actions of certain youth subcultures to the dominant culture. The unfettered anarchic power of youth, without the restraints of any social responsibility, acts as a warning in the text, a warning to mainstream culture that if youth continues to be misrepresented and marginalized, an alienated group will be produced that, in its attempt to construct its own marginalized identity, will lash out violently at other marginalized groups.

MacInnes's response to this potentially destructive subculture involves a crucial re-inclusion of the vibrancy and liberatory eclecticism of his own vision of teenage culture into a new decent 'English' (or even 'post-English') society that incorporates, rather than rejects, the new forces of youth. Towards the end of the novel the teenager initially plans to leave England as a response to what he sees as the widespread racism existing there. This is a moment of defeat for the teenager, but also a moment of rejection of his responsibility, of leaving the country to the white racists and the darker teenage subculture as represented by Wizard. However, the teenager ultimately decides to stay: to accept a social responsibility for his 'race', and for his teenage subculture, and to fight for an emergent, vibrant, multicultural Englishness. The end of the novel is therefore poignant, as the teenager goes off to embrace new arrivals from Africa: "'Welcome to

London! Greetings from England! Meet your first teenager! We're all going up to Napoli to have a ball!'" (235).

Ultimately, therefore, the text rejects the complete irresponsibility and non-productive excesses of the jazz subcultural world in favour of the advocacy, on the part of its central character, of a form of 'responsible' political action. The 'jazz' existence is significantly constructed as a site that exists outside of the normal time-frame of dominant society, a momentary escape from its prejudices and inconsistencies. It is precisely because the jazz world is *sub*cultural that it cannot engage in a context of wider social conscience: the radicalism it offers is contained in the restricted space of the jazz club. It is a place of escape, but also a space where the teenager is allowed to renege his social responsibilities. However, the outside world gradually invades the teenager's 'jazz' existence, forcing him to take responsibility for his social, cultural and national identity, challenging his independent and individualized identity. The passage at the end of section three of the novel highlights the way in which the teenager's Edenic jazz world is about to be invaded by exterior socio-political forces:

> They rose to her at the end – all those hundreds of English boys and girls, and their friends from Africa and the Caribbean – and they practically had to gouge us all out of that auditorium. Cats I didn't know from Adam said, hadn't it been great, and one cat in particular then said, had I heard about the happenings at St. Ann's Well, up in Nottingham, last evening? I asked him, what happenings? not taking very much in (because I was still back there with Maria Bethlehem), when I realized he was saying there'd been rioting between whites and coloured, but what could you expect in a provincial dump out there among the sticks? (189)

This passage represents the moment of expulsion from the utopian world as rumours of the 'race riots' from Nottingham are about to impinge on the teenager's life closer to home, finally cementing his sense of responsibility for the actions of his 'race'.

Ultimately, then, the teenager is forced to take responsibility for both his subcultural and his national identity. His desire tends towards total irresponsibility, but the ideological movement of the text forces the hero to confront the implications of his subcultural status. In the context of fifties social critique, the teenager is forced into a position of expressing a specific political and social commitment. The text invokes him to move from a position of individualistic rejection of mainstream culture to an acceptance that he must fight within his culture to try and change it for the better. This commitment is signifycantly distanced from a Marxist focus on class issues and projected onto a discourse of youth, ethnicity and nation. As the teenager comments: 'I'm just not interested in the whole class trap that seems to needle you and all the tax-payers' (41). The teenager's style of commitment is articulated through engagement in a specific localized form of politicized discourse in response to specific events: the 1958 riots. In terms of the contemporaneous debates about literature and commitment, therefore, the text constructs its own alternative form of committed literature that distances itself from a communist or Marxist discourse, but maintains a commitment based on attacking social prejudice in terms of age and 'race' and thereby constructs its own alternative model of (radical) community.

Cruel Britannia: 'Race' and Identity in *City of Spades*

MacInnes's contradictory representations of English national identity and youth are also reproduced in his representation of black subcultures. In *City of Spades*, MacInnes attempts to record, again deploying an 'authentic' narrative voice, a faithful representation of the culture and specific concerns of the emergent black communities in fifties London. In part, the text attempts to re-address the misrepresentation of these identities in the media and in the mainstream 'structure of feeling' amongst the white population towards ethnic minorities from commonwealth and decolonized countries.[37] As argued in chapter three above, the main channel of intellectual social critique in the 1950s, as represented by the New Left, failed to identify the specific

---

37   I am again deploying Raymond Williams's concept of 'structures of feeling' here; Williams, *The Long Revolution*, p.48.

concerns of black minority groups. As Paul Gilroy has argued, the reason for this gap in discourses of 'race' was the privileging of class as a category of analysis.[38]

City of Spades represents the black subcultures existent in London in the fifties through the deployment of the first-person narrative of Johnny Fortune, a black African student, who shares the narrative with the white civil servant, Montgomery Pew. Fortune's discourse is represented linguistically as close to Pew's Standard English with a few discrepancies that function as an attempt to represent the 'authenticity' of Fortune's African-English. Therefore, the text allows Fortune to speak in his own voice: in Gayatri Spivak's terms, the text allows the 'subaltern' narrative to speak for itself.[39] As with youth subcultures in *Absolute Beginners*, this strategy avoids the distancing of fifties New Left discourses on ethnicity that tended to position the black subject as an 'other' who is spoken *for*, and thereby disallowed from voicing his or her specific concerns directly. *City of Spades*, therefore, is radical in its attempts to produce a textual space in which these marginalized discourses could be articulated. However, MacInnes's novel is problematic in its representation of black identity, as it engages in the artificial *construction* of a black 'other' that reinscribes many of the racial and cultural stereotypes it claims to disperse.

In the final section of *Absolute Beginners*, MacInnes represents mainstream attitudes to 'race' through the discussion of an article in what the teenager calls 'Mrs Dale's Daily', by the fictional journalist Ambrose Drove, representative of dominant cultural attitudes towards immigrant and black individuals (193–7). The 'Ambrose Drove' article serves to highlight several specific racial prejudices and misrepresentations, such as: the dangerous irresponsibility of unrestricted immigration; the positioning of immigrant cultures as underdevel-

38   Paul Gilroy, '"Race", Class and Agency', in *There Ain't No Black in the Union Jack: The Cultural Politics of Race and Nation* (London and New York: Routledge, 1987), pp.15–42. Also see the discussion of Gilroy in chapter three above.

39   Gayatri Spivak, 'Can the Subaltern Speak?', in *Marxism and the Interpretation of Culture*, ed. by Cary Nelson and Lawrence Grossberg (London: Macmillan, 1988), pp.271–313.

oped, and lacking in ethical and moral frameworks comparable to the (white) British population; anti-social and excessive behaviour; sexual promiscuity; and criminality, especially in the practice of 'living off the immoral earnings of white prostitutes' (195). The fictional article places the responsibility for the incidents of racial violence in the Nottingham and Notting Hill riots on the immigrants, implying that the racist reaction of the Teds is understandable though 'entirely alien to our way of life' (196).

City of Spades opens up a range of issues that engage with this dominant (mis)construction and stereotyping of black identity. For example, the text foregrounds the misreading of 'black' immigrants as a unified homogenous group by identifying the distinctions between separate black cultural identities resident in Britain in the 1950s, especially in the cultural differences between Caribbean, African and African American identities, and also in distinctions within those categories such as Gambian, Nigerian, and so on. Each sub-group is given its own specific identity in the text that is representative of specific national/cultural identities. The novel is also concerned to redress the dominant (white) cultural belief that black individuals are culturally, morally and intellectually inferior. This is achieved in two ways: firstly, through the narrative strategy of delivering half of the narrative from the perspective of Johnny Fortune; and secondly, through the characterization, which establishes a moral and ethical equality in terms of the practices and actions of individual characters, irrespective of cultural history and skin colour.

As Paul Gilroy has argued, discourses of the nation and 'race' have been articulated together in post-war Britain.[40] Therefore, anxieties about the declining status of the nation are presented through discourses of racial prejudice that serve to focus the blame of national decline on 'alien' individuals and cultures. As Gilroy writes: 'Alien cultures come to embody a threat which, in turn, invites the conclusion that national decline and weakness have been precipitated by the arrival of blacks.'[41] In the 1950s, the impact of decolonisation intensified this racial discourse. Gilroy also identifies that this con-

---

40 Gilroy, *There Ain't No Black*, p.56.
41 Ibid., p.46.

nection of ethnicity and nation was specifically articulated in the fifties through a discourse of criminality in which: 'issues of sexuality and miscegenation were often uppermost'.[42] *City of Spades* attempts to emphasize, contextualize and contest these discourses of criminality and sexuality. The dominant cultural charge of excessive criminality amongst black immigrant cultures is foregrounded through the representation of the underworld activities of Billy Whispers and his followers. The emphasis throughout the text is on the sociological causes of the reliance on criminal activity amongst black subcultures, representing a survival strategy in response to an institutionally racist culture that limits the economic opportunities for black individuals. This position challenges the view that criminality is an intrinsic racial characteristic of immigrant lifestyle, as suggested in the Ambrose Drove article in *Absolute Beginners*. This is evidenced in the trajectory of Fortune's progress in the novel. He arrives in London as an optimistic and ambitious student but through his encounters with the racist attitudes of the 'landladies', employers and the police, he ultimately quits college and resorts to illicit gambling and selling 'weed' to make a living.

MacInnes also engages with the trope of miscegenation as identified by Gilroy. In *Absolute Beginners*, MacInnes records this fear of miscegenation in the Ambrose Drove article:

> To begin with, he [Ambrose Drove] said, mixed marriages – as responsible coloured persons would be the very first to agree themselves – were most undesirable. They led to a mongrel race, inferior physically and mentally, and rejected by both of the unadulterated communities. (194–5)

This cultural anxiety is represented in *City of Spades* through the various sexual relationships Johnny Fortune has with white women. This can be seen, for example, in the heterodiegetic passage discussed earlier where Fortune and his white lover Muriel take a boat trip on the Thames. The possibility of a 'mixed marriage' between the two characters is proposed, and the idyllic surroundings of this episode make this anticipated future a tangible possibility. The escape from

42   Ibid., p.79.

central London in this section thereby represents an escape from the dominant social and cultural mores that would make such marriage difficult. This escape, however, is only temporary as it becomes clear that the pleasure steamer is on a non-stop round trip jettisoning the couple back into the very social and cultural environment that would oppose their relationship:

> Muriel called out to the helmsman. 'Can't we get off?'
> 'Get off, miss? No, we don't stop.'
> 'But it said it was an excursion to Greenwich Palace.'
> 'This is the excursion, miss. We take you there and back, to see it, but you get off where you came from in the City.' (106)

This journey represents a tantalizing glimpse of the possibility of a non-racist future that is, nevertheless, prohibited for the two lovers in the present. The text goes on to describe how the pressures of society gradually and stealthily undermine the possibility of this 'mixed-race' relationship. This aspect of the novel represents a negotiation of the cultural anxieties of dominant white society through the perspective of a heterosexual 'mixed-race' couple. The narrative thus reflects these anxieties back towards the culture from which they are produced, 'denaturalizing' concerns of miscegenation prevalent in dominant cultural discourse. The text also challenges the dominant cultural stereotype of black individuals as sexually promiscuous by projecting sexual desire onto the white female characters of the text, in particular Theodora Pace, Dorothy and Muriel, and away from Fortune himself.

However, despite the attempts to redress the misconceptions and prejudices observed in dominant white culture towards marginalized immigrant cultures, the text also engages in a discourse of 're-orientalizing' black identity through the process of exoticizing and eroticizing black individuals, revealing an ambivalent attitude to constructions of a black 'other'.[43] In this sense, the text reinforces rather than challenges the Euro-centric cultural practice of projecting white exotic and erotic desire onto the imagined bodies of oriental and black indi-

43   I am referring, here, to Edward Said's theory of the orientalizing effects of much Western art and culture; see his *Orientalism: Western Conceptions of the Orient* (London: Penguin, 1991).

viduals. This process, although on the surface challenged by the novel, is re-inscribed through a double move it makes in relation to the representation of black identity. The description of the discrete subcultural world of the immigrants is exoticized in the text through the perspective of Montgomery Pew's exploration of the 'dangerous' spaces of this subculture. For example, Pew's decision to visit the 'Moorhen Public House, the Cosmopolitan dance hall, or the Moonbeam club' that represent the spaces of black subcultural existence, is initially prohibited by the governmental department's guidelines on 'Bad People and Places to Avoid' (11). Pew's visit to these prohibited spaces is, therefore, represented as a transgression from the homogeneous forces of dominant society into the heterogeneous world of London's black subcultures. This transgression is celebrated in the text, but the implication that black culture inherently represents transgression is maintained rather than challenged, reinforcing, rather than negating, the process of orientalizing black identity from the perspective of the white observer. Black subcultural practice is re-inscribed in the text as a representation of a white desire to engage in the exotic/erotic world of the black 'other'.

As with the representation of youth subcultures and national identity in *Absolute Beginners*, *City of Spades* represents a 'janus-faced' construction of black identity, which reveals both the anxieties and desires of fifties culture in relation to the construction of the racial other. MacInnes's text constitutes a double perspective of representation. On the one hand, it provides an attempt to record or 'speak' in the authentic voice of a 1950s London black subcultural identity, removing the 'silence' of this discourse both in dominant cultural discourse and in New Left writing. On the other hand, that representation is presented from the perspective of white cultural analysis, resulting in a paradoxical artificial construction of an 'authentic' black voice. Perhaps this is as far as MacInnes could go in terms of the representation of a culture that remains 'other' to the projected implied readership or interpretive community of the text, which would have been predominantly white. Despite its shortcomings, however, the text (and *Absolute Beginners*) represent a celebration of the possibility of an emergent form of national identity that is plural, multicultural and heterogeneous, rejecting univocal constructions of

260

Englishness based on past myths of English imperial greatness. It is to Sam Selvon that we must turn to discover a form of writing that further experiments with the difficulties of representing an authentic subcultural black voice in the context of the English novel.

Chapter Eight
Sam Selvon: *The Lonely Londoners*

Sam Selvon was one of a group of writers that moved to Britain from the Caribbean in the fifties. This group included George Lamming, V.S. Naipaul, Andrew Salkey, Derek Walcott and E.K. Brathwaite, and they began to make an impact on the London literary scene in the latter half of the decade, so much so that Francis Wyndham, in a 1958 review of Selvon's *Ways of Sunlight*, speculates on the emergence of a 'West Indian "school"'.[1] These writers represent a small sub-section of the large number of Caribbeans moving to Britain during the decade, but they are crucial in the articulation of that experience.[2] Selvon's novels and short stories in particular represent the experience of this diaspora. His first two novels, *A Brighter Sun* and *An Island is a World*, are set in Trinidad, Selvon's home country, while his later *The Lonely Londoners* and half of the short stories collected in *Ways of Sunlight* are set in fifties London. Despite Selvon's connection with this group of Caribbean writers, however, it is also important to stress his difference from them. His work is distinctive in its concern with the experiences of young, black, working-class males trying to establish economic and cultural security in 1950s London. This concern with working-class experience distinguishes his work from that of Naipaul, Walcott and Lamming. *The Lonely Londoners*, for example, is a novel that includes individual stories of several working-class black and Asian immigrants to Britain from the Caribbean. The two main characters are Moses Aloetto, who is considered a veteran, having been in London for nearly a decade, and Sir Galahad, who, as

---

1   Francis Wyndham, 'Ways of Sunlight', in *The Spectator*, 28 February 1958, p.273.
2   Margaret Byron has calculated that between 1951 and 1961 the Caribbean population residing in England rose from 17, 218 to 173, 659; Margaret Byron, *Post-War Caribbean Migration to Britain: The Unfinished Cycle* (Aldershot: Avebury, 1994), p.78.

the novel opens, has just arrived. In addition, the text weaves in the exploits of several other immigrants, which taken together presents the reader with a collective narrative of subcultural experience in fifties London.

Most of the criticism on Selvon to date has focused on his position as a Caribbean writer, but it is also important to read his work against the dominant trends and groups in 1950s British writing, such as the Movement, the Angry Young Men, the New Left, and the debates around the relationship between specific literary forms and the ideological assumptions those forms carried with them.[3] Selvon's work intersects with contemporary debates in the fifties novel concerning authenticity, representation of marginalized subcultures, commitment in the novel in relation to the literary modes of realism and modernism, and specific sub-genres of the novel such as the 'documentary' novel. As Mark Looker has stressed, it is important to read Selvon contextually, 'from the perspective of post-war British fiction in general'.[4] It is necessary, therefore, to identify the way in which his fiction engages with these contexts, and how they produce an implicit commentary on them from a 'postcolonial' position. Most of the critical work on *The Lonely Londoners* has focused on his 'experiment' with narrative technique and language from a Caribbean perspective. Much of the criticism interprets Selvon's fiction in terms of its relationship to realist modes of writing, and Selvon's experimentation within a realist tradition, which has been exported and reformulated through the geographical distancing of the (post)colonial experience of Caribbean culture and identity. Too often, though, terms such as realism, modernism, authenticity and commitment have been applied to Selvon's work without specific reference to the contextual and ideological signification attached to these concepts in 1950s cultural debate. As we saw in chapter two above, the understanding of a writer's work in relation to the concepts of realism and experimentalism was shot through with ideological significance during the

---

3   See the discussion of these issues in the first part of this book above.
4   Mark Looker, *Atlantic Passages: History, Fiction and Language in the Fiction of Sam Selvon* (New York: Peter Lang, 1996), p.19.

period, and an awareness of this helps to open up Selvon's novels to their historical and literary contexts.

In this chapter, I contextualize Selvon's fiction, not only in terms of a postcolonial writing, but also in relation to dominant trends in the British writing of the period. This is particularly relevant given the fact that Selvon (as did many of the Caribbean writers of the period) felt his work could only be legitimized if it was presented through the colonial and cultural 'centre' of London's literary institutions. Most of his fifties fiction was first published in London, and many writers identify the importance of the BBC's radio series, *Caribbean Voices*, to provide a platform for Caribbean writing during the period.[5] Within this cultural framework, howebver, his writing represents an engagement with dominant literary practice in the West. As we shall see, Selvon's understanding of his literary project negotiates models of postcolonial writing that, on the one hand, produce a culturally specific 'resistance' literature, whilst on the other, claims a right to be judged against, and ultimately incorporated into, the universalizing discourses of literary value imposed by the dominant institutions of literature in the West.

I discuss three main aspects of Selvon's fiction, each of which is connected. Firstly, I relate *The Lonely Londoners* to the 1950s literary and cultural debates concerning the relationship between realism and experimentalism. Secondly, I discuss the way Selvon uses narrative and linguistic techniques that represent the marginalized otherness of the immigrant experience in a postcolonial context. This section will focus, in particular, on the attempt by Selvon to produce a written expression of a traditional oral form: the Caribbean calypso, and how this strategy challenges the cultural and ideological assumptions attached to the English realist novel. Thirdly, I explore some of the problematics of representation that Selvon's writing produces: problematics that are themselves indicative of cultural assumptions about the representation of subcultural identity in a racial context. In this section, I also explore the relationships between Selvon's articulation

5   See Looker, *Atlantic Passages*, p.7. Looker identifies the irony of the power of the BBC to 'legitimize' these marginalized voices, not only for a British (and international) audience, but also in the Caribbean.

of the experiences of black working-class males in London in the 1950s and other marginalized groups in terms of class and gender.

Informing the whole chapter is the argument that Selvon's fiction constructs two distinct groups of 'addressee'. Following Steven Connor's model of the addressivity of literary texts[6], I argue that Selvon's novel projects a dual model of anticipated readership: firstly, the Caribbean subcultural groups establishing a distinct black British identity in the late 1950s; and secondly, a mainstream white audience that receives the text as a kind of reportage novel, recording an essentially alien experience through the articulation of otherness.[7] As Selvon has commented concerning *The Lonely Londoners*: 'I wrote a modified dialect which could be understood by European readers, yet retain the flavour and essence of Trinidadian speech.'[8] This geographical and cultural opposition lies at the heart of understanding Selvon's fiction, and offers a way of interpreting the various experimental narrative, and linguistic, techniques he deploys. As with the fiction of Sillitoe and MacInnes, Selvon's texts are constructed in such a way as to offer a dual function in terms of representation. It is because of this dual model of addressivity that some of the problematics and ambivalences of the text's representations are produced.

Although we need to be wary, as Kenneth Ramchand has pointed out, of applying Western critical models to Selvon's work, it is fruitful to discuss *The Lonely Londoners* in relation to several Western theorists. In particular, Selvon's narratives produce resonances with concepts and models developed by Mikhail Bakhtin, Gilles Deleuze and Félix Guattari, and Walter Benjamin, as well as postcolonial approaches to narrative theory by Bill Ashcroft, Gareth Griffiths, Helen Tiffin and Homi Bhabha. In this chapter, therefore, I explore the connections between these theorists and Selvon's fiction. In particular,

6   Steven Connor, *The English Novel in History 1950–1995* (London and New York: Routledge, 1996), pp.8–13.

7   Connor makes reference to Emmanuel Levinas's concept of the 'vocativity' of discourse by which the 'opening towards the Other [...] is at work in all language', ibid., p.9.

8   Michel Fabre, 'Samuel Selvon: Interviews and Conversations', in *Critical Perspectives on Sam Selvon*, ed. by Susheila Nasta (Washington D.C.: Three Continents Press, 1988), pp.64–76, (p.66).

I discuss Benjamin's definition of 'oral' narrative and the role of the storyteller in relation to Selvon's utilization of 'calypsonian' techniques; the connection between Deleuze and Guattari's concept of 'deterritorialization' in relation to the 'minor literature' that Selvon produces; and in relation to Bakhtin, the multiple or 'heteroglossic' voices that Selvon deploys in his fiction. I will also discuss the way in which Selvon's fiction exemplifies a negotiation of realism in the novel, a characteristic that engages with Homi Bhabha's identification of the mode as a culturally specific, Westernized literary form. In addition, I discuss the ways in which Selvon's experimentation with language represents many of the definitions of postcolonial literatures as produced by Ashcroft, Griffiths and Tiffin.

Selvon in Context:
Realism, Modernism and the Caribbean Novel

As discussed in chapter two above, one of the main debates in the novel in the 1950s was the oppositional relationship between the literary modes of realism and modernism (the latter often being defined as 'experimentalism' in the fifties). This opposition was expressed in terms of both method and implied ideological assumptions.[9] In interview with Michel Fabre, Selvon has commented on his approach in *The Lonely Londoners* in terms of both realism and experimentalism. When asked about his use of dialect in the novel, he replies: 'I just attempted to write the way people spoke and to render their language out of a desire for verisimilitude, or realism'. However, he goes on to suggest that this process was 'an experimental attempt'.[10] Somewhat paradoxically then, Selvon's articulation of 'authentic' Caribbean speech as a realist project represented a form of experimentalism in the context of the mainstream British novel. This

9   See the discussion of the debate on the aesthetic and ideological characteristics of specific literary forms in the fifties in chapter two above.
10   Fabre, 'Samuel Selvon: Interviews and Conversations', pp.65–6.

paradox, however, is produced by the shortcomings in the oppositional model rather than as a failing on Selvon's part. In fact, his texts
disrupt the opposition between realism and experimentalism dominant
in the fifties.

Realist modes carried with them a series of ideological assumptions in the 1950s related to two distinct discourses: one broadly
political, and one in terms of national identity. The realist novel was
understood by Georg Lukàcs, for example, to be a mode that was
conducive to a politically committed literature that intended to awaken
readers to specific political inconsistencies, or to critique specific
abuses of power in the contemporary culture.[11] There was a parallel
discourse being produced at the time, especially amongst novelists
connected to the Movement, that realism, as a mode, represented a
traditional English form, as distinct from the 'foreigness' of modernism.[12] Selvon is particularly interesting because his novels engage
with both these contemporary understandings of the ideological function of the realist mode. His engagement with 'realism' reveals a
writer who is questioning those assumptions both in a political sense,
and in terms of the correspondence of particular literary modes and
the construction of an (English) national identity. His texts, therefore,
represent radical articulations of the inconsistencies within the appropriation of the realist form to the construction of a discourse of
national identity. Selvon reclaims the realist tradition from a discourse
of the nation and re-focuses it through a postcolonial perspective. In
doing so, however, he problematizes the definition of realism itself.

This can be further identified in the way in which *The Lonely
Londoners* appears to combine realism with techniques traditionally
associated with modernism. In interview, Selvon has described his
narrative technique in terms usually associated with modernism:

> I think I can say without a trace of modesty that I was the first Caribbean writer
> to explore and employ dialect in a full-length novel where it was used in both

11 Georg Lukàcs, *The Meaning of Contemporary Realism*, trans. by John and
    Necke Mander (London: Merlin Press, 1963), first published 1957. See the
    discussion of Lukàcs and the ideology of realism in chapter two above.
12 Anthony Easthope, *Englishness and National Culture* (London and New York:
    Routledge, 1999), pp.87–114.

narrative and dialogue. I was boldfaced enough to write a complete chapter in a stream-of-consciousness style.[13]

The use of stream of consciousness in a fifties novel would be interpreted as a modernist technique, and therefore would produce associations with certain ideological assumptions about the kind of readership the novel anticipated. William Cooper, for example, defined experimental writing as an attack 'on intellect in general, made by intellectuals so decadent that they no longer mind if intellect persists'.[14] According to Cooper, 'experimental' writing, by which he also means modernism, anticipates a range of addressee that excludes the working class and other marginalized groups, projecting towards a particular socio-cultural group characterized by educational privileges.

However, Selvon's use of stream of consciousness is used to articulate, without irony, the thoughts of a black, working-class character. The technique, therefore, would seem to reject the association of modernism to a specific readership educated within a white, middle-class, Western culture. In fact, the stream of consciousness section functions to emphasize the construction by dominant white culture of black identity reflected back through the consciousness of the alienated black individual. This is written through stereotypical and culturally produced images of black sexuality:

> the cruder you are the more the girls like you you can't put on any English accent for them or play ladeda or tell them you studying medicine in Oxford or try to be polite and civilise they don't want that sort of thing at all they want you to live up to the films and stories they hear about black people living primitive in the jungles of the world.[15]

The lack of punctuation and the flow of language representing the immediacy of thought are standard stream of consciousness tech-

---

13   Sam Selvon, 'A Note on Dialect', in Nasta, *Critical Perspectives on Sam Selvon*, p.69.
14   William Cooper, 'Reflections on Some Aspects of the Experimental Novel', in *International Literary Review*, No.2, ed. by John Wain (London: John Calder, 1959), pp.29–36, (p.36). I also refer to this quotation on page 58 above.
15   Sam Selvon, *The Lonely Londoners* (Harlow, Essex: Longman, 1985), first published 1956, p.108.

niques.[16] The use of these techniques in Selvon, however, articulates the alienation felt by the black immigrant in the alien environment of London in the 1950s.[17] The use of 'modernist' techniques supports the progressive content of the novel and, therefore, undermines the argument that these techniques are restricted to the articulation of middle and upper-middle-class experience, reclaiming the form for a marginalized subcultural group. The text also disrupts the claim that modernism represents an inherently isolationary and individualistic discourse as defined by Lukàcs.[18] In fact, as Clement H. Wyke argues, the use of stream of consciousness style by Selvon represents a liberating and ultimately empowering technique for the representation of black identity.[19]

In the context of the 1950s, the combination of narrative techniques (such as representations of identifiable characters and locales, the deployment of non-linear or episodic narrative structures, and the use of free indirect discourse) that correspond to contemporary definitions of both realism and modernism appear to be contradictory, but it is within this opposition that the radical nature of Selvon's fifties writing lies. In effect, Selvon produces a form that incorporates elements of both realism and modernism to produce a politically engaged writing. *The Lonely Londoners*, therefore, is an example of what Andrzej Gasiorek identifies as a type of postwar British novel that problematizes the oppositional discourse between the modes of real-

---

16 Abrams defines 'stream of consciousness' as: 'a special mode of narration that undertakes to reproduce, without a narrator's intervention, the full spectrum and the continuous flow of a character's mental process, in which sense perceptions mingle with conscious and half-conscious thoughts, memories, expectations, feelings, and random associations', M.H. Abrams, *A Glossary of Literary Terms*, 6th edition (Fort Worth: Harcourt Brace College Publishers, 1993), p.202.

17 This articulation of the sense of alienation experienced through modernist form corresponds to Raymond Williams's reading of modernist technique in 'The Metropolis and the Emergence of Modernism' in *Modernism/Postmodernism*, ed. by Peter Brooker (London: Longman, 1992), pp.82–94.

18 Lukàcs, *The Meaning of Contemporary Realism*.

19 Clement H. Wyke, *Sam Selvon's Dialectical Style and Fictional Strategy* (Vancouver: University of British Columbia Press, 1991), p.47.

ism and experimentalism.[20] Selvon's position as an outsider from mainstream formal/ideological conventions thereby allows him to produce a writing that disrupts those conventions. This disruption is produced in two distinct ways: firstly, in Selvon's experimental and engaged manipulation of language, and secondly, the strategies he deploys in terms of the narrative structure of the text. In the following sections, I discuss these two distinctions.

'As the Ballad Goes On': Writing the Caribbean Calypso[21]

One of the methods by which a diasporic culture articulates its position of otherness in a dominant culture is through a celebration of its popular forms. This is often problematized, however, by the appropriation and repackaging of those forms by the dominant culture. As Imruh Bakari argues, referring to the importation of black music styles to Britain:

> Fuelled by iconoclastic narratives of sexual exploits and drug usage, Black music [...] was established in the popular consciousness with a certain attractive deviancy. Yet for [...] Black people [...] the perspective on this music and its associated behaviour was much more sophisticated than the stereotyped image implied.[22]

In the 1950s, both these processes can be identified in relation to the Caribbean calypso. The calypso is a popular oral form, developed especially in Selvon's own Caribbean region of Trinidad and Tobago, which expresses the preoccupations, anxieties and subjugation of a

20   Andrzej Gasiorek, *Post-War British Fiction: Realism and After* (London: Edward Arnold, 1995).
21   Sam Selvon, *Ways of Sunlight* (London and New York: Longman, 1987) first published in 1957, p.139.
22   Imruh Bakari, 'Exploding Silence: African-Caribbean and African-American Music in British Culture Towards 2000', in *Living Through Pop*, ed. by Andrew Blake (London and New York: Routledge, 1999), pp.98–111, (p.100).

colonized people.[23] Its essential modes are popular lyrical expression, comedy and satire. As Peter Manuel defines them: 'calypso texts, as expressions of popular sentiment, often acquire the nature of important political statements to be discussed in Parliament and the news media'.[24] In the 1950s, the calypso form was exported to Britain with the Caribbean diaspora, and through the dominant cultural institution of the BBC gained air play (although with a politically watered-down version of the form), resulting in the success in the British pop market of artists such as Harry Belafonte.[25] This phenomenon provided British culture with an expression of a cultural 'otherness' that identified a colonial connection, but articulated that 'otherness' in a form palatable for a mainstream white audience. It represented another expression of a desire for an 'authentic' popular art form, which, as we have seen, was a preoccupation of fifties culture.[26] However, in relation to the black Caribbeans beginning to settle in Britain during the period, the calypso offered an ambivalent form of cultural expression. In one sense, it defined black culture for both black and white audiences, but

23   See Gordon Rohlehr's discussion of the importance of the calypso in Caribbean culture in his 'Images of Men and Women in the 1930s Calypsos', in *Gender in Caribbean Development*, ed. by P.Mohammed and C. Shepard (St. Augustine, Trinidad: University of the West Indies, 1988).

24   Peter Manuel, *Popular Musics of the Non-Western World* (New York and Oxford: Oxford University Press, 1988), p.80.

25   Colin MacInnes makes reference to the unusual popularity of the 'coloured' pop artist Belafonte in a 1958 article for *The Twentieth Century*, where he describes Belafonte's interpretation of the calypso as a 'sentimental rendition of West Indian calypso'; Colin MacInnes, 'Pop Songs and Teenagers', in *England, Half English* (London: Chatto and Windus, 1993), pp.45–59, (p.53).

26   This was identified primarily in terms of British (white/male) working-class culture in the work of Hoggart, Williams and fictionally in Sillitoe's work. It is also significant in the identification of an authentic teenage voice in MacInnes. Selvon's text can therefore be identified as part of a series of radical novels in the fifties which attempt to represent an 'authentic' voice, and to construct a collective identity for a particular marginalized subculture or ethnic group. Other examples from the period in relation to issues of 'race' include George Lamming's *In the Castle of My Skin* (London: Joseph, 1953) and *The Emigrants* (London: Joseph, 1959); Andrew Salkey's *A Quality of Violence* (London: Hutchinson, 1959); and Chinua Achebe's *Things Fall Apart* (London: Heineman, 1958).

the sanitized version of calypso broadcast by the BBC problematized the construction of an autonomous black Caribbean identity for the immigrants.

It is in this cultural context that Selvon's novel is produced, and many critics have identified parallels between Selvon's writing and the form and subject matter of the traditional Caribbean calypso.[27] Kenneth Ramchand has described *The Lonely Londoners*, citing the importance of the calypso form, as a novel that is 'an admirable illustration of how writing can feed on oral literature and on the stuff that oral literature itself draws upon without losing its identity as writing'.[28] This linkage is significant in relation to four characteristics of narrative technique in *The Lonely Londoners*. First, the novel's attempt to reconstitute an oral tradition in a form recognizable to English literary culture. Second, the episodic structure of the novel corresponds to the calypso's use of disconnected narratives. Third, the calypso is characterized by its use of comic situations, exaggerated events, picaresque characters and carnival sensibilities and excesses, all of which are features of Selvon's novel. Lastly, the calypso, through its use of satirical comment, produces a politically engaged form that challenges dominant political and cultural codes and practices, again, a parallel concern in *The Lonely Londoners*. In addition, the distinctive role of the calypso singer is reproduced in Selvon's novel through his experimental use of an idiosyncratic extradiegetic narrative voice.

Walter Benjamin, for one, has stressed the importance of oral narratives in the expression of proletarian identity and culture. In 'The Storyteller' he discusses the process by which the Western, bourgeois novel form gradually displaced older forms of oral narrative that were grounded in artisan culture. He identifies the oral tradition as the terri-

27 See for example Nasta, *Critical Perspectives on Sam Selvon*, p.10; Michel Fabre, 'From Trinidad to London: Tone and Language in Samuel Selvon's Novels', in Nasta, *Critical Perspectives on Sam Selvon*, pp.213–22; Wyke, *Sam Selvon's Dialectical Style*, p.49; Jane Grant, 'Introduction', in Selvon, *Ways of Sunlight*, p.xii; John Thieme, '"The World Turned Upside Down": Carnival Patterns in "The Lonely Londoners"', *The Toronto South Asian Review*, 1986, Vol. 5, Summer, pp.191–204.
28 Kenneth Ramchand, 'Introduction', in Selvon, *The Lonely Londoners*, p.10.

tory of the 'resident tiller of the soil, and the [...] trading seaman'. This tradition he distinguishes from the novel, which he defines as an essentially middle-class form centred on the 'solitary individual'.[29] These distinctions correspond to Selvon's work in that they represent an attempt to integrate the novel form with an oral tradition.[30] In that sense, *The Lonely Londoners*, as John Thieme notes, 'subvert[s] the norms of the novel genre', and this is achieved through the disruption of the conventional novel's representation of individualized middle-class experience through an articulation of the collective experience of black working-class life.[31] Benjamin, of course, is primarily concerned with European literature, but in relation to Selvon's novel, the representation of 'word of mouth' narratives corresponds to the culturally specific form of the Caribbean calypso. In effect, the figure of the black exile in fifties London corresponds partly to both of Benjamin's definitions: the 'peasant' working-class individual and the exiled 'sailor', both of whom are figures who rely on oral narratives to communicate their experiences, and thereby articulate their individual and collective identities. It is also significant in this context that George Lamming refers to Selvon as a 'peasant' writer, one who is concerned to represent the life of the 'peasant' in fictional form.[32]

In Selvon's novel, however, the oral narratives describe figures who are displaced in the metropolitan centre of 1950s London. Selvon's writing represents a negotiation of Benjamin's narrative paradigms: the 'peasant' narrator, in that his narratives are located in the working class; and the 'sailor', who records stories of distant

29   Walter Benjamin, 'The Storyteller: Reflections on the Works of Nikolai Leskov', in *Illuminations*, ed. by Hannah Arendt, trans. by Harry Zohn (London: Fontana, 1992) p.84, and p.87.

30   Given Selvon's essentially middle-class background, Lamming is identifying a tendency in the novels rather than specifying Selvon's identity. See George Lamming, *The Pleasures of Exile* (London: Michael Joseph, 1960), p.45.

31   John Thieme, 'Rama in Exile: The Indian Writer Overseas', in *The Eye of the Beholder: Indian Writing in English*, ed. by Maggie Butcher (London: Commonwealth Institute, 1983), p.72.

32   Lamming, *The Pleasures of Exile*, pp.38–9. See also F. Gordon Rohlehr's discussion of Lamming's comments on Selvon in 'The Folk in Caribbean Literature', in Nasta, *Critical Perspectives on Sam Selvon*, pp.29–43.

places and the experience of nomadic existence. In addition, Selvon's narrative articulates the oral narratives of 'solitary individuals', whilst also attempting to produce a collective narration through the presentation of disparate and anecdotal stories of the Caribbean emigrant. The writing of these narratives thereby becomes its own legitimizing process. The inscription of the 'other' is established through the negotiation of difference from, and similarity to, preconceived constructions of black identity formed by dominant white culture.

The Lonely Londoners presents the reader with a number of larger than life characters and their stories – comic descriptions of their experiences as alienated exiles in the metropolitan centre. Much of the humour is produced through the encounter between a romantic and naive Caribbean sensibility and the harsh realities of life in London. However, these comic narratives have a serious function in foregrounding the alienated lifestyle of the emigrants they describe, chronicling their encounters with prejudice, racism and the dominant constructions of black identity by mainstream white culture. The following passage, for example, describes one of the central characters, Galahad, and his address to the colour 'Black' as an abstract entity:

> So Galahad talking to the colour Black, as if is a person, telling it that is not *he* who causing botheration in the place, but Black, who is a worthless thing for making trouble all about. 'Black, you see what you cause to happen yesterday? I went to look at that room that Ram tell me about in the Gate, and as soon as the landlady see you she say the room let already. She ain't even give me a chance to say good morning. Why the hell can't you change colour?'. (88-89)

This passage serves to emphasize issues of black identity and its construction by dominant white culture. It dramatizes the exiled immigrant's gradual awareness of his constructed image. Galahad, by projecting 'blackness' as an external category, highlights the artificiality of the construction of racial identity by foregrounding the colour as something external to the consciousness of the 'black' individual.

Galahad, in this sense, only recognizes his black identity as it is projected onto him from a white perspective.[33]

The Lonely Londoners presents the reader with fragmented narratives of individuals such as Galahad as an expression of individual experience. Many critics have identified the episodic nature of the novel, and the deployment of this narrative technique has a dual function in the novel.[34] First, it represents the experience of alienation as fragmented expression, incorporated into the structure of the text. Second, it produces, through the accumulation of these disparate narratives, a collective narration of minority representation, what Deleuze and Guattari call a 'collective assemblage of enunciation'.[35] This technique, therefore, serves to empower black identity through a process of accumulation by which individual experiences contribute to the expression of the communal experience of exile, focused on the central themes of alienation, racial prejudice and survival.

However, as Ramchand has argued, despite the episodic form there is a clear progression in terms of the trajectory of the narrative.[36] Ramchand identifies this in terms of the development of the central characters Moses and Galahad as they move through the text. He discusses the last section of the novel in particular as a point to which

33   Galahad's conception of racial politics is 'innocent' here, but this innocence does not necessarily equate to a naiveté. Rather, as Stefano Harney argues: 'Selvon is confident of Caribbean innocence, itself a kind of superiority'; Stefano Harney, 'Samuel Selvon and the Chronopolitics of a Diasporic Nationalism', in *Nationalism and Identity: Culture and the Imagination in a Caribbean Diaspora*, (London and New Jersey: Zed Books, 1996), p.107.

34   See Fabre, 'Samuel Selvon: Interviews and Conversations', p.66; Kenneth Ramchand, 'Song of Innocence, Song of Experience: Samuel Selvon's *The Lonely Londoners* as a Literary Work', in Nasta, *Critical Perspectives on Sam Selvon*, 1988, pp.223–33, (p.227); Wyke, *Sam Selvon's Dialectical Style*, p.34.

35   Deleuze and Guattari, in their book on Kafka, identify the creation of a 'minor' literature produced by writers from a marginalized social group living within a dominant culture. This literature tends to develop a voice that represents a collective expression of marginalized communal identity. Gilles Deleuze, and Felix Guattari, *Kafka: Toward a Minor Literature*, trans. by Dana Polan (Minneapolis: University of Minnesota Press, 1986), p.18. See the further discussion of this below.

36   Kenneth Ramchand, 'Introduction', p.13.

it has been moving in terms of Moses's greater understanding of his exiled position. The novel, therefore, negotiates a linear *and* episodic narrative structure to produce a hybrid form that reveals its connection both to Western modes of realism in the novel and to the Caribbean oral tradition. Formally, *The Lonely Londoners* represents a radical style that negotiates different modes and traditions of writing: realistic, modernist/experimental and oral. This hybrid form is again related to the double sense of addressee the text projects and indicates Selvon's awareness of the need for a complex narrative style to articulate the specific concerns of a postcolonial literature.

This can be exemplified in Selvon's experiment with linguistic styles. He has described his decision to use a form of Creolized expression in the extradiegetic third-person narrative as a crucial and liberating stage in the writing of *The Lonely Londoners*:

> when I started to work on my novel *The Lonely Londoners* I had this great problem with it that I began to write it in Standard English and it would just not move along [...] It occurred to me that perhaps I should try to do both the narrative and the dialogue in this form [Trinidadian form of the language ...] I started to experiment with it and the book just went very rapidly along [...] With this particular book I just felt that the language that I used worked and expressed exactly what I wanted it to express.[37]

Here, Selvon relates the liberating effect of his decision to write the extradiegetic narrative voice in the same Creolized style used by the central characters of the novel. This marks a 'release' from Standard English as a technique incorporated into the narrative, as well as linguistic, structure of the text. The removal of distance between the omniscient narrative voice and the characters it describes, or, in Catherine Belsey's terms, the rejection of a 'hierarchy of discourses', represents an empowering expression of collective identity that rejects the positioning of authority produced by having the narrator speak in Standard English whilst the characters use dialect.[38]

---

37 Peter Nazareth, 'Interview with Sam Selvon', in *World Literature Written in English*, Vol. 18, 1979, pp.420–37, (p.421).
38 Catherine Belsey, *Critical Practice* (London and New York: Routledge, 1980), pp.70–2.

This aspect of Selvon's experiment with language establishes his position as a postcolonial writer. As Ashcroft, Griffiths and Tiffin have argued, language is one of the key sites in which postcolonial writers express their cultural distance from the literature of the colonizing power. Manipulation of linguistic forms is an important means by which Caribbean writers proclaim their sense of place (and displacement), and construct a distinct identity in terms of difference to a dominant construction of Englishness. In literary texts, this is often negotiated through a manipulation of, and experimentation with, Standard English: 'The crucial function of language as a medium of power demands that postcolonial writing define itself by seizing the language of the centre and re-placing it in a discourse fully adapted to the colonized place.'[39] The style adopted for the extradiegetic[40] voice in *The Lonely Londoners* represents this apsect of the postcolonial manipulation of language:

> And this sort of thing was happening at a time when the English people starting to make rab about how too much West Indians coming to the country: this was a time, when any corner you turn, is ten to one you bound to bounce up a spade. (24)

In terms of representing immigrant identity, the use of elision, West Indian slang words (such as 'rab'), and the manipulation of Standard English syntax ('people starting to make'; 'bounce up a spade') provide an 'authentic' flavour to the narration. The use of non-Standard English also serves to disrupt the linguistic authority of the colonial centre through the importation of alternative forms of syntax and vocabulary. This replicates, in a linguistic form, the radical presence of the (post)colonized individual in the (old) colonial centre.

This strategic manipulation of Standard English corresponds to the function of heteroglossia as suggested by Mikhail Bakhtin, in

39 Bill Ashcroft, Gareth Griffiths and Helen Tiffin, *The Empire Writes Back: Theory and practice in Post-Colonial Literatures* (London and New York: Routledge, 1989), p.38. (Henceforward referred to as Ashcroft et al.).

40 I am again referring to the typology of narrative levels as identified in Gerard Genette, 'Voice', in *Narrative Discourse*, trans. by Jane E. Lewin (Oxford: Basil Blackwell, 1980), pp.212–68.

which 'centripetal' and 'centrifugal' forces work simultaneously in the use of language in practice. Bakhtin argues that while there is a constant pressure exerted by the dominant culture to standardize language into a structured framework, there is, simultaneously, a reverse impulse, a 'centripetal' force that counters the homogenizing process by subverting and rejecting standardized usage. For Bakhtin, the novel is a site in which this contest is fought out:

> Heteroglossia, as organized in these low genres, was not merely heteroglossia vis-à-vis the accepted literary language [...] that is, vis-à-vis the linguistic center of verbal-ideological life of the nation and the epoch, but was a heteroglossia consciously opposed to this literary language.[41]

In *The Lonely Londoners*, the use of Creolized speech represents a heteroglossia opposed to the 'linguistic center of verbal-ideological life of the nation', in this case, Standard English. The use of this kind of utterance, therefore, carries within it the negotiation of a connection with, and distance from, the language of the centre, and subsequently acts as an expression of opposition to the cultural and ideological frameworks of that central culture. As Cliff Lashley argues, in a Jamaican context, this manipulation of language represents a political comment that implicitly challenges the dominant system of cultural assumptions, and the power relationships between the colonizer and the colonized.[42]

Another linguistic technique used by Selvon is the incorporation of Creole slang words within the 'English' of the text. This strategy again foregrounds the distance between two cultures. The use of untranslated words without gloss or explanation provided by the author represents an image of cultural distance, and, as Ashcroft et al. argue,

---

41   M.M. Bakhtin, *The Dialogic Imagination*, ed. by Michael Holquist, trans. by Caryl Emerson and Michael Holquist (Austin: University of Texas Press, 1981), pp.272–3.

42   Cliff Lashley, 'Towards a Critical Framework for Jamaican Literature: A Reading of the Fiction of Victor Stafford Reid and Other Jamaican Writers', PhD Dissertation (St. Augustine, Trinidad,: University of the West Indies, 1984) See the discussion of Lashley's argument in Ashcroft et al., 1989, p.48.

represents the gap and silence between the colonizing and the post-colonial cultures:

> untranslated words [...] have an important function in inscribing difference [...] they are directly metonymic of that cultural difference which is imputed by the linguistic variation [...] It is the 'absence' which occupies the gap between the contiguous inter/faces of the 'official' language of the text and the cultural difference brought to it. Thus the alterity in that metonymic juncture establishes a silence beyond which the cultural Otherness of the text cannot be traversed by the colonial language.[43]

In Selvon's case, the use of untranslated words metonymically represents the displacement experienced by the characters of the text, and the unwritten colonial history that conditions the presence of these black immigrants in London at this specific historical juncture. The distance, therefore, between the 'English' of Moses, Galahad and the other characters in *The Lonely Londoners* linguistically represents the history of colonialism at the same time as it proclaims a distinct sub-cultural identity. The subversion of the language is emblematic of a wider subversion of cultural domination by the colonizing power over the colonized subject.

This use of Creolized expression by the extradiegetic narrator has led many critics to suggest that Moses is in fact the unnamed narrator of the novel. This argument is based on the last few paragraphs of the book, in which there appears to be a self-reflexive reference to the possibility of Moses writing a book such as *The Lonely Londoners*:

> Daniel was telling him [Moses] how over in France all kinds of fellars writing books what turning out to be best-sellers. Taxi-driver, porter, road-sweeper – it didn't matter [...] He watched the tugboat on the Thames wondering if he could ever write a book like that, what everybody would buy. (141)

This passage suggests that Moses has in fact realized his ambitions and the novel we are reading is his own composition. This logically explains the narrator's use of Creolized language as consistent with

---

43   Ashcroft et al., *The Empire Writes Back*, pp.53–4.

Moses's own style of language. Mark Looker, for example, suggests that:

> Moses's quest is finally to write his own narrative, and his narrative is infinitely bound up with the invention of Black London [...] In fact by the end of the novel Moses has become the narrator of his own life and that of his people.[44]

Looker is right to suggest that *The Lonely Londoners* is involved in the creation of a 'Black London', but his insistence on foregrounding Moses as the creative force behind this construction seems to reveal a specifically Western desire for the marking of individual authorship.furthermore, this argument tends to assume that the novel as a form is superior to the oral narratives of Caribbean aesthetic expression. I would prefer to suggest that the novel constructs a form of collective narration by re-introducing what Roland Barthes posits as a 'shamanistic' function of oral narratives, one which was displaced by the emergence of the bourgeois realist novel, and its insistence on individual authorship.[45] The extradiegetic narrative voice, therefore, is not representative of an individual character but of a collective expression for this particular subculture. This corresponds to Deleuze and Guattari's model of the process of constructing a 'minor literature' from a marginalized geographical and cultural position within a dominant language system.[46] In particular, they identify this process at work in Kafka's writing, which reveals his cultural position as a Jewish Czech writing in German. They write:

> A minor literature doesn't come from a minor language; it is rather that which a minority constructs within a major language [...] The three characteristics of minor literature are the deterritorialization of language, the connection of the individual to a political immediacy, and the collective assemblage of enunciation. (16–18)

44   Looker, *Atlantic Passages*, p.79.
45   This point is made by Roland Barthes in 'The Death of the Author', in *Image, Music, Text*, trans. by Stephen Heath (London: Fontana, 1977), pp.142–8.
46   Deleuze, *Kafka*, pp.16–27.

The process of 'deterritorialization' (and 'reterritorialization') can be identified in Selvon's writing as a marginalized black Caribbean writing in English, and resident in the colonial centre.[47] The process of creating a minority literature or collective narration is therefore a process of political empowerment through the creation of representative and identity-forming narratives that simultaneously reject the cultural centrality of Englishness and proclaim the validity of marginalized voices within the privileged site of the novel form. As Rohlehr writes: 'In *The Lonely Londoners* it is the group that has a full self, that faces the wilderness and survives; not to belong is to be lost in the void.'[48] This is represented structurally through the accumulation of different stories recording the experiences of several exiled Caribbean individuals in fifties London, such as Moses, Sir Galahad, Tolroy, Big City, the Cap and Bart. The collection of these individual stories ultimately combines to produce a collective subcultural 'enunciation'.

Another element of Selvon's text that links to the thematic connection with the calypso form is the use of comedy. This appears at the level of both character construction and the reported events of the novel. In interview, Selvon has stressed the importance of comedy as a political strategy of empowerment, and as a means by which to access serious problems within the black experience: 'The comedy element has always been there among black people from the Caribbean. It is their means of defence against the sufferings and tribulations that they have to undergo.'[49] The reliance on the comic situation, therefore, becomes a strategy for survival for the marginalized group. Selvon's strategic use of comedy resonates with Bakhtin's concept of the Carnival in literature, by which a politically marginalized and disempowered group can strategically deploy comic and exaggerated situations and forms to challenge the authority of domin-

---

47   Looker identifies the connection between Selvon's fifties writing and Deleuze and Guattari's concept of deterritorialization but does not go on to identify this as an example of a 'collective' element of a 'minor literature'; Looker, *Atlantic Passages*, p.74.

48   Rohlehr, 'The Folk in Caribbean Literature', p.41.

49   Nazareth, 'Interview with Sam Selvon', p.424.

ant power structures.[50] Selvon manipulates the comic encounters of the alienated black characters, out of their depth in the colonial centre, to foreground the painful alienation of the exile. As Mark Looker argues, the 'evaporation of satire' in Selvon ultimately leads the reader to associate with, rather than mock, the comic situations in which the black exiles find themselves.[51] The comedy tends toward the absurd: the absurdity of the racial prejudice experienced by displacement of the black settlers in their alien environment, and of the encounter with dominant white culture.

As we have seen, the political aspects of Selvon's work is articulated through the written expression of the calypso form. However, the politics of representation in Selvon's texts are problematic in terms of the representation of black identity and it is with this issue that the next section will deal.

Black London:
The Ideology of Representation in *The Lonely Londoners*

Mark Looker's chapter on *The Lonely Londoners*, entitled 'Inventing Black London', suggests that Selvon was the first black writer to construct a representation of the experiences and lives of black immigrants in London in the 1950s. This process necessarily involves, as Looker argues, an element of experimental inventiveness in terms of the construction of a specific subcultural identity, and he is right to focus upon the importance of Selvon's position as probably the first

---

50 Mikhail M. Bakhtin, *Rabelais and His World*, trans. by Helene Iswolsky (Cambridge MA: The MIT Press, 1968). Significant here is the Carnival tradition developed in Trinidad in the nineteenth and twentieth centuries. One of the predominant forms in Carnival is the calypso, and this connection supplies Selvon with a thematic structure for his text. See Manuel, *Popular Musics of the Non-Western World* for a discussion of the importance of Carnival in Trinidad.
51 Looker, *Atlantic Passages*, pp.77–8.

novelist to record the experiences of this particular subcultural group. However, this process inevitably involves the negotiation of pre-conceived images of black identity and practices that reproduce, rather than challenge, many of the stereotypes present in mainstream white culture. Therefore, the process of description, recording and empowering black identity becomes problematic in terms of the selected elements of black cultural practice Selvon chooses to foreground.

The novel engages directly with the construction of black identity as formed through the perspective of dominant culture in Britain in the 1950s. In this sense, the novel negotiates the anxieties in mainstream fifties culture Paul Gilroy has identified as operating through discourses of criminality, sexuality and miscegenation that ultimately threaten to exceed the boundaries of homogenous white culture.[52]

The Lonely Londoners approaches these constructions with ambivalence, despite representing them through a black perspective. Selvon's characters engage in criminal activity, and are portrayed as sexually promiscuous, often supporting the stereotypical image created by dominant white culture. However, these character traits are represented in the text as crucial in the process of identity-formation that distinguishes Caribbean culture. Representation of criminality and sexuality in practice needs to be contextualized within a specific set of socio-cultural conditions that construct such practice as a response to marginalization. The celebration of criminality and sexuality, therefore, becomes another strategy of empowerment gesturing towards a Bataillean excess that privileges the heterogeneous over the homogenizing forces of society.[53] The reader, however, is forced to negotiate the ideological implications of the construction of black identity in these terms. The discourse of excess is empowering, but it can

52   Paul Gilroy, *There Ain't No Black in the Union Jack: The Cultural Politics of Race and Nation* (London and New York: Routledge, 1992), pp.79–85. See the discussion of Gilroy in chapter seven above.

53   Georges Bataille, 'The Psychological Structure of Fascism', in *Visions of Excess: Selected Writings, 1927–1939*, ed. and trans. by Allan Stoekl (Minneapolis: University of Minnesota Press, 1985), pp.137–60.

simultaneously reproduce a stereotypical association of excess with black identity.

This construction of black identity is represented in the text through formal experimentation, and can be identified in the 'stream of consciousness' section (101–10) that describes the liberation of the Caribbean immigrants from the harsh London winter to the excesses of summer:

> Oh what a time it is when summer come to the city and all them girls away heavy winter coat and wearing light summer frocks so you could see the legs and shapes that was hiding away from the cold blasts and you could coast a lime in the park and negotiate ten shillings or a pound with the sports as the case may be. (101)

The use of stream of consciousness in this particular section represents the release of the language from the syntactical conventions of Standard English, which emblematically represents release from the restrictions that dominant white British culture places on the black individual. Here, the excess of the form is deployed functionally to mirror the excess involved in culturally and ideologically distancing the speaking voice from dominant discourses. In addition to this, the summer setting is deployed to symbolize this empowering release in terms of climatic differentiation. As Homi Bhabha has identified, description of the weather is a strategy often used in postcolonial texts to represent the distance between 'cold' English culture, with its emotional connotations, and the heat of tropical and desert climates, with its connotations of chaos, mystery and excess.[54] It is culturally significant, therefore, that the feelings of release experienced through the collective narration at this point in *The Lonely Londoners* takes place in the British summer. This contrasts to the opening of the novel, which foregrounds the cold 'fog sleeping restfully over London' (23) as strange and alien, reflecting on the alienation felt by Moses in the unfamiliar cold climate. This release is also specifically introduced through images of sexuality: the description of the women's bodies in the quoted passage is focused through the per-

---

54   Homi K. Bhabha, 'DissemiNation', in *Nation and Narration*, ed. by Homi Bhabha (London and New York: Routledge, 1990), pp.291–322, (p.319).

spective of black working-class men and foregrounds the anxieties concerning black/white relationships as identified by Gilroy, articulated here in a universalizing frame.

Descriptions of excess are also prevalent in the section that describes the minor character Harris's party, mainly through the stereotypical association of black subcultural activity with the use of illegal drugs. Harris represents a character who has attempted to enter dominant British society by mimicking its cultural practices and rejecting those of his Caribbean upbringing. However, Harris's cultural aspirations (he claims to have 'really distinguished people' at his dance) are ultimately rejected in the text through the character of 'Five', who sees through Harris's pretensions: 'Is only since you hit Brit'n that you getting on so English' (113). Five is a character who survives through involvement in illegal drugs, again activating dominant constructions of black identity in the fifties:

> Is a funny thing, but sometimes you walking down the road and all them who you pass say the same thing. They like the weed more than anybody else, and from the time they see you black they figure that you know all about it, where to make contact and how much to pay. (120)

The text goes on to suggest that most of the Caribbean immigrants smoke 'weed', but very few are involved as dealers. This serves to foreground this stereotypical image, whilst simultaneously challenging the foundations on which it is based. It does this by projecting Five as a type, whilst distancing the other Caribbean characters from him, and this serves to undermine the stereotype by reproducing it as an individual, rather than a racial or subcultural characteristic.

The issue of representation, however, remains ambiguous. Selvon is ultimately ambivalent in relation to these racially defined constructions because his text projects two distinct addressees in fifties British society. For the black addressee the cultural practices the text describes represent an empowering framework of cultural differentiation and celebration. But for an addressee belonging to dominant white culutre the text re-activates the very stereotypes it claims to challenge. Of course, this is not the fault of Selvon's novel, but reveals the specificity of the cultural understanding and con-

286

struction of racial identities in the fifties. The text displays these (sub)
cultural practices without projecting value judgements upon them,
thereby persuading the reader to make his/her own value judgements
and ultimately to analyze the bases on which those judgements are
made. The concept of empowerment, therefore, becomes problematic,
as the very aspects of cultural practice Selvon celebrates in black
culture could very easily be used by dominant white culture to con-
firm prejudices about black identity.

In addition to this ambivalence in the ideology of representation,
the text is problematic in terms of its representation of women. The
concentration on the social cohesion of black, working-class male
identity in Selvon's novel (the male characters are repeatedly referred
to as the 'boys') tends to exclude expression of black female experience and identity. In an interview with Selvon, Alessandra Dotti
remarks on the tendency in *The Lonely Londoners* for the male characters to construct a sense of their marginalized and subcultural
identity through an assertion of their masculinity.[55] Dotti identifies an
important aspect of the text here, which again intersects with dominant themes in British fifties culture in general. The empowerment of
male marginalized groups in terms of class, youth and ethnicity is
often produced at the expense of a recognition of a 'chain of equivalence' with the marginalized position of women.[56] In *The Lonely
Londoners*, women characters are portrayed as either comic sources of
restriction on the male characters or as sexual objects. Significantly, it
tends to be black women who represent the former, and white women
the latter. This re-marginalization of women in Selvon's writing can

55   John Thieme and Alessandra Dotti, '"Oldtalk": Two Interviews with Sam
      Selvon', in *Caribana*, Vol.1, 1990, pp.71–84. See also Paola Loreto's essay on
      Selvon's representation of women, 'The Male Mind and the Female Heart:
      Selvon's Ways to Knowledge in the "Tiger Books"', in Mark Zehnder (ed.)
      Something Rich and Strange: Selected Essays on Sam Selvon (Leeds: Peepal
      Tree, 2003) pp.39–51.
56   This again relates to the concept of a 'chain of equivalence' between working-
      class politics and other marginalized groups in Laclau and Mouffe's model of a
      post-Marxist political project. Ernesto Laclau and Chantal Mouffe, *Hegemony
      and Socialist Strategy: Towards a Radical Democratic Politics* (London:
      Verso, 1985).

be seen in his short story 'Brackley and the Bed' from *Ways of Sunlight*. In this story, the central character Brackley is forced to change his reprobate ways by the arrival from Tobago of his abandoned fiancé Teena:

> 'I see you make yourself at home,' he [Brackley] say maliciously.
> 'And what you think?' Teena flares.
> 'The boys does come here sometimes for a little rummy.'
> 'None of that now.'
> 'And sometimes a girl-friend visit me.'
> 'None of that now.'
> 'So you taking over completely.'[57]

Teena is portrayed as domineering and manipulative, reproducing a stereotypical image of the strong-willed Caribbean woman. Although Brackley is also portrayed as a comic figure, the reader's sympathies are with him due to Selvon's deployment of narrative perspective. Teena thus becomes an emblematic threat to the independence of the male individual.[58] This pattern re-emerges in *The Lonely Londoners* in its various black female figures, such as Tolroy's 'ma', and especially Tanty, who is a caricature of the matriarchal Caribbean woman. This aspect of the text also corresponds to the appropriation of the calypso form, which traditionally produces negative images of women.[59]

The white female characters in the novel often remain unnamed and are described through the perspective of Caribbean male characters as love or sex objects. These women occupy peripheral positions to the text's primary concern of recording the experience of the male immigrants. Again, this element of Selvon's work is part of a process of empowerment for black male immigrants in the fifties. The 'conquering' of white women by black males in the text operates to

---

57   Selvon, *Ways of Sunlight*, p.142.

58   Brackley and Teena are also characters in *The Lonely Londoners*. The connection between the short stories set in London in *Ways of Sunlight*, and the episodic narratives of the novel show a strong inter-connection between these two fifties works.

59   As Peter Manuel argues, 'The sexism of calypso songs is remarkable even by traditional standards', Manuel, *Popular Musics of the Non-Western World*, p.81.

foreground provocatively the threat felt within racist elements of the dominant white male population in the fifties. This also reveals the text's engagement with contemporary anxieties concerning miscegenation. However, this raises ambiguities in the representation of sexuality in the novel. To a certain extent, the text re-imposes stereotypical constructions of black identity through this emphasis on interracial sexuality. Selvon describes these sexual encounters without offering moral judgement, but to a fifties readership they dramatize the prejudices involved in the construction of racial stereotypes. Furthermore, the marginalized position of women remains silent in the text through the reproduction of dominant masculine and racial discourses. This again corresponds to similar processes at work in the novels of Sillitoe and MacInnes and to a characteristic of fifties subcultural, or male marginalized fiction, as identified by Lynne Segal.[60]

The lack a chain of equivalence between differing marginalized groups in fifties British culture can also be shown in terms of class in Selvon's novel. Selvon *does* identify links between the marginalized position of the black settlers in Britain in the fifties and the white working class, most forcefully in terms of the ghettoization of these groups into specific areas:

> The place where Tolroy and the family living was off the Harrow road, and the people in that area call the Working-class. Wherever in London that it have Working-class, there you will find a lot of spades [...] The houses around here old and grey and weatherbeaten [...] and some of the walls of the buildings have signs painted like Vote Labour and Down with the Tories. (73–4)

This reference to the political contexts of fifties working-class areas in London is made as a detached observation by the extradiegetic narrator, and therefore emphasizes the distance felt by the black immigrants to the politics of class. The reference to the Labour and Tory parties is projected as external to the concerns of this subcultural group, emphasizing their lack of political representation. There is a

---

60   Lynne Segal, 'Look Back in Anger: Men in the Fifties', in *Male Order: Unwrapping Masculinity*, ed. by Rowena Chapman and Jonathan Rutherford (London: Lawrence and Wishart, 1988), pp.68–96.

reference to Moses canvassing for the Labour Party (134), but this appears to be an isolated practice, not general amongst the group.

For the most part, however, the text presents differences rather than similarities between white and black working-class cultures, stressing a cultural and institutional racism that crosses class boundaries. For example, in the section in the novel where Moses and Galahad visit the Labour Exchange, Selvon begins by foregrounding the despair of unemployment in non-racialized terms: 'It ain't have no place in the world exactly like a place where a lot of men get together to look for work and draw Money form the Welfare State while they ain't working' (45). This inclusive description of the labour exchange seems to describe the culturally translated experience of the international working classes, but Selvon goes on to focus on the doubly marginalized position of the black experience of unemployment in 1950s Britain:

> Now on all the records of the boys, you will see mark on top in red ink. J-A, Col. That mean you from Jamaica and you black. So that put the clerks in the know right away, you see. Suppose a vacancy come and they want to send a fellar, first they will find out if the firm want coloured fellars before they send you. That save a lot of time and bother, you see. (46)

This passage shows the culturally specific practice in the fifties of racial discrimination perpetuated by the institutionalized system of employers and the government employment agency. This practice serves to divide the working classes in racial terms, and therefore makes it more difficult to organize a working-class political movement that includes racial distinctions.

The Lonely Londoners also records the lack of organized political struggle within the black subcultural group.The various characters depend rather on strategies of survival focused on individualistic, hustling, anti-authority practices, rather than a collectivized politics. This factor is symptomatic of the lack of awareness amongst Labour Party and other left-wing movements in Britain in the fifties of the specific concerns of these subcultural groups, and a privileging in left politics of class concerns over issues of ethnicity. Black individuals are, therefore, marginalized not only from mainstream white culture, but also from the primary bodies of political opposition to dominant power frameworks. The lack of equivalence between the marginalized discourses of class and 'race' is thereby projected by the text as indicative of the lack of political articulation amongst black subcultural groups.

The novel, then, foregrounds the problematics of an ideology of representation contextualized in terms of dominant literary and cultural debates in the fifties. This does not mean, however, that the text does not produce its own political emphases. Selvon has rejected the idea of his fiction as 'committed' in an overtly political sense. As he has commented in interview:

> Being a committed writer does not appeal to me because it often amounts to limiting your scope and range. Freedom of topics, of perspectives, of style is essential to the writer [...] Too often so-called commitment restricts the quality and universal scope of the work.[61]

Here, Selvon returns to the image of the 'committed' writer, established in the late fifties, as one who neglects quality of writing in the pursuit of a political imperative.[62] This politicized function of the novel was identified in the fifties as connected to the broadly left political agenda of socialist and Marxist discourse. Selvon rejects this partly because that discourse tended to exclude issues of ethnicity and postcolonial identity. However, Selvon's rejection is related to his perception of a committed literature represented in the fifties by a didacticism often associated with socialist realism. He thereby reveals a disillusionment with a certain *form* of committed literature, not with the general *concept* of a literature that engages with political issues. It is apparent that despite his rejection of a 'commitment' label, *The*

---

61   Michel Fabre, 'Samuel Selvon: Interviews and Conversations', p.71.
62   Selvon's position here again reveals a contradiction in his fictional project in terms of whether he feels his writing represents, on the one hand, a culturally specific 'resistance' literature, or, on the other, that it should be judged against (and incorporated into), 'universalizing' models of the dominant (Western) literary canon. Of course, postcolonial theory has shown the inconsistencies of the 'universal' criteria by which the institution of literature in the West values literary texts, but Selvon's awareness of this remains ambiguous.

Lonely Londoners does produce its own form of political commentary on the social and cultural experience of black individuals in London in the fifties. This is an issue, therefore, that relates to literary form and the treatment of subject, rather than to ideological positions. Selvon's sense of commitment is in fact closer to a Benjaminian model, which supports the imperative to reclaim specific marginalized 'histories', and to avoid that collective experience 'disappear[ing] irretrievably'.[63]

In conclusion, it is apparent that in addition to Selvon's position as a postcolonial or Caribbean writer, his fifties fiction engages directly with specific cultural and literary debates in Britain. His writing articulates the experiences of the black settlers during the period by deploying narrative techniques and strategies to produce a distinct subcultural identity in terms of 'race' similar to those used by Sillitoe and MacInnes in relation to categories of class and youth. Selvon's writing is radical in the sense that it produces a discourse previously unwritten in the English novel, and it achieves this by disrupting the dominant formal debates of the period concerning the realism/experimentalism opposition and the ideological connotations attached to those forms.

63   Walter Benjamin, 'Theses on the Philosophy of History', in *Illuminations*, ed. by Hannah Arendt, trans. by Harry Zohn, (London: Fontana, 1973), pp.245–55, (p.247).

Conclusion
Identity Parades

As we have seen, the radical novels of the 1950s were concerned with articulating the concerns and experiences of emergent and marginalized identities whilst at the same time engaging with a range of contemporaneous social and cultural debates such as the new frameworks of class, gender and ethnicity, the construction of national identity, the theoretical and practical goals of Marxism and socialism, and the crisis in the role of the novel. The belief that the current models of representation for these identities and communities in mainstream cultural sites, and by the New Left, were inadequate produced a desire to develop competing constructions of identity in the novels. However, the process of representing these identities in fiction produced its own complexities and problems. The novels discussed in the second part of this book reveal a dual function: firstly, to record the existence of *a priori* marginalized identities or subcultures, while simultaneously constructing those identities through the medium of literary fiction. This often produced a contradiction in terms of the aims to represent and to create simultaneously.

In their own way, each of the texts was concerned to engage with a kind of subculture. This leads us to investigate further the models of subculture in cultural theory. The concept of subcultures has predominantly been associated with youth, but analysis of the novels in this book have suggested that this model can be translated to other categories, in particular, of class, 'race' and gender. Alan Sinfield writes:

> Subcultures [...] afford to those who live them stories of their own identities and significance [...] We notice subcultures most when they disconcert the system, but even then the element of resistance is often incoherent or implicit. For resistance is first of all a way of retaining a degree of collective identity and

individual self-esteem in the face of the humiliation and frustration suffered by people within the prevailing relations of production.[1]

For Sinfield, subcultures establish their identities through the construction of 'stories', emphasizing their imaginary, symbolic and fictional character. This fictive or imaginary character is produced through a variety of cultural texts, but the novel represents a particularly powerful form of expression in this context. This relates to Sinfield's further point that subcultures articulate collective identities and individual self-esteem. However, the relationship between these two functions needs further analysis. The novels are concerned to articulate collective identities, but they also represent personalized and individualized perspectives on subcultural groups. The combination of collective and personal narratives, therefore, complicates the articulation of subcultural identity. Furthermore, although collective identities are represented in the novels, individual readers respond to them in different ways, and a model of pluralized addressivity has proved valuable in this context. Adapting Steven Connor's model of addressivity for the fifties radical novel has shown that there is a range of possible addressees written into the texts that produce multiple interpretations of the subcultural identities they record.[2] There are, of course, no guarantees concerning the way in which these narratives of emerging or subcultural identities are read or interpreted by individuals encountering them, and some of this ambivalence is incorporated into the narrative techniques and strategies the texts deploy. There is a simultaneous process of association and difference put into play when an individual engages with the construction of subcultural identities, and this factor informs many of the ambivalences and contradictions of the novels discussed in this book. The simultaneous elements of transgression and acceptance of specific aspects of the dominant culture marks the complex relationship of the subculture to its 'others', and identifies Sinfield's point on the often incoherent characteristic of subcultural 'resistance'.

1   Alan Sinfield, *Literature, Politics and Culture in Postwar Britain* (Oxford: Basil Blackwell, 1989), p.153.
2   Steven Connor, *The English Novel in History 1950–1995* (London and New York: Routledge, 1996), pp.8–13.

The six novelists discussed in part two of the book, although they have similar characteristics, articulate these concerns differently. Amis and Wain are both concerned with articulating the frustrations of an emergent group of lower-middle-class, university educated individuals who find their path blocked to the higher levels of society by entrenched class prejudice. Although they both emphasize the individualistic outlook of this group, they still, to a certain extent represent, a kind of subculture. Spark is also interested in several aspects of marginalized identity in relation to gender, class, age and ethnicity and shows the way in which disruptive forces can challenge the hegemonies on which prevailing identities rest. Sillitoe is engaged in constructing a heterogeneous model of working-class culture that competes both with mainstream media representations of the working class and with the tendency in the New Left to produce a homogenizing and nostalgic image of working-class culture. MacInnes is involved in countering constructions of youth and black subcultures produced in the media and by the New Left. Again, the tendency is to pluralize the model of marginalized identity dominant in those discourses in terms of multiple levels and a variety of distinct (sub-) subcultures within both youth and black identities. In addition, MacInnes's attempt to articulate a new or emergent model of Englishness is produced through constructions of alternative collective identities that negotiate older images of national identity. Selvon's novels are concerned to provide an empowering discourse of collective identity for black émigrés to England in the 1950s, and to record the process of transition for these communities as they move from emigrant to settler status. This process of constructing a collective, though marginalized, identity is concerned to counter the effects and anxieties of alienation for the black individual coming to Britain in the fifties.

However, each of the novels produces ambivalences and inconsistencies in relation to other marginalized identities. Comparison with Bataille's theories to each of the novels discussed in part two identifies this element of ambivalence. Bataille discusses the unrationalized and incoherent nature of transgressive behaviour that can express itself either as a revolutionary or reactionary force dependent on the specific cultural situation in which it occurs.[3] This is represented by the incoherent and uncontrollable manifestation of excess in the texts: the irresponsible and anti-social behaviour of Amis, Wain and Sillitoe's characters; the tendency of some of Spark's characters to destabilize conventional codes of belief and behaviour; the cultural and utopian excess of the jazz world in MacInnes; and Selvon's negotiation of stereotypical images of sexuality and criminality attributed to black identity in the 1950s.

This leads us to the issue of correspondence between the various expressions of resistance and transgression the texts articulate. In the 'Third Space', Homi Bhabha summarizes his model of cultural difference by examining his use of the concepts of 'translation' and 'incommensurability'. He suggests that because all cultures engage in similar strategies of construction and differentiation to other cultures the possibility of a 'translation' of concerns between different cultures is possible. This 'translation', however, operates in terms of an internal distancing between itself and its projected 'other':

> cultures are only constituted in relation to that otherness internal to their own symbol-forming activity which makes them decentred structures – through that displacement or liminality opens up the possibility of articulating *different*, even incommensurable cultural practices and priorities.[4]

The possibility of this translation is increased when dealing with marginalized identities, in that each of these has 'structural' similarities in its position *vis a vis* a dominant or central culture. This allows the potential for the construction of a 'chain of equivalence', as Laclau and Mouffe have identified it, between marginalized groups.[5] The intersection in fifties Britain between working-class, youth, black and female subcultures suggests the possibility of a radical translation

3   Georges Bataille, 'The Psychological Structure of Fascism', in *Visions of Excess: Selected Writings 1927–1939*, ed. by Allan Stoekl, trans. by Allan Stoekl and others (Minneapolis: University of Minnesota Press, 1985), pp.137–60.

4   Homi Bhabha, 'The Third Space: Interview with Homi Bhabha', in *Identity: Community, Culture, Difference*, ed. by Jonathan Rutherford (London: Lawrence and Wishart, 1990), pp.207–21, (p.210–11).

5   Ernesto Laclau and Chantal Mouffe, *Hegemony and Socialist Strategy: Towards a Radical Democratic Politics* (London and New York: Verso, 1985).

in their collective resistance to the dominant culture in terms of power. However, Bhabha also identifies the structural relationship of 'incommensurability' between cultures, in the sense that divisions between certain cultural groups or theoretical models are so irreconcilable that they cannot be translated into a combined force. The distinctions between discourses of class, age, ethnicity and gender are therefore rendered incommensurable as the prioritizing of certain issues and cultural practices undermines the connection with alternative 'others'. In Amis and Wain, the emphasis on the frustrations of lower middle-class 'scholarship boys' fails to recognize a commensurable sense of injustice for the working class and women. In Sillitoe's texts this can be seen in the relationship between white working-class male culture and its negotiation of its 'parent' culture, of women and of black identity. MacInnes's concentration on jazz youth cultures and collective black identities establishes oppositions, not only with the dominant culture, but also with the working-class Teds and with women. Selvon's privileging of black, male identity produces ambivalences in relation to other marginalized groups, in particular, the white working class and women of all ethnicities. Only Spark, perhaps, provides the questioning framework that, potentially at least, signals a correspondence between the subaltern positions of women, youth, the working class and other ethnicities. Although, even in her work, the 'otherness' of certain characters like Caroline Rose, Robison and Dougal Douglas serves to reinstate rather than challenge their marginalized status.

The texts, then, produce inconsistencies and contradictions in terms of their specific political and cultural agendas. However, it is clear that they each are concerned to engage ideologically and politically in the key concerns and anxieties of fifties culture. The model that has emerged in this book suggests that the texts are engaged in identifying a politics of difference, a politics that accepts the simultaneous and equal existence of different forms of oppositional and resistance (sub-) cultures as a negotiation of translation and incommensurability. As Jonathan Rutherford writes:

> We can use the word difference as a motif for that uprooting of certainty. It represents an experience of change, transformation and hybridity, in vogue

because it acts as focus for all those complementary fears, anxieties, confusions and arguments that accompany change. But as an approach to cultural politics it can help us make sense of what is happening: it can be a jumping off point for assembling new practices and languages, pulling together a diversity of theories, politics, cultural experiences and identities into new alliances and movements. Such a politics wouldn't need to subsume identities into an under-lying totality that assumes their ultimately homogeneous nature. Rather it is a critique of essentialism and mono-culturalism, asserting the unfixed and 'overdetermined' character of identities. The cultural politics of difference recognises both the interdependent and relational nature of identities, their elements of incommensurability and their political right of autonomy.[6]

Two issues can be taken from this definition of the politics of differ-ence that have direct relevance for the position of the radical novel in relation to competing forms of oppositional discourse in the 1950s.

First, that a more complex model of identity emerges that ex-ceeds the prioritizing of class and economic issues in traditional Marxist and socialist theory. As Stuart Hall writes: 'Identities are never completed, never finished; [...] they are always as subjectivity itself is, in process.'[7] Rutherford develops this fluid model of identity in terms of marginalized communities:

> when the margin resists and discovers its own words, it not only decentres the dominant discourses and identities that have suppressed it, but also transforms its own meaning. Just as it invades the centre with its own difference, so it too is opened up to its internal differences [...] Identity then is never a static lo-cation, it contains traces of its past and what it is to become. It is contingent, a provisional full stop in the play of differences and the narrative of our own lives.[8]

Adapting this model to the 1950s, the articulation of marginalized and subcultural identity in the radical novels produces an awareness of the internal contradictions within the construction of those identities, at

6   Jonathan Rutherford, 'A Place Called Home: Identity and the Cultural Politics of Difference', in *Identity: Community, Culture, Difference*, ed. by Jonathan Rutherford (London: Lawrence and Wishart, 1990), pp.9–27, (p.10).
7   Stuart Hall, 'Old and New Identities, Old and New Ethnicities', in *Culture, Globalization and the World-System*, ed. by Anthony D. King (Houndmills and London: Macmillan, 1991), pp.41–68, (p.47).
8   Rutherford, 'A Place Called Home', pp.23–4.

the same time as it states its opposition to dominant culture. This helps to explain some of the ambiguities in the representations they produce.

Second, Rutherford goes on to suggest that the politics of difference replaces the 'binarism' of Marxist and socialist politics that traditionally prioritizes white working-class masculine identities against the 'bourgeoisie' as the primary concern for its oppositional discourse. In response to the debilitating effects of this binarism, the politics of difference emphasizes the pluralization of radicalism across other marginalized categories of 'race', gender and sexuality. Although Rutherford sites this process in the 1980s,[9] it can be seen that it also informs the late fifties. The crisis in Marxism and socialism, re-articulated in the early New Left, finds a competing radicalized politics in the emergence of collective identities, articulated in the novels of Amis, Wain, Spark, Sillitoe, MacInnes and Selvon.

However, the concept of cultural difference, and the model of identity on which it relies, has increasingly come under scrutiny.[10] Lawrence Grossberg argues that: '[the] logic of difference, in which the other is defined by its negativity, can only give rise to a politics of resentment'.[11] Grossberg regards cultural difference as a model grounded in modernity, and suggests its aims of producing hybridized, mutually co-existing identities is, in fact, a re-instatement of a politics of division. He attempts to replace this with: 'alternative logics of otherness [...that] suggest the concept of a belonging without identity, a notion of what might be called *singularity*' (Grossberg's italics) as a basis for an alternative cultural politics. Grossberg develops this concept of singularity to explore the relationship between the individual and a community to which that individual might belong. Following Giorgio Agamben's model of the relationship between an 'example'

9   In particular, Rutherford, cites the Miner's Strike as the last moment of the traditional Left's policy of aggressively oppositional politics, ibid., pp.17–19.

10   Vivek Dhareshwar, 'Toward a Narrative Epistemology of the Postcolonial Predicament', in *Inscriptions*, No.5, 1989; Renato Rosaldo, *Culture and Truth: The Remaking of Social Analysis* (Boston: Beacon Press, 1989); and Aijaz Ahmed, *In Theory: Classes, Nations, Literatures* (London: Verso, 1992).

11   Lawrence Grossberg, 'Identity and Cultural Studies', in *Questions of Cultural Identity*, ed. by Stuart Hall and Paul du Gay (London: Sage, 1996), pp.87–107, (p.97).

and its 'set', Grossberg identifies the structural relationship between individuals in a collective community:

> the example functions as an example not by virtue of some common property which it shares with all the other possible members of the set, but rather by virtue of its metonymical (understood both literally and spatially) relation to the set itself.[12]

This model proves valuable in understanding the processes involved in the articulation of marginalized and subcultural identity in literary fiction and especially in the novels discussed in the second part of this book. With different nuances and priorities, the texts by the six authors covered attempt to negotiate distinctions between singularity and difference, in the sense that Grossberg uses the terms. Furthermore, the representation of individual voices that 'belong' to subcultural communities should be seen as metonymically representing their group identity, whilst avoiding being subsumed into a contained expression of that subculture. Grossberg's model retains the singularity of the individual, whilst simultaneously producing, as Deleuze and Guattari would put it, a 'collective assemblage of enunciation'.[13] Andrew Gibson develops this point by suggesting that ethically: 'The novelist [in general] presents us with individuality and diversity alike without any attempt to reduce either to the terms of a singular scheme or totality.'[14] The negotiation of singularity and identification of difference is achieved formally through the use of either of first-person narratives, or narratives that are focalized through one character, in most of the novels discussed in part two of this book. This type of narration produces a fluctuation between identification with the singularity of the speaking voice and the collective identity of the relationship the individual has to his/her (sub)cultural group. As Gibson has identified, following Levinas, first-person narration by characters involved in the events of the story (extradiegetic-homodiegetic

---

12   Ibid., p.104.
13   Gilles Deleuze and Felix Guattari, *Kafka: Toward a Minor Literature*, trans. by Dana Polan (Minneapolis: University of Minnesota Press, 1986), p.18.
14   Andrew Gibson, *Postmodernism, Ethics and the Novel: From Leavis to Levinas* (London and New York: Routledge, 1999), p.8.

narration)[15] produces a complex and radical representation of otherness that attempts to explode the distance between the self and other, whilst maintaining the separation of the two entities.[16] It is significant that the representation of subcultural identity in Sillitoe, MacInnes and Selvon, for example, is articulated through the deployment of first-person (and collective second-person in the case of *Saturday Night and Sunday Morning*) narratives. This formal technique reproduces the complexities of representation identified in Grossberg's model of singularity, while also re-negotiating a politics of difference.

This play between difference and singularity also relates to formal characteristics. Although each novel retains its singularity of formal technique, together they represent a body of fiction that negotiates the genres of realism and modernism without finally resting on either of them. The politics of difference, therefore, is articulated in a literary form that resists the realism versus experimentalism opposition informing much literary criticism of the period.[17] Furthermore, the formal characteristics of these novels are representative of a desire to move from a class-based approach in cultural and critical analysis to one that is pluralized across different marginalized categories. The incorporation of oral traditions, collective narratives and culturally specific forms (such as the calypso in Selvon) serves both to distance the novels from established literary styles, and to represent a heterogeneous model of form that resists the attempt by some literary criticism to polarize formal technique into a binary, oppositional model.

The radical novel of the 1950s, then, represents a moment of transition and transgression. Its articulation of new collective and individual identities manifests itself in a manipulation and negotiation of established literary forms. The novels discussed in this book reflect this process, although similar approaches and techniques can be traced in various other novels written during the period. In addition, the presence of alternative 'foreign' literary models in terms of the re-

---

15   See Gerard Genette, *Narrative Discourse*, trans. by Jane E. Lewin (Oxford: Blackwell, 1980), p.248.
16   Gibson, *Postmodernism, Ethics and the Novel*, pp.25–9.
17   Although it has to be said that this applies more to Spark, Sillitoe, MacInnes and Selvon than it does to Amis and Wain.

lationship between formal technique and ideological significance adds to the range of difference affecting fifties writing. All this shows that the 1950s novel is far more heterogeneous than the traditional readings of the period have tended to suggest.

Bibliography

Primary Texts

1. Literary

Achebe, Chinua, *Things Fall Apart* (London: Heineman, 1958)

Amis, Kingsley, *Lucky Jim* (Harmondsworth: Penguin, 1961), first published 1954

—— *That Uncertain Feeling* (London: Gollancz, 1955)

Arden, John, *Sergeant Musgrave's Dance: An Un-Historical Parable* (London: Eyre Methuen, 1960)

Beckett, Samuel, *The Beckett Trilogy* (London: Picador, 1979), first published 1959

Berger, John, *The Foot of Clive* (London: Methuen, 1962)

Braine, John, *Room at the Top* (Harmondsworth: Penguin, 1959), first published 1957

Braithwaite, E.R., *To Sir, With Love* (London: Four Square, 1962), first published 1959

Camus, Albert, *The Outsider*, trans. by Joseph Laredo (Harmondsworth: Penguin, 1982), first published 1942, in English translation, 1946

—— *The Rebel: An Essay on Man in Revolt*, trans. by Anthony Bower (Harmondsworth: Penguin, 1962), first published in French 1951

Conrad, Joseph, *Heart of Darkness* (Harmondsworth: Penguin, 1973), first published in 1902

Durrell Lawrence, *The Alexandrian Quartet* (London: Faber & Faber, 1968), first published between 1957–60

Golding, William, *Lord of the Flies* (London: Faber & Faber, 1954)

—— *The Inheritors* (London: Faber & Faber, 1955)

—— *Pincher Martin* (London: Faber & Faber, 1956)

Greene, Graham, *The End of the Affair* (London: Heineman, 1951)

Harrison, Tony, 'On Not Being Milton', in *Selected Poems*, 2nd edn. (Harmondsworth: Penguin, 1987), 112

Kersch, Gerald, *Fowlers End* (London: Heineman, 1958)

Lamming, George, *In the Castle of My Skin* ((London: Michael Joseph, 1953)
—— *The Emigrants* (London: Michael Joseph, 1959)
—— *The Pleasures of Exile* (London: Michael Joseph, 1960)
Larkin, Philip, *Jill* (London: Faber & Faber, 1975), first published 1946
—— *A Girl in Winter* (London: Faber & Faber, 1975), first published 1947
—— *Collected Poems* (London: Faber & Faber, 1988)
Lessing, Doris, *In Pursuit of the English* (London: MacGibbon and Kee, 1960)
—— *The Golden Notebook* (London: Grafton, 1973), first published 1962
—— *The Four-Gated City* (Frogmore, St. Albans: Panther, 1972), first published in 1969,
MacInnes, Colin, *City of Spades* (London and New York: Allison and Busby, 1980), first published 1957
—— *Absolute Beginners* (Harmondsworth: Penguin, 1964), first published 1959
Orwell, George, *The Clergyman's Daughter* (London: Gollancz, 1935)
—— *The Road to Wigan Pier* (London: Gollancz, 1937)
—— *Down and Out in Paris and London* (Harmondsworth: Penguin, 1940)
—— *Animal Farm: A Fairy Story* (Harmondsworth: Penguin, 1945)
—— *Nineteen-Eighty-Four* (Harmondsworth: Penguin, 1949)
Osborne, John, *Look Back in Anger* (London: Faber & Faber, 1957)
The Penguin Book of the Beats, ed. by Ann Charters (Harmondsworth: Penguin, 1992)
Salinger, J.D., *The Catcher in the Rye* (Harmondsworth: Penguin, 1958), first published 1951
Salkey, Andrew, *A Quality of Violence* (London: Hutchinson, 1959)
Sartre, Jean-Paul, *Nausea*, trans. by L. Alexander (London: Hamilton, 1962)
Selvon, Sam, *The Lonely Londoners* (Harlow, Essex: Longman, 1985), first published 1956
—— *Ways of Sunlight* (London and New York: Longman, 1987), first published 1957
—— *I Hear Thunder* (London: MacGibbon and Kee, 1963)
—— *Moses Ascending* (London: Davis Poynter, 1975)
Sigal, Clancy, *Weekend in Dinlock* (London: Secker and Warburg, 1960)
Sillitoe, Alan, *Saturday Night and Sunday Morning* (London: Flamingo, 1994), first published 1958
—— *Saturday Night and Sunday Morning* (London and New York: W.H. Allen, 1973)
—— *Saturday Night and Sunday Morning* (London: Pan, 1960)

—— *The Loneliness of the Long Distance Runner* (London: Panther, 1985), first published 1959

—— *Key to the Door* (London: W.H. Allen, 1961)

—— *Birthday* (London: Flamingo, 2001)

Spark, Muriel, *The Comforters* (London: Macmillan, 1957)

—— *Robinson* (London: Macmillan, 1958)

—— *Memento Mori* (Harmondsworth: Penguin, 1961), first published 1959

—— *The Ballad of Peckham Rye* (London: Macmillan, 1960)

Storey, John, *This Sporting Life* (Harmondsworth: Penguin, 1962), first published 1960

Toynbee, Philip, *The Garden to the Sea* (London: MacGibbon and Kee, 1953)

Trocchi, Alexander, *Young Adam* (Edinburgh: Rebel Inc., 1996), first published 1954

Wain, John, *Hurry On Down* (Harmondsworth: Penguin, 1960), first published 1953

Waterhouse, Keith, *Billy Liar* (London: Michael Joseph, 1959)

Waugh, Evelyn, *Men at Arms* (London: Chapman and Hall, 1952)

—— *Officers and Gentlemen* (London: Chapman and Hall, 1955)

Wilson, Angus, *Anglo-Saxon Attitudes* (Harmondsworth: Penguin, 158) first published 1956

Wilson, Colin, *The Outsider* (London: Pan, 1978), first published 1956

Williams, Raymond, *Border Country* (London: Chatto and Windus, 1960)

2. Literary/Cultural Criticism

Allcorn, Derek, 'The Unnoticed Generation', in *Universities and Left Review*, No.4, 1958, 54–58

Amis, Kingsley, *Socialism and the Intellectuals*, Fabian Tract No.304 (London: The Fabian Society, 1957)

Anderson, Lindsay, 'Commitment in Cinema Criticism', in *Universities and Left Review*, No.1, 1957, 44–8

Annan, Noel, 'The Intellectual Aristocracy', in *Studies in Social History*, ed. by J.H. Plumb (London: Longman, 1955), 241–87

Armstrong, Michael, 'Commitment in Criticism', in *Universities and Left Review*, No.2, 1957, 65–66

Bell, Daniel, *The End of Ideology* (Glencoe: Free Press, 1960)

Benjamin, Walter, 'The Author as Producer', in *Understanding Brecht*, trans. by Anna Bostock (London: NLB, 1966), 85–104

Brecht, Bertolt, 'Against Georg Lukacs', trans. by Stuart Hood, in *Aesthetics and Politics*, ed. by Ronald Taylor and others (London: New Left Books, 1977), 68–85

The Communist Party of Great Britain, *The British Road to Socialism*, second draft (London: 1958)

Conquest, Robert (ed.), *New Lines: An Anthology* (London: Macmillan, 1957)

Cooper, William, 'Reflections on Some Aspects of the Experimental Novel', in *International Literary Review*, No.2, ed. by John Wain (London: John Calder, 1959), 29–36

Cox, Idris, 'New Factors in the Struggle Against Imperialism', in *Marxism Today*, Vol.2, No.1, January 1958, 5–12

Crosland, Anthony, *The Future of Socialism* (London: Cape, 1956)

Crossman, R.H.S. (ed.), *New Fabian Essays* (London: Turnstile Press, 1952)

Curran, Charles, 'The New Estate in Great Britain', in *The Spectator*, January 1956, 72

de Beauvoir, Simone, *The Second Sex* (New York: Bantam Books, 1961)

de Franscia, Peter, 'Commitment in Art Criticism', in *Universities and Left Review*, No.1, 1957, 49–51

Fiedler, Leslie, 'The Middle Against Both Ends', in *Encounter*, 5 August 1955, 16–23

Fraser, G.S., *The Modern Writer and His World* (London: Andre Deutsch, 1964), first published 1953

Freud, Sigmund, 'The Uncanny', in *The Standard Edition of the Complete Psychological Works of Sigmund Freud*, ed. and trans. by James Strachey, Vol. XVII (London: Hogarth, 1953), 219–52

Fyvel, T.R. 'The Stones of Harlow: Reflections on Subtopia', in *Encounter*, June 1956, 15

Galbraith, J.K., *The Affluent Society* (London: Andre Deutsch, 1958)

Gomulka, V., 'The Cultural Revolution, Revisionism and the Party', in *Marxism Today*, Vol.2, No.3, April 1959, 119–122

Hall, Stuart, 'A Sense of Classlessness', in *Universities and Left Review*, No.5, 1958, 50–52

—— and others 'The Habit of Violence', in *Universities and Left Review*, No.5, 1958, 4–5

—— 'The Big Swipe', in *Universities and Left Review*, No.7, 1959, 50–52

—— 'Absolute Beginnings', in *Universities and Left Review*, No.7, 1959, 17–25

—— 'Commitment Dilemma', in *New Left Review*, No.10, July/August 1961, 67–69

—— and Paddy Whannel, *The Popular Arts* (London: Pantheon, 1964)

Hartley, Anthony, *A State of England* (London: Hutchinson, 1963)

Hoggart, Richard, *The Uses of Literacy* (Harmondsworth: Penguin, 1958), first published 1957

Holloway, John, 'New Lines in English Poetry', in *Hudson Review*, No.9, 1956, 592–97

Howe, Irving, 'The Worker as a Young Tough', in *New Republic*, No.24, August 1958, 27–8

Jackson, Brian and Dennis Marsden, *Education and the Working-class* (Harmondsworth: Penguin, 1966), first published 1962

Karl, Frederick R., *A Reader's Guide to the Contemporary English Novel* (New York: Octagon Press, 1972)

Kettle, Arnold, *An Introduction to the English Novel: Volume 1* (London: Arrow Books, 1962), first published 1951

Klugmann, Jack, 'The Road to Socialism', in *Marxism Today*, Vol.2, No.2, February 1958, 42

Kullman, Michael, 'The Anti-Culture Born of Despair', in *Universities and Left Review*, No.4, 1958, 51–54

Larkin, Philip, 'Interview' (1964), in *Twentieth Century Poetry*, ed. by Graham Martin and P.N. Furbank (Milton Keynes: Open University Press, 1975), 243–54

—— *Required Writing: Miscellaneous Pieces 1955–1982* (London: Faber & Faber, 1983)

Lehmann, John, 'Foreword', *London Magazine*, December 1955, 11–13

—— (ed.), *The Craft of Letters in England* (London: Cresset Press, 1956)

Lessing, Doris, 'A Small Personal Voice', in *Declaration*, ed. by Tom Maschler (London: MacGibbon and Kee, 1957), 11–27

Lukàcs, Georg, *The Meaning of Contemporary Realism*, trans. by John and Necke Mander (London: Merlin Press, 1963), first published in German 1956

MacInnes, Colin, *England, Half English* (London: Chatto and Windus, 1986), first published 1961

—— 'Young England, Half English', in *England, Half English* (London: Chatto and Windus, 1986), first published 1961, 11–19

—— 'Pop Songs and Teenagers', in *England, Half English* (London: Chatto and Windus, 1986), first published 1961, 45–59

307

—— 'A Taste of Reality', in *England, Half English* (London: Chatto and Windus, 1986), first published 1961, 205–07

Macmillan, Harold, 'Address given to Members of both Houses of the Parliament of the Union of South Africa', in *Pointing the Way, 1959–1961* (London: Macmillan, 1972), 473–82.

Mailer, Norman, 'The White Negro', in Charters, *The Penguin Book of the Beats*, 582–605, first published 1957

Mander, John, *The Writer and Commitment* (London: Secker and Warburg, 1961)

Mann, B.R., 'The Fight of African Nations to Self-Determination', in *Marxism Today*, Vol.3, No.1, January 1959, 16–21

Maschler, Tom (ed.), *Declaration* (London: MacGibbon and Kee, 1957)

Maugham, Somerset, 'Books of the Year – I', in *Sunday Times*, 25 December 1955.

Orwell, George, *Collected Essays* (London: Secker and Warburg, 1961)

—— 'England Your England', in *England Your England* (London: Secker and Warburg, 1953), 192–224, first published 1941

Pollitt, Harry, *The Political Report to the 21st Congress of the Communist Party* (London: Communist Party, 1949)

Pothekin, I., 'The Formation of Nations in Africa', in *Marxism Today*, Vol.2, No.10, October 1958, 308–14

Robbe-Grillet, Alain, *Snapshots and Notes Towards a New Novel*, trans. by Barbara Wright (London: Calder and Boyars, 1965), first published 1956

Samuel, Raphael, 'Class and Classlessness', in *Universities and Left Review*, No.6, 1959, 44–50

Sartre, Jean-Paul, *What is Literature?*, trans. by Bernard Frechtman (London: Methuen & Co., 1967), first published in English translation 1950

—— 'Preface', in Frantz Fanon, *The Wretched of the Earth*, trans. by Constance Farrington (Harmondsworth: Penguin, 1967), 7–26; first published in French 1961, first published in English translation 1965

Sigal, Clancy, 'Nihilism's Organizational Man', in *Universities and Left Review*, No.6, 1958, 59–65

Sillitoe, Alan, 'Johnny Livens Up Grim Schooldays', in *Reynold's News*, No.31 January 1960, 11

—— 'Introduction', in *Saturday Night and Sunday Morning*, ed. by David Craig (London: Longmans, 1968), vii–xii

Snow, C.P., 'New Trends in First Novels', in *Sunday Times*, 27 December 1953, 3

Spender, Stephen, *The Struggle of the Modern* (London: Hamish Hamilton, 1963)

Strachey, John, *Contemporary Capitalism* (London: Gollancz, 1956)

Taylor, Charles, 'Alienation and Community', in *Universities and Left Review*, No.5, 1958, 11–18

Thomas, Hugh, *The Establishment* (London: Anthony Blond, 1959)

Thompson, E.P., 'Commitment in Politics', in *Universities and Left Review*, No.6, 1959, 50–55

—— *The Making of the English Working-class* (Harmondsworth: Penguin, 1968), first published 1963

Toynbee, Philip, 'Experiment and the Future of the Novel', in *The Craft of Letters in England*, ed. by John Lehmann (London: Cresset Press, 1956), 60–73

Tynan, Kenneth, *Tynan on Theatre* (Harmondsworth: Penguin, 1964)

van Ghent, Dorothy, *The English Novel: Form and Function* (New York: Harper and Row, 1961)

Wain, John, 'Possible Worlds', in *The Observer*, 12 October 1958, 20

—— (ed.) *Essays on Literature and Ideas* (London: MacMillan, 1963)

—— 'The Conflict of Forms in Contemporary English Literature', in *Essays on Literature and Ideas* (London: Macmillan, 1963), 1–55

Watt, Ian, *The Rise of the Novel: Studies in Defoe, Fielding and Richardson* (London: Hogarth Press, 1987), first published 1957

Williams, Raymond, *Culture and Society 1780–1950* (London: Hogarth, 1987), first published 1957

—— *The Long Revolution* (London: Chatto and Windus, 1961)

Wyndham, Francis, 'Twenty-five Years of the Novel', in *The Craft of Letters in England*, ed. by John Lehmann (London: Cresset Press, 1956), 44–59

Young, M, and P Wilmot, *Family and Kinship in East London* (London: Routledge and Kegan Paul, 1957)

Young, Wayland, 'Return to Wigan Pier', in *Encounter*, June 1956, 5

Secondary Texts

1. General: Cultural, political, literary criticism

Ahmed, Aijaz, *In Theory: Classes, Nations, Literatures* (London: Verso, 1992)

Althusser, Louis, 'Ideology and Ideological State Apparatuses', in *Lenin and Philosophy and Other Essays*, trans. by Ben Brewster (London: New Left Books, 1971), 122–73

Anderson, Benedict, *Imagined Communities* (London: Verso and New Left Books, 1983)

Ashcroft, Bill, Gareth Griffiths and Helen Tiffin, *The Empire Writes Back: Theory and Practice in Post-Colonial Literatures* (London and New York: Routledge, 1994)

Bakari, Imruh, 'Exploding Silence: African-Caribbean and African-American Music in British Culture Towards 2000', in *Living Through Pop*, ed. by Andrew Blake (London and New York: Routledge, 1999), 98–111

Bakhtin, Mikhail M., *Rabelais and His World*, trans. by Helene Iswolsky (Cambridge MA: The MIT Press, 1968)

—— 'Discourse in the Novel' in *The Dialogic Imagination: Four Essays by M.M. Bakhtin*, ed. by M. Holquist, trans. by Carl Emerson and Michael Holquist (Austin: University of Texas Press, 1981), 259–422

Balibar, Etienne, and Pierre Macherey, 'On Literature as an Ideological Form', in *Untying the Text: A Post-Structuralist Reader*, ed. by Robert Young (London and New York: Routledge and Kegan Paul, 1981), 79–99

Barthes, Roland, *Writing Degree Zero* trans. by Annette Lavers and Colin Smith (New York: Hill and Wang, 1977

—— 'Introduction to the Structural Analysis of Narratives', in *Image, Music, Text*, trans. by Stephen Heath (London: Fontana, 1977), 79–124

—— 'The Death of the Author', in *Image, Music, Text*, 142–8

—— *The Rustle of Language* (London: Blackwell, 1986), first published 1967

—— *S/Z*, trans. by Richard Miller (Oxford: Basil Blackwell, 1990)

Bataille, Georges, *Visions of Excess: Selected Writings 1927–1939*, ed. by Allan Stoekl, trans. by Allan Stoekl and others (Minneapolis: University of Minnesota Press, 1985)

Baudrillard, Jean, *The Mirror of Production*, trans. by Mark Poster (St. Louis: Telos Press, 1975)

—— 'The Evil Demon of Images and the Precession of Simulacra', in *Postmodernism: A Reader*, ed. by Thomas Doherty (Hemel Hempstead: Harvester Wheatsheaf, 1993), 194–99

Belsey, Catherine, *Critical Practice* (London and New York: Routledge, 1980)

Benjamin, Walter, 'The Storyteller: Reflections on the Works of Nikolai Leskov', in *Illuminations* ed. by Hannah Arendt, trans. by Harry Zohn (London: Fontana, 1973), 83–107

—— 'Theses on the Philosophy of History', in *Illuminations*, 245–55

Bergonzi, Bernard, 'The Novel No Longer', in *The Situation of the Novel* (London: Macmillan, 1970), 11–34

—— *Wartime and Aftermath: English Literature and its Background 1939–1960* (Oxford: Oxford University Press, 1993

Bhabha, Homi K. (ed.), *Nation and Narration* (London and New York: Routledge, 1990)

—— 'Introduction', in Bhabha, *Nation and Narration* (London and New York: Routledge, 1990), 1–7

—— 'The Third Space: Interview with Homi Bhabha', in *Identity: Community, Culture, Difference*, ed. by Jonathan Rutherford (London: Lawrence and Wishart, 1990), 207–21

Birbalsingh, Frank (ed.), *Frontiers of Caribbean Literature in English* (London and Basingstoke: Macmillan Education, 1996)

Blair, Sara, 'Modernism and the Politics of Culture', in *The Cambridge Companion to Modernism*, ed. by Michael Levenson (Cambridge: Cambridge University Press, 1999), 157–73

Botting, Fred and Scott Wilson (eds), *The Bataille Reader* (Oxford: Blackwell, 1997)

Bradbury, Malcolm, *The Modern British Novel 1878–2001*, Revised Edition, (Harmondsworth: Penguin, 2001)

Brannigan, John, *Literature, Culture and Society in Postwar England, 1945–1965* (New York: Edward Mellen Press, 2002)

Brennan, Timothy, 'The National Longing for Form', in Bhabha, *Nation and Narration*, 44–70

Brook, Susan, 'Engendering Rebellion: The Angry Young Man, Class and Masculinity' in *Posting the Male: Masculinities in Post-War and Contemporary Literature*, ed. by Daniel Lea and Berthold Schone (Amsterdam: Rodopi, 2003), 19–34

Brooker, Peter (ed.), *Modernism/Postmodernism* (London: Longman, 1992)

Byron, Margaret, *Post-War Caribbean Migration to Britain: The Unfinished Cycle* (Aldershot: Avebury, 1994)

Carpenter, Humphrey, *The Angry Young Men: A Literary Comedy of the 1950s* (London: Penguin 2002)

Chapman, Rowena. and Jonathan Rutherford (eds), *Male Order: Unwrapping Masculinity* (London: Lawrence and Wishart, 1988)

Charters, Ann (ed.), *The Penguin Book of the Beats* (Harmondsworth: Penguin, 1992)

Chatman, Seymour, *Story and Discourse: Narrative Structure in Fiction and Film* (Ithaca and London: Cornell University Press, 1978)

Childs, David, *Britain Since 1945: A Political History* (London and New York: Routledge, 1997)

Chun, Lin, *The British New Left* (Edinburgh: Edinburgh University Press, 1993)

Clarke, Gary, 'Defending Ski-Jumpers: A Critique of Theories of Youth Subcultures', in *The Subcultures Reader*, ed. by Ken Gelder and Sarah Thompson (London and New York: Routledge, 1997), 175–80

Clarke, John, Chas Critcher and Richard Johnson (eds), *Working-class Culture: Studies in History and Theory* (London: Hutchinson, 1979)

Clarke, Simon et al., *One-Dimensional Marxism: Althusser and the Politics of Culture* (London and New York: Allison & Busby, 1980)

Cohen, Phil, 'Subcultural Conflict and Working-Class Community', in *The Subcultures Reader*, ed. by Ken Gelder and Sarah Thornton (London and New York: Routledge, 1997), 90–99

Connor, Steven, *The English Novel in History 1950–1995* (London and New York: Routledge, 1996

Craig, Cairns, *Yeats, Eliot, Pound and the Politics of Poetry* (London and Canberra: Croom Helm, 1982)

—— *The Modern Scottish Novel: Narrative and the National Imagination* (Edinburgh: Edinburgh University Press, 1999)

Craig, David (ed.), *Marxists on Literature: An Anthology* (Harmondsworth: Penguin, 1975)

Critcher, Chas, 'Sociology, Cultural Studies and the Post-War Working-class', in Clarke, John, Chas Critcher and Richard Johnson (eds), *Working-class Culture: Studies in History and Theory* (London: Hutchinson, 1979), 13–40

Dabydeen, David, 'On Not Being Milton: Nigger Talk in England Today', in Davis, *Crisis and Creativity in the New Literatures in English*, 61–74

Dhareshwar, Vivek, 'Toward a Narrative Epistemology of the Postcolonial Predicament', in *Inscriptions*, No.5, 1989

Davey, Kevin, *English Imaginaries* (London: Lawrence and Wishart, 1999)

Davis, Geoffrey V. and Hena Maes-Jelinek (eds), *Crisis and Creativity in the New Literatures in English* (Amsterdam and Atlanta: Rodopi, 1990)

D'Costa, Jean, 'The West Indian Novelist and Language: A Search for a Literary Medium', in *Studies in Caribbean Literature*, ed. by the Carrington Society for Caribbean Linguistics (St. Augustine, Trinidad: University of the West Indies Press, 1983)

Deleuze, Gilles and Felix Guattari, *Kafka: Toward a Minor Literature*, trans. by Dana Polan (Minneapolis: University of Minnesota Press, 1986)

—— *A Thousand Plateaus: Capitalism and Schizophrenia* (London and New York: Continuum, 2004)

Derrida, Jacques, *Margins of Philosophy*, trans. by Alan Bass (Chicago: University of Chicago Press, 1982)

—— *Acts of Literature*, ed. by Derek Attridge (London and New York: Routledge, 1992)

——'"This Strange Institution Called Literature": An Interview with Jacques Derrida', trans. by Geoffrey Bennington and Rachel Bowlby, in Attridge, *Acts of Literature*, 33–75

—— *Specters of Marx: The State of the Debt, the Work of Mourning, and the New International*, trans. by Peggy Kamuf (London and New York: Routledge, 1994)

Dollimore, Jonathan, *Radical Tragedy: Religion, Ideology and Power in the Drama of Shakespeare and his Contemporaries* (Hemel Hempstead: Harvester Wheatsheaf, 1984)

—— 'Introduction: Shakespeare, Cultural Materialism and the New Historicism', in Dollimore, Jonathan, and Alan Sinfield (eds), *Political Shakespeare: New Essays in Political Shakespeare* (Manchester: Manchester University Press, 1985), 2–17

Doyle, Brian, *English and Englishness* (London and New York: Routledge, 1989)

Dummett, Ann and Andrew Nicol, *Subjects, Citizens, Aliens and Others: Nationality and Immigration Law* (London: Weidenfeld and Nicolson, 1990)

Dworkin, Dennis, *Cultural Marxism in Postwar Britain: History, the New Left, and the Origins of Cultural Studies* (Durham and London: Duke University Press, 1997)

Eagleton, Terry, *Criticism and Ideology* (London: Verso, 1976)

—— *Ideology: An Introduction* (London and New York: Verso, 1991)

—— (ed.), *Ideology* (London and New York: Longman, 1994)

Easthope, Anthony, *Englishness and National Culture* (London and New York: Routledge, 1999)

Fanon, Frantz, *The Wretched of the Earth*, trans. by Constance Farrington (Harmondsworth: Penguin, 1967)

Feenberg, Andrew, *Lukacs, Marx and the Sources of Critical Theory* (Oxford: Martin Robertson, 1981)

Ferrebe, Alice, *Masculinity in Male-Authored Fiction 1950–2000* (Houndmills, Basingstoke and New York: Palgrave, 2005)

Foucault, Michel, *The Order of Things: An Archaeology of the Human Sciences*, trans. by Alan Sheridan Smith (New York and London: Routledge, 1970)

—— 'Nietzsche, Genealogy, History', in *Language, Counter-Memory, Practice* (Oxford: Blackwell, 1977), 139–64

—— 'Discipline Three: Panopticism', in *Discipline and Punish: The Birth of the Prison*, trans by Alan Sheridan (London and New York: Vintage, 1995), pp.195–228.

Furst, Lilian R. (ed.), *Realism* (Harlow: Longman, 1992)

Gasiorek, Andrzej, *Post-War British Fiction: Realism and After* (London: Edward Arnold, 1995)

Genette, Gerard, *Narrative Discourse*, trans. by Jane E. Lewin (Oxford: Basil Blackwell, 1980)

—— *Figures of Literary Discourse*, trans. by Alan Sheridan (New York: Columbia University Press, 1982)

Gibson, Andrew, *Towards a Postmodern Theory of Narrative* (Edinburgh: Edinburgh University Press, 1996)

—— *Postmodernism, Ethics and the Novel: From Leavis to Levinas* (London and New York: Routledge, 1999)

Gilbert, Sandra and Susan Gubar, The Madwoman in the Attic: The Woman Writer and the Nineteenth-Century Literary Imagination (New Haven and New York: Yale University Press, 1979)

Giles, Judy and Tim Middleton (eds), *Writing Englishness 1900–1950* (London and New York: Routledge, 1995)

Gilroy, Paul, *There Ain't No Black in the Union Jack: The Cultural Politics of Race and Nation* (London: Hutchison, 1987)

—— *Small Acts: Thoughts on the Politics of Black Cultures* (London: Serpent's Tail, 1993)

—— 'British Cultural Studies and the Pitfalls of Identity', in *Black British Cultural Studies: A Reader*, ed. by Huston A. Baker, Manthia Diawara and Ruth M. Lindeborg (Chicago and London: University of Chicago Press, 1996), 223–39

314

Gould, Tony, Inside Outsider: The Life and Times of Colin MacInnes (London: Allison and Busby, 1993)

Gramsci, Antonio, *Selections from Prison Notebooks*, ed. and trans. by Quintin Hoare and Geoffrey Smith (London: Lawrence and Wishart, 1971)

—— '[The Intellectuals]', in *A Gramsci Reader: Selected Writings 1916–1935*, ed. by David Forgacs (London: Lawrence and Wishart, 1988), 301–11

Grossberg, Lawrence, 'Identity and Cultural Studies', in *Questions of Cultural Identity*, ed. by Stuart Hall and Paul du Gay (London: Sage, 1996), 87–107

Hall, Stuart and others (eds), *Resistance Through Rituals: Youth Subcultures in Postwar Britain* (London: Hutchinson, 1976)

—— 'A Critical Survey of the Theoretical and Practical Achievements of the Last Ten Years', in *Literature, Society and the Sociology of Literature*, ed. by F. Barker and others (Essex: University of Essex, 1977), 1–7

—— and others (eds), Culture, Media and Language: Working Papers in Cultural Studies, 1972–79 (London: Routledge, 1980)

—— 'Encoding/Decoding', in *Culture, Media, Language*, ed. by Stuart Hall and others(London: Hutchinson, 1980), 128–38

—— 'The "First" New Left: Life and Times', in *Out of Apathy: Voices of the New Left 30 Years On*, ed. by The Oxford University Socialist Discussion Group(London and New York: Verso, 1989), 11–38

—— 'Old and New Identities, Old and New Ethnicities', in *Culture, Globalization and the World-System*, ed. by Anthony D. King (Houndmills and London: Macmillan, 1991), 41–68

—— 'Cultural Studies and its Legacies', in *Cultural Studies*, ed. by Lawrence Grossberg, Lawrence, Cary Nelson and Paula A. Treichler (London and New York: Routledge, 1992), 277–94

—— 'The Question of Cultural Identity', in *Modernity and Its Futures* (London: Polity, 1992), 274–99

—— 'Gramsci's Relevance for the Study of Race and Ethnicity', and 'New Ethnicities', both in *Stuart Hall: Critical Dialogues in Cultural Studies*, ed. by David Morley and Kuan-Hsing Chen (London and New York: Routledge, 1996), 411–49

—— and Paul du Gay (eds), *Questions of Cultural Identity* (London: Sage, 1996).

Hand, Sean (ed.), *The Levinas Reader* (Oxford UK & Cambridge USA: Blackwell, 1989)

Hartmann, Heidi, 'The Unhappy Marriage of Marxism and Feminism: Towards a More Progressive Union', in *Post-Marxism: A Reader*, ed. by Stuart Sim (Edinburgh: Edinburgh University Press, 1998), 156–68

Head, Dominic, *The Cambridge Introduction to Modern British Fiction, 1950–2000* (Cambridge: Cambridge University Press, 2002)

Heaney, Seamus, 'Englands of the Mind', in *Preoccupations: Selected Prose 1968–1978* (London and Boston: Faber & Faber, 1980), 150–69

Heath, Stephen, *The Nouveau Roman: A Study in the Practice of Writing* (London: Elek, 1972)

Hebdige, Dick, *Subculture: The Meaning of Style* (London and New York: Routledge, 1979)

—— *Hiding in the Light: On Images and Things* (London and New York: Routledge, 1988)

Hewison, Robert, *In Anger: Culture in the Cold War 1945–60* (London: Weidenfeld and Nicolson, 1981)

—— *Too Much: Art and Society in the Sixties 1960–75* (London: Methuen, 1986)

Hill, John, *Sex, Class and Realism: British Cinema 1956–1963* (London: BFI Publishing, 1986)

Hill, Tracey, and William Hughes (eds), *Contemporary Writing and National Identity* (Bath: Sulis Press, 1995)

Holland, R.F., *European Decolonization 1918–1981: An Introductory Survey* (London: Macmillan, 1985)

Hough, Graham, *Reflections on a Literary Revolution* (Washington D.C.: The Catholic University of America Press, 1960)

Howe, Irving, 'Mass Society and Postmodernist Fiction', in *Decline of the New* (London: Victor Gollancz, 1971), 204–05

Jenkins, Keith (ed.), *The Postmodern History Reader* (London and New York: Routledge, 1997)

Karl, Frederick R., *A Reader's Guide to the Contemporary English Novel* (New York: Octagon Press, 1972)

Keating, J.P., *The Working-Class in Victorian Fiction* (London: Allen and Unwin, 1971)

Kellner, Hans, *Language and Historical Representation* (Madison: University of Wisconsin Press, 1989)

Kemp, Peter, *Muriel Spark* (London: Peter Elek, 1974)

Kenny, Michael, The First New Left: British Intellectuals After Stalin (London: Lawrence and Wishart, 1995)

Laclau, Ernesto and Chantal Mouffe, *Hegemony and Socialist Strategy: Towards a Radical Democratic Politics* (London and New York: Verso, 1985)

Laing, Stuart, *Representations of Working-class Life 1957–1964* (London: Macmillan, 1986)

Lashley, Cliff, 'Towards a Critical Framework for Jamaican Literature: A Reading of the Fiction of Victor Stafford Reid and Other Jamaican Writers', PhD Dissertation (St. Augustine, Trinidad,: University of the West Indies, 1984)

Laurie, Peter, *The Teenage Revolution* (London: Anthony Blond, 1965)

Leech, Kenneth, *Youthquake: The Growth of a Counter Culture Through Two Decades* (London: Sheldon Press, 1973)

Lessing, Doris, *Walking in the Shade: Part Two of My Autobiography 1949–1962* (London: Harper Collins, 1997)

Livingstone, Marco, 'A Big Sensation', in *Pop Art*, ed. by Royal Academy of Arts (London: Weidenfeld and Nicolson, 1991), 146–62

Lodge, David, *The Modes of Modern Writing: Metaphor, Metonymy and the Typology of Modern Literature* (London: Edward Arnold, 1979)

—— *Working With Structuralism* (London: Routledge and Kegan Paul, 1981)

Lovell, Terry, *Consuming Fiction* (London: Verso, 1987)

Lucas, John, *Writing and Radicalism* (London and New York: Longman, 1996)

Lukàcs, Georg, *The Lukàcs Reader*, ed. by Arpad Kadarkay (Oxford UK & Cambridge USA: Blackwell 1995)

MacCabe, Colin, *James Joyce and the Revolution of the Word* (London: Macmillan, 1979)

MacDonald, J.S. and L.D. MacDonald, 'Chain Migration: Ethnic Neighbour-hood Formations and Social Networks', in *Millbank Memorial Fund Quarterly*, No.42, 1964, 82–97

McQuillan, Martin, and others (eds), *Post-Theory: New Directions in Criticism* (Edinburgh: Ediburgh University Press, 1999)

—— (ed.), *The Narrative Reader* (London and New York: Routledge, 2000)

MacRobbie, Angela and Jenny Barber, 'Girls and Subcultures: An Explanation', in *Resistance Through Rituals: Youth Subcultures in Postwar Britain*, ed. by Stuart Hall and Tony Jefferson (Birmingham: Hutchinson (CCCS), 1975) 209–22.

McRobbie, Angela, *Postmodernism and Popular Culture* (London and New York: Routledge, 1994)

317

Manuel, Peter, *Popular Musics of the Non-Western World* (New York and Oxford: Oxford University Press, 1988)

Marx, Karl, *A Reader*, ed. by Jon Elster (Cambridge: Cambridge University Press, 1986)

Mendras, Henri with Alistair Cole, *Social Change in Modern France: Towards a Cultural Anthropology of the Fifth Republic* (Cambridge: Cambridge University Press, 1991)

Morrison, Blake, *The Movement: English Poetry and Fiction of the 1950s* (London and New York: Methuen, 1980)

Morley, David and Kuan-Hsing Chen (eds), *Stuart Hall: Critical Dialogues in Cultural Studies* (London and New York: Routledge, 1996)

Moore-Gilbert, Bart, and John Seed, *Cultural Revolution?: The Challenge of the Arts in the 1960s* (London and New York: Routledge, 1992)

Mungham, Geoff and Geoff Pearson (eds), *Working-class Youth Culture* (London: Routledge and Kegan Paul, 1976)

Nairn, Tom, *The Break-up of Britain* (London: New Left Books, 1977)

The Oxford English Dictionary, 2nd Edition (Oxford: Clarendon Press, 1989) Vol. vi, 78–81; and Vol. xiii, 91–93

The Oxford University Socialist Discussion Group (eds), *Out of Apathy: Voices of the New Left 30 Years On* (London and New York: Verso, 1989)

Platt, J., *Social Research in Bethnal Green* (London: Macmillan, 1971)

Pope, Rob, *The English Studies Book: An Introduction to Language, Literature and Culture*, 2nd Edition (London: Routledge, 2002)

Rabinovitz, Rubin, *The Reaction Against Experiment in the English Novel 1950–1960* (New York and London: Columbia University Press, 1967)

Rainey, Lawrence, 'The Cultural Economy of Modernism', in *The Cambridge Companion to Modernism*, ed. by Michael Levenson (Cambridge: Cambridge University Press, 1999), 33–69

Renato, Rosaldo, Culture and Truth: The Remaking of Social Analysis (Boston: Beacon Press, 1989)

Rimmon-Kenan, Shlomith, *Narrative Fiction; Contemporary Poetics* (London: Methuen, 1983)

Ritchie, Harry, *Success Stories: Literature and the Media in England, 1950–1959* (London and Boston: Faber & Faber, 1988)

Rivkin, Julie and Michael Ryan (eds), *Literary Theory: An Anthology* (Malden, Massachussets and Oxford: Blackwell, 1998)

Rohlehr, Gordon, 'Images of Men and Women in the 1930s Calypsos', in *Gender in Caribbean Development*, ed. by Mohammed, and C. Shepard (St. Augustine, Trinidad: University of the West Indies, 1988)

Rosaldo, Renato, *Culture and Truth: The Remaking of Social Analysis* (Boston: Beacon Press, 1989)

Rowbotham, Sheila, *Women, Resistance and Revolution* (New York: Vintage, 1974)

Rutherford, Jonathan (ed.), *Identity: Community, Culture, Difference* (London: Lawrence and Wishart, 1990)

—— 'A Place Called Home: Identity and the Cultural Politics of Difference', in Rutherford, 1990, 9–27

Said, Edward, *Orientalism: Western Conceptions of the Orient* (Harmondsworth: Penguin, 1991), first published 1978

Sargent, Lydia (ed.), *The Unhappy Marriage of Marxism and Feminism: A Debate on Class and Patriarchy* (London and Sydney: Pluto Press, 1981)

Sartre, Jean-Paul, 'Materialism and Revolution', in *Literary and Philosophical Essays*, trans. by Annette Michelson (London: Radius Book/ Hutchinson, 1968), 189–239

Sedgwick, Eve Kosofsky, *Between Men: English Literature and Homosocial Desire* (New York: Columbia University Press, 1985)

Sedgwick, Peter, 'Introduction: Farewell, Grosvenor Square', in *The Left in Britain: 1956–1968*, ed. by David Widgery (Harmondsworth: Penguin, 1976), 19–41

Segal, Lynne, 'Look Back in Anger: Men the 1950s', in *Male Order: Unwrapping Masculinity*, ed. by Rowena Chapman and Jonathan Rutherford (London: Lawrence and Wishart, 1988), 68–96

Sim, Stuart (ed.), *Post-Marxism: A Reader* (Edinburgh: Edinburgh University Press, 1998)

Sinfield, Alan, *Literature, Politics and Culture in Postwar Britain* (Oxford: Basil Blackwell, 1989)

Snow, C.P., *Public Affairs* (London: Macmillan, 1971)

Spanos, Walter V., 'Overture in the Recursive Mode', in *Repetitions: The Postmodern Occasion in Literature and Culture* (Baton Rouge and London: Louisiana State University Press, 1987), 1–12

Spivak, Gayatri, 'Can the Subaltern Speak?', in *Marxism and the Interpretation of Culture*, ed. by Cary Nelson and Lawrence Grossberg (London: Macmillan, 1988), 271–313

Stevens, Frances, *The New Inheritors* (London: Hutchinson Educational, 1970)

Strinati, Dominic, *An Introduction to Theories of Popular Culture* (London and New York: Routledge, 1995)

Taylor, D.J., *After the War: The Novel and England Since 1945* (London: Flamingo, 1993)

Todd, Emmanuel, The Making of Modern France: Ideology, Politics and Culture (Oxford: Blackwell, 1991)

Worpole, Ken, *Dockers and Detectives: Popular Reading, Popular Writing* (London: Verso, 1983)

—— 'Scholarship Boy', in *The Bloodaxe Critical Anthologies 1: Tony Harrison*, ed. by Neil Astley (Newcastle: Bloodaxe, 1991), 61–7

Widgery, David (ed.), *The Left in Britain: 1956–1968* (Harmondsworth: Penguin, 1976)

Williams, Raymond, *Orwell* (Glasgow: Collins/Fontana, 1971)

—— *Marxism and Literature* (Oxford: Oxford University Press, 1977)

—— *Politics and Letters: Interviews with the New Left Review* (London: New Left Books, 1979)

—— *Problems in Materialism and Culture* (London: Verso, 1980)

—— 'Base and Superstructure in Marxist Cultural Theory', in *Problems in Materialism and Culture* (London: Verso, 1980), 37–45

—— 'The Metropolis and the Emergence of Modernism', in Brooker, *Modernism/Postmodernism*, 82–94

Young, Iris, 'Beyond the Unhappy Marriage: A Critique of Dual Systems Theory', in Sargent, *The Unhappy Marriage of Marxism and Feminism*, 43–69

Young, Robert (ed.), *Untying the Text: A Post-Structuralist Reader* (London and New York: Routledge and Kegan Paul, 1981

—— White Mythologies: Writing History and the West (London and New York: Routledge, 1990)

2. Kingsley Amis and John Wain

Bradford, Richard, *Kingsley Amis* (London: Edward Arnold, 1989)

Hague, Angela, 'Picaresque /structure and the Angry Young Novel', *Twentieth Century Literature*, 32, No.2 (1986) 209–20

Keulks, Gavin, *Father and Son: Kingsley Amis, Martin Amis, and the British Novel Since 1950* (Madison, Wisconsin: University of Wisconsin Press, 2003)

McDermott, John, *Kingsley Amis: An English Moralist* (London: Macmillan, 1989)

Salwak, Dale, *Kingsley Amis, Modern Novelist* (New York: Harvester Wheatsheaf)

Schaffer, Brian W., 'Kingsey Amis's *Luck Jim* (1953)', in *Reading the Novel in English* 1950–2000 (Oxford: Blackwell, 2005), 35–53

3. Muriel Spark

Bradbury, Malcolm, 'Muriel Spark's Fingernails', *Critical Quarterly*, No.14 (1972), 242–3

Brian Cheyette *Muriel Spark* (Plymouth: Northcote Press, 2000)

Idle, Jeremy, 'Muriel Spark's Uselessness', in McQuillan, *Theorizing Muriel Spark*, 141–54

Kane, Richard C., *Iris Murdoch, Muriel Spark and John Fowles: Didactic Demons in Modern Fiction* (London and Toronto: Associated University Presses, 1988)

Peter Kemp, *Muriel Spark* (London: Paul Elek, 1974)

Kermode, Frank, 'Muriel Spark', in *Modern Essays* (London: Fontana, 1990), 267–83

McQuillan, Martin (ed.) *Theorizing Muriel Spark: Gender, Race, Deconstruction* (London: Palgrave, 2002

—— 'Introduction: "I Don't Know Anything About Freud": Muriel Spark Meets Contemporary Criticism', in McQuillan, *Theorizing Muriel Spark*, 1–31

Ohmann, Carol B., 'Muriel Spark's *Robinson*', *Critique: Studies in Modern Fiction* VIII, Fall 1965, 70–84

Patricia Stubbs, *Muriel Spark* (Harlow: Longman, 1973)

Ruth Whittaker, *The Faith and Fiction of Muriel Spark* (London: Macmillan Press, 1982)

4. Alan Sillitoe

Atherton, Stanley S., *Alan Sillitoe: A Critical Assessment* (London: W.H. Allen, 1979)

Barber, Michael, 'Love on a Slag Heap', Radio Four broadcast, May 22, Part 2 of *The Angry Decade*, 1987

Craig, David, 'The Roots of Sillitoe's Fiction', in *The British Working-class Novel*, ed. by Jeremy Hawthorn (London: Edward Arnold, 1984), 95–110

Gray, Nigel, 'Life is What You Make It', in *The Silent Majority: A Study of the Working-class in Post-War British Fiction* (London: Vision, 1973), 101–32

Hitchcock, Peter, *Working-Class Fiction in Theory and Practice: A Reading of Alan Sillitoe* (Ann Arbor/London: UMI Research Press, 1989)

Hutchings, William, 'Proletarian Byronism: Alan Sillitoe and the Romantic Tradition', in Allan Chavkin (ed.), *English Romanticism and Modern Fiction* (New York: AMS Press, 1993), 83–112

Leonardi, Susan, 'The Long Distance Runner (The Loneliness, Loveliness, Nunliness of)', in *Tulsa Studies in Women's Literature*, Vol.13, 1994, 57–85

Nardella, Anna Ryan, 'The Existential Dilemmas of Alan Sillitoe's Working-class Heroes', in *Studies in the Novel* 5, winter 1973, 469–82

Paul, Ronald, *'Fire in Our Hearts': A Study of the Portrayal of Youth in a Selection of Post-War British Working-Class Fiction* (Gothenburg: Acta Universitatis Gothoburgensis, 1982)

Rothschild, Joyce, 'The Growth of a Writer: An Interview with Alan Sillitoe', in *Southern Humanities Review*, spring 1986, 20:2, 127–40

Taylor, Christopher, 'Realism and the Language of Realism in the Works of Alan Sillitoe', in *Four Fits of Anger: Essays on the Angry Young Men*, ed. by Brady and others (Zeta Universita: Campanotto Editore, 1986), 100–49

Vaverka, Ronald Dee, *Commitment as Art: A Marxist Critique of a Selection of Alan Sillitoe's Political Fiction* (Stockholm: Uppsala University Press, 1978)

West, Anthony, 'On the Inside Looking In', in *New Yorker*, 5 September 1959, 99–100

5. Colin MacInnes

Ferrebe, Alice, 'A Teenage Ball', in Ferrebe, *Masculinity in Male-Authored Fiction*, 139–51

Gould, Tony, *Inside Outsider: The Life and Times of Colin MacInnes* (London: Allison and Busby, 1983)

Blodgett, Harriet, 'City of Other Worlds: The London Novels of Colin MacInnes', in *Critique: Studies in Modern Fiction*, 18:1, 1976, 105–18

6. Sam Selvon

Ariel: A Review of International English Literature, 'Sam Selvon: A Celebration', Special Edition on Sam Selvon, Vol.27, No.2, April 1996

Fabre, Michel, 'Samuel Selvon: Interviews and Conversations', in Nasta, 1988, 64–76

—— 'From Trinidad to London: Tone and Language in Samuel Selvon's Novels', in Nasta, 1988, 213–22

Grant, Jane, 'Introduction', in Sam Selvon, *Ways of Sunlight*, Selvon, 1987, v–xxx

Harney, Stefano, 'Samuel Selvon and the Chronopolitics of a Diasporic Nationalism', in *Nationalism and Identity: Culture and the Imagination in a Caribbean Diaspora* (London and New Jersey: Zed Books, 1996), 91–117

Looker, Mark, *Atlantic Passages: History, Fiction and Language in the Fiction of Sam Selvon* (New York: Peter Lang, 1996)

Loreto, Paola, 'The Male Mind and the Female Heart: Selvon's Ways to Knowledge in the "Tiger Books"', in Zehnder, *Something Rich and Strange*, 39–51

Nasta, Susheila (ed.), *Critical Perspectives on Sam Selvon* (Washington D.C.: Three Continents Press, 1988)

—— and Anna Rutherford (eds), *Tiger's Triumph: Celebrating Sam Selvon* (Armidale: Dangaroo, 1995)

Nazareth, Peter, 'Interview with Sam Selvon', in *World Literature Written in English*, Vol.18, 1979, 420–37

Ramchand, Kenneth, 'Sam Selvon Talking: A Conversation with Kenneth Ramchand', in *Canadian Literature*, No.95, 1982, 56–64

—— 'An Introduction to this Novel', in Sam Selvon, *The Lonely Londoners* (Harlow, Essex: Longman, 1985), 3–20

—— 'Song of Innocence, Song of Experience: Samuel Selvon's *The Lonely Londoners* as a Literary Work', in Nasta, 1988, 223–33

Rohlehr, Gordon, 'The Folk in Caribbean Literature', in Nasta, 1988, 29–43

Selvon, Sam, 'A Note on Dialect', in Nasta, 1988, 63

Thieme, John, '"The World Turned Upside Down": Carnival Patterns in "The Lonely Londoners"', in *The Toronto South Asian Review,* Vol.5, summer 1986, 191–204

—— 'Rama in Exile: The Indian Writer Overseas', in *The Eye of the Beholder: Indian Writing in English*, ed. by Maggie Butcher (London: Commonwealth Institute, 1983)

—— and Alessandra Dotti, '"Oldtalk": Two Interviews with Sam Selvon', in *Caribana*, Vol.1, 1990, 71–84

Wyke, Clement H., *Sam Selvon's Dialectical Style and Fictional Strategy* (Vancouver: University of British Columbia Press, 1991)

Wyndham, Francis, 'Ways of Sunlight', in *The Spectator*, 28 February 1958, 273

Zehnder, Mark (ed.) *Something Rich and Strange: Selected Essays on Sam Selvon* (Leeds: Peepal Tree, 2003)

Index